AF262801

Approaching the Buddha

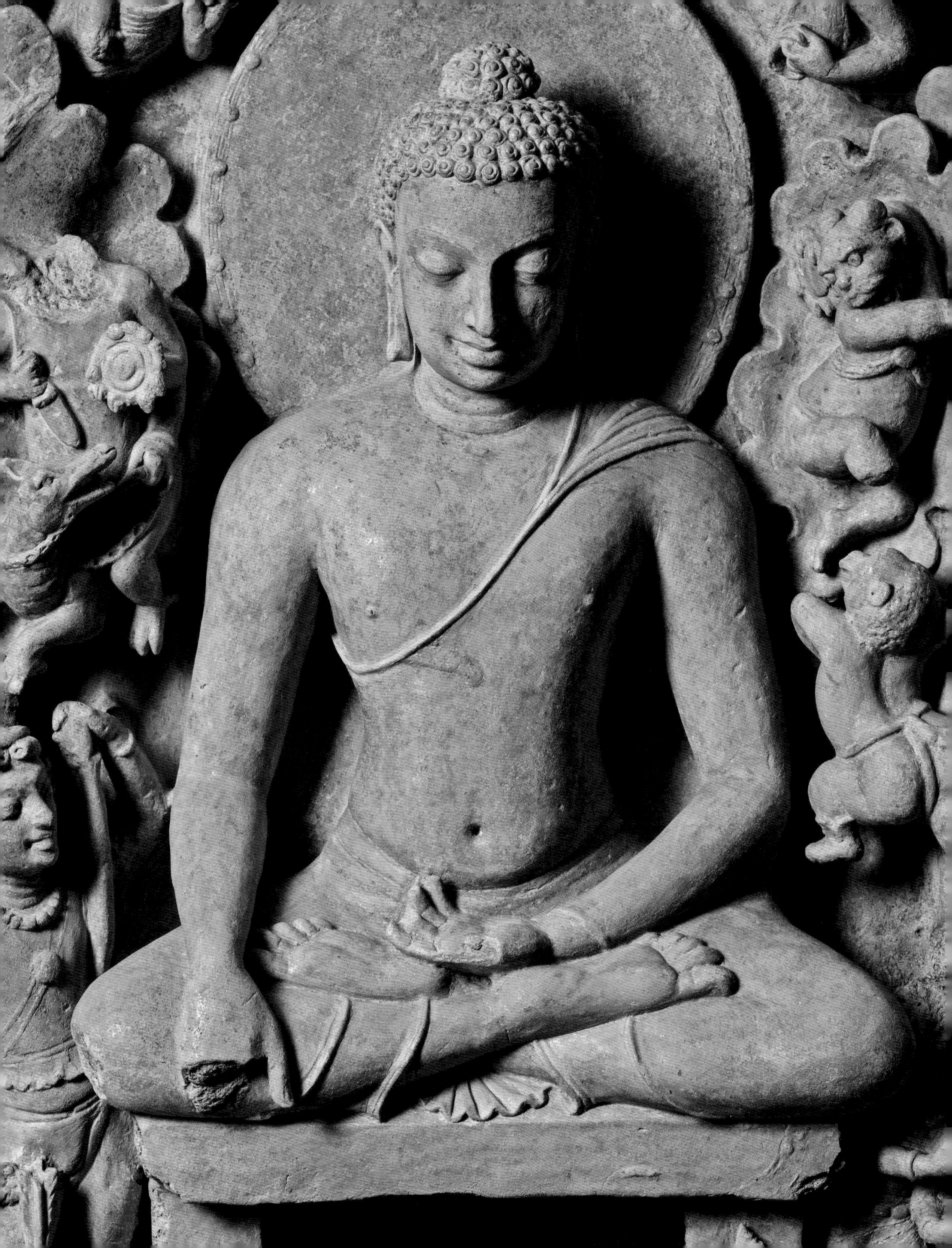

Approaching the
Buddha
Transmission and Transformation

Hao Sheng

**with contributions by Jane Casey, Susan L. Huntington,
Karen Hwang, Michael Knight, Donald S. Lopez, Donna K. Strahan,
John Twilley, and David Weldon**

The Museum of Fine Arts, Houston
Distributed by Yale University Press, New Haven and London

Contents

Director's Foreword
by Gary Tinterow
7

Acknowledgments
by Hao Sheng
9

Collector's Statement
11

Approaching the Buddha
TRANSMISSION AND TRANSFORMATION
by Hao Sheng
13

Creating Merit
ART IN BUDDHIST PRACTICE
by Susan L. Huntington
22

Maitreya
by Donald S. Lopez
29

Found in Translation
EARLY CHINESE BUDDHIST SCULPTURE (FIRST CENTURY–849 CE)
by Michael Knight
32

Featured Works
39

TECHNICAL CASE STUDY
A Tang Dynasty Hollow-Core Lacquer Buddha Head
by Donna K. Strahan
113

**From the Twelfth Century to the Present,
a Gilded Wisdom Buddha**
by John Twilley
118

Bibliography
124

Contributors
127

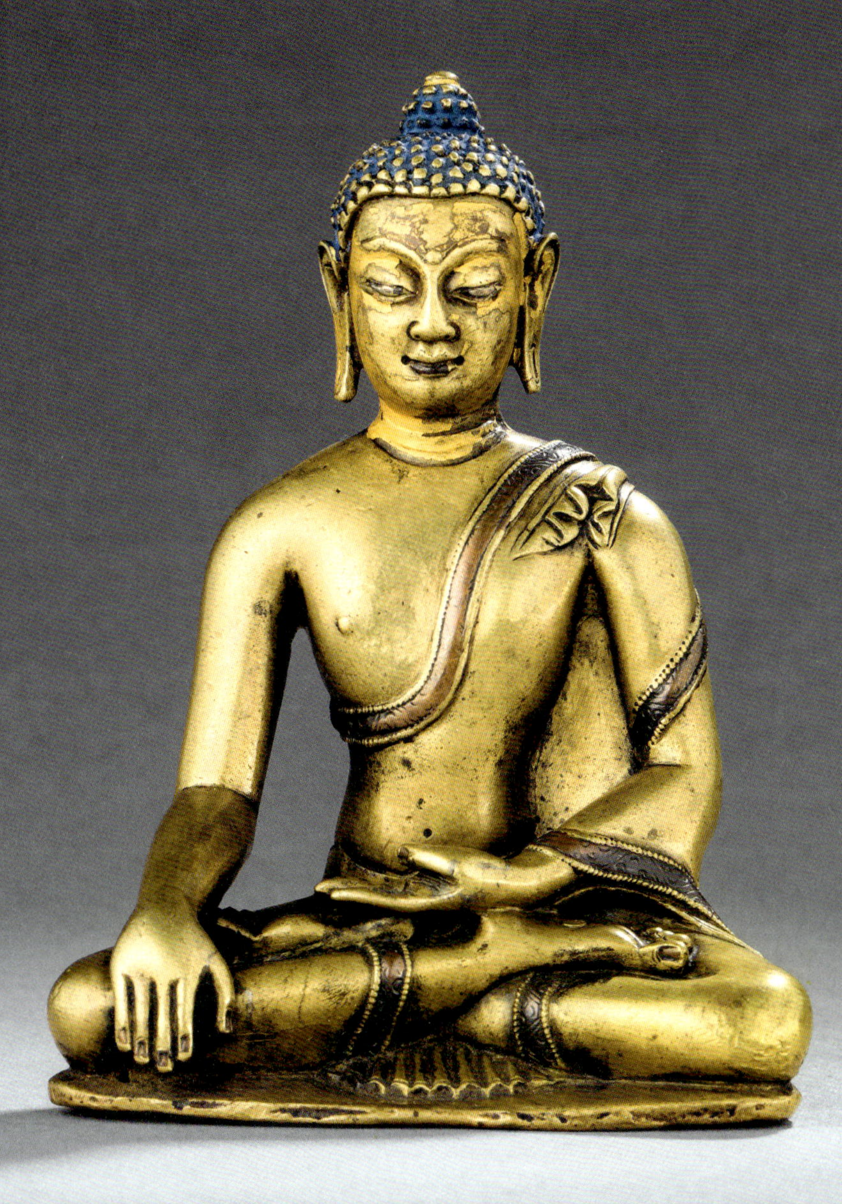

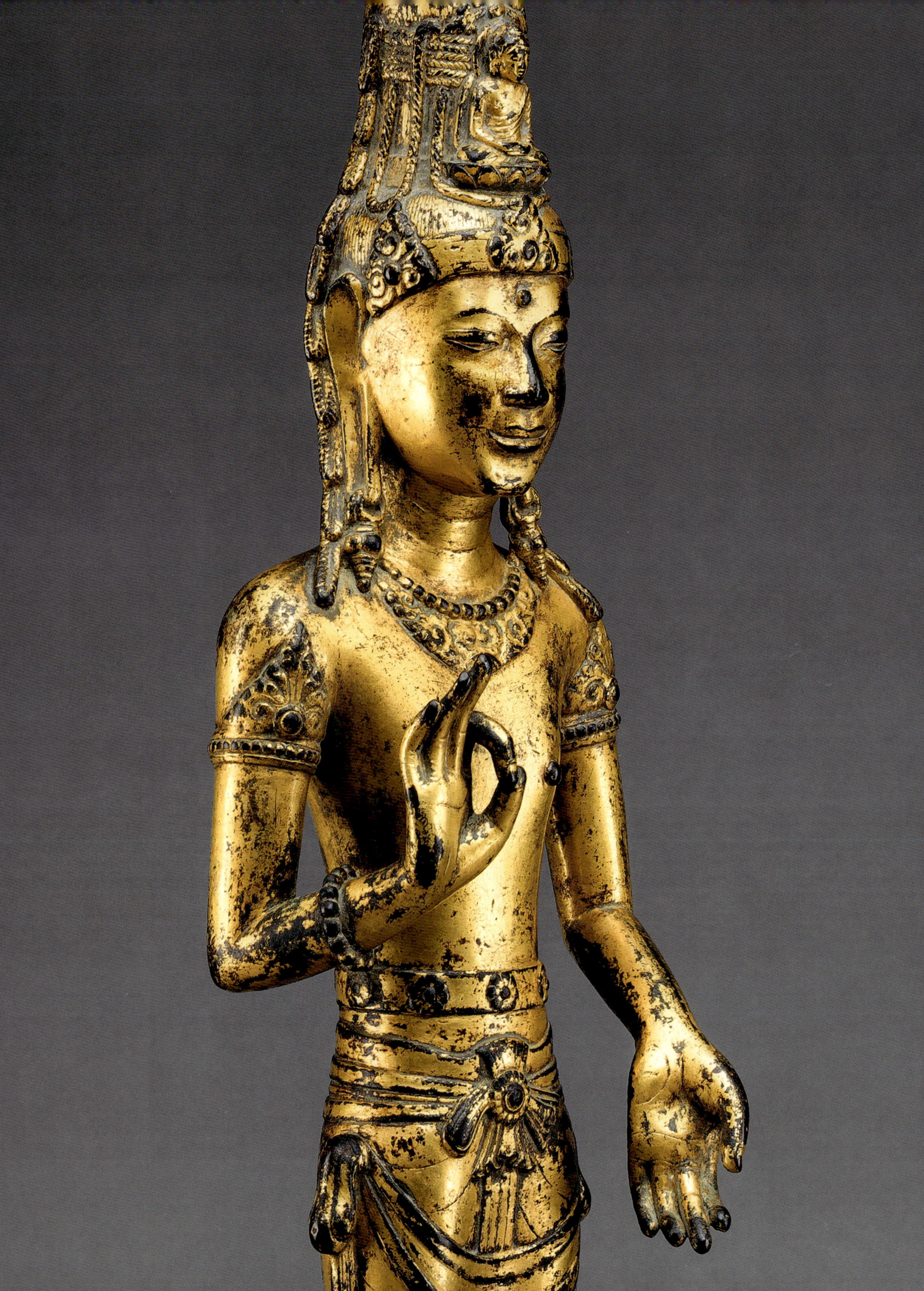

Director's Foreword

For much of this century, a private collector with a scholarly sensibility and a keen eye for quality has pursued the most outstanding Buddhist images available on the international art market. Calling it the Xuzhou Collection of Buddhist Art, the collector generously placed twenty-eight works of art on long-term loan at the Museum of Fine Arts, Houston, in 2021. Shown together in public for the first time, these works, which span more than a millennium and represent the major Buddhist cultures across Asia, have transformed our presentations of Asian art and more specifically deepened our representation of the magnificent art that this influential faith inspired.

Since its arrival in Houston, the Xuzhou Collection has been integrated into the Museum's permanent collection galleries, significantly enhancing the displays representing East Asia, Southeast Asia, and the Indian subcontinent. In addition, the Xuzhou Collection was a central component of the 2024 exhibition *Living with the Gods: Art, Beliefs, and Peoples*, where a selection of seven sculptures conveyed the story of the Buddha and illuminated Buddhist beliefs. That exhibition was a manifestation of the Museum's *World Faiths Initiative*, made possible by a grant from Lilly Endowment Inc., which seeks to reveal how faith, religion, and spirituality have inspired art throughout all of human history.

Approaching the Buddha: Transmission and Transformation celebrates this collaboration and documents the Xuzhou Collection's artistic excellence and historical significance. Each sculpture bears the imprint of countless encounters — from the artists and craftspeople who created these forms to the pilgrims who acquired them, to the practitioners who wore down their surfaces through centuries of reverent touch. These sculptures were created as devotional instruments — powerful mediators between the human and the divine — whose effectiveness was increased by the artistic beauty that they displayed.

We are all deeply grateful to the collector, who humbly wishes to remain anonymous. His generosity has made this publication possible, thereby enabling the images of the Buddha to exert a salutary influence through the world. I am grateful to the distinguished scholars who have contributed to this catalogue; their scholarship and insights illuminate the multiple dimensions of these sculptures, from their technical achievement to their spiritual significance. It is a pleasure to record my special gratitude to Life Trustee Dr. Anne Chao; her diplomacy was instrumental in securing the long-term loan of the collection for Houston.

I am very proud to acknowledge the remarkable staff of the Museum of Fine Arts, Houston, whose expertise and commitment have brought exhibitions and this publication to fruition, in particular Hao Sheng, our consulting curator, and Heather Brand, our publisher in chief. By serving as custodians of these precious works and making them accessible to the public, both the collector and the Museum participate in the tradition of sharing Buddhist wisdom — not only with those who have embraced Buddhism but also with those for whom it opens a new world of understanding.

Gary Tinterow
Director
The Margaret Alkek Williams Chair
The Museum of Fine Arts, Houston

Acknowledgments

I would like to express my sincere gratitude to Gary Tinterow, Director, the Margaret Alkek Williams Chair, for his leadership in exhibiting sacred art at the Museum of Fine Arts, Houston (MFAH). The inclusion of the Xuzhou Collection in our Asian galleries, as well as in the centennial exhibition *Living with the Gods: Art, Beliefs, and Peoples,* is a direct result of his vision, which invites visitors to experience these Buddhist masterpieces as continuing sources of wisdom, compassion, and personal transformation in our contemporary world. This mission also guides the exhibition *Buddha | Nature,* presented at the MFAH in the spring of 2026, in which the Xuzhou Collection is seen anew through the framework of our pressing environmental concerns. Our gratitude goes to the Jerold B. Katz Foundation for its leadership support of this exhibition.

I remain deeply grateful to the collector, whose discernment and passion have built this extraordinary collection. His commitment to support scholarship, to share the collection with the public, and to make historical art relevant to today's concerns has been the driving force behind both the exhibitions and this publication.

I am profoundly thankful to the distinguished scholars of art history, Buddhism, and conservation science who contributed generously to this catalogue: Jane Casey, Susan L. Huntington, Karen Hwang, Michael Knight, Donald S. Lopez, Donna K. Strahan, John Twilley, and David Weldon. Many of them have guided the collection since its inception, and their continued research and discoveries have elevated this publication immeasurably. I will always treasure the privilege of viewing and discussing these works together with them and remember their warmth and wisdom.

I would like to thank my colleagues in the Asian art department: Bradley Bailey, the Ting Tsung and Wei Fong Chao Curator of Asian Art, Amy Poster, consulting curator, and Sumin Park, curatorial assistant, as well as our dedicated Asian art subcommittee, particularly our chair, Dr. Anne Chao, whose visit to the collection in Asia was instrumental in bringing these treasures to the Museum.

The publications team deserves my deepest appreciation: Heather Brand, publisher in chief, for refining the manuscripts and for her sage advice throughout the process; Megan Smith, managing editor, for keeping this project on track, and Katie Horrigan, senior graphic designer, for fine-tuning the catalogue's images.

I want to thank the catalogue's designer, Roy Brooks of Fold Four, Inc., for his sensitivity to the Buddhist material and his creative vision, as well as Mark French for photography, and Will Michels, senior collection photographer at the Museum, for the stunning portrait of the *Buddha Head* pictured on the cover.

I am grateful to our conservation team — Per Knutås, chairman of conservation, and conservators Jane Gillies, Nick Pedemonti, and Szilvia Revesz — for their meticulous care of these precious works. Our extraordinary library staff members Rebekah Scoggins and Emma Jackson, along with their network of library colleagues, provided timely assistance with resources for this catalogue. Additionally, my colleagues in registration and preparations, Julie Bakke, Kim Pashko, Dale Benson, Ken Beasley, Michael Kennaugh, and Frances Trahan, made essential contributions to this project.

Finally, I would like to thank my family, Ray and Clyde.

Hao Sheng
Consulting Curator of Asian Art
The Museum of Fine Arts, Houston

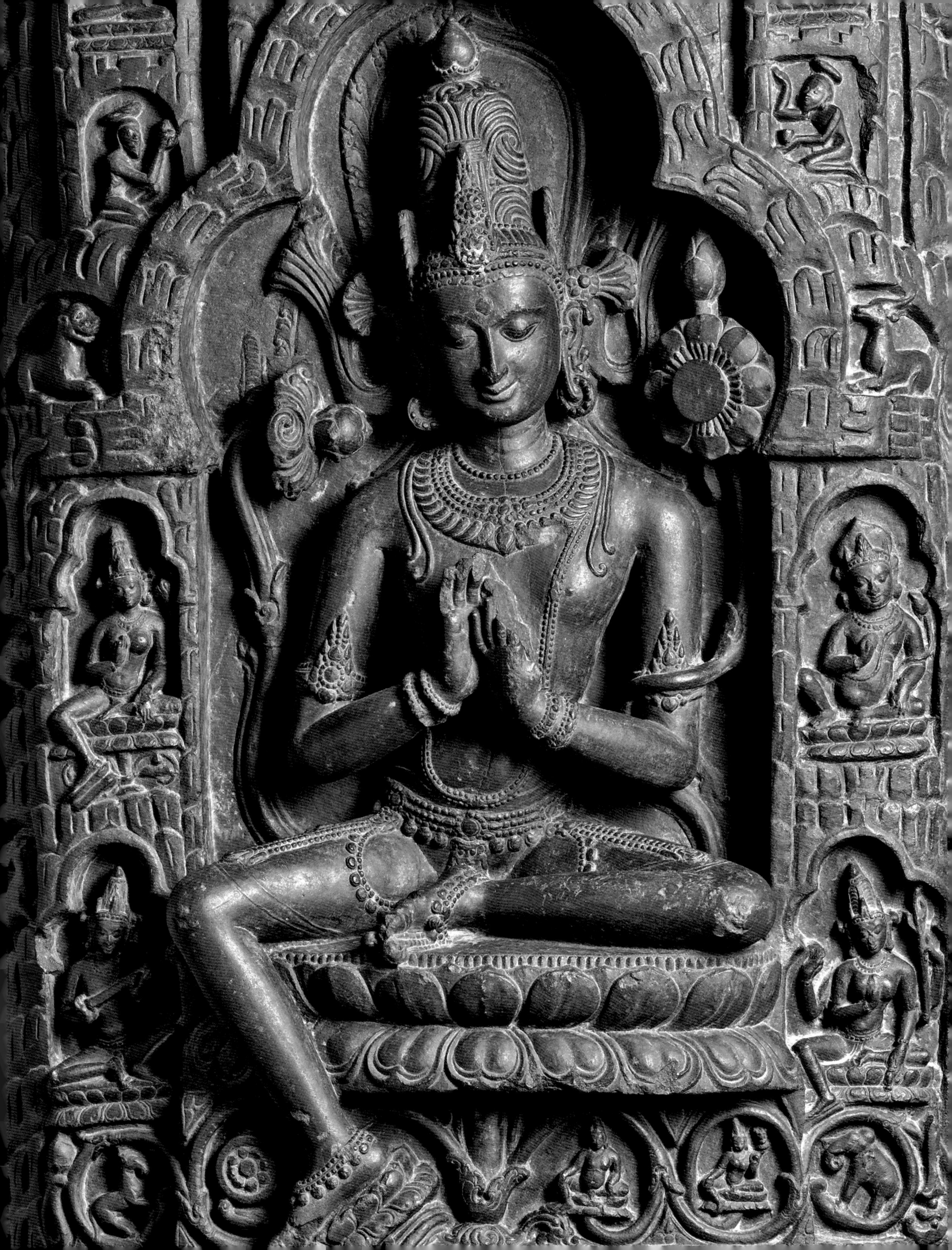

Collector's Statement

Buddhism has often used the raft as a metaphor to describe its teachings, a useful tool to help one cross the river of ignorance to reach enlightenment, only to be discarded afterward. The Xuzhou Collection (*Xuzhou* meaning "empty raft" in Chinese) extends this idea to Buddhist art, which can serve as a vehicle carrying the viewer toward an understanding of Buddhist wisdom. I chose this name, rather than my own, preferring to remain anonymous so that viewers might focus on the purpose of the collection rather than the identity of the collector.

My exploration of Buddhist practice over the years has profoundly shaped my relationship with Buddhist art. As my practice has evolved, I have come to see these works not merely as aesthetic objects, or devotional items to help deepen my practice, but also as material witnesses to Buddhism's remarkable ability to adapt and flourish across different cultural and historical settings while maintaining its essential teachings.

The collection, assembled over the past two decades, reflects this pan-Asian perspective. Each piece serves as a reminder of Buddhism's vast historical and cultural reach, from its birthplace in North India, through the Himalayas to Tibet; west to Gandhara and Central Asia; east to China, Korea, and Japan; and south to Sri Lanka and the Indonesian islands. I am fascinated by how each culture interpreted Buddhist teachings through its own artistic vocabulary, while maintaining that ineffable quality that marks true Buddhist art — the clear embodiment of Dharma.

I hesitate to call my "collection" a collection, because my collecting journey is less deliberate and intentional and is more often spontaneous and opportunistic. Nevertheless, with the Xuzhou Collection, I've evolved from seeking representative pieces from each tradition to focusing on works with exceptional quality and provenance. I believe the best pieces come to you when the timing is right. There is an element of karma in collecting. Beyond aesthetic and historical significance, I look for objects that also possess an

undefinable quality of presence that speaks across time. The small Tibetan earth-touching Buddha with its lapis lazuli hair is an example (see cat. 15). Despite its size, it commands attention, its nose worn smooth and its surface bearing the patina of countless hands. It was a cherished devotional item, likely carried personally, that connects us to generations of practitioners and speaks to Buddhism's scope and endurance.

Sharing these works with the public is essential to me. These objects are meant to be seen, not hidden away. I hope visitors, especially those encountering Buddhist art for the first time, will appreciate Buddhism's rich history, cultural diversity, and varied traditions. Buddhism has been a tolerant unifying force across Asia while adapting to local contexts. In today's world of cultural erasure and religious tensions, preserving and sharing this heritage becomes increasingly vital.

Although these sculptures are no longer consecrated ritual objects, they retain a refined aesthetic that can guide viewers toward both internal and social transformation. They are vessels awaiting activation through an encounter with sympathetic viewers. In this way, they continue to serve their original purpose as vehicles for enlightenment, offering insights and representing values deeply needed in today's world.

Avalokiteshvara Seated on Mount Potala (detail), Bangladesh, ancient Vikrampura region (Dhaka district), 11th century, black stone, 35 ⅝ × 17 ¹¹⁄₁₆ × 5 ⅛ in. (90.5 × 45 × 13 cm), Xuzhou Collection of Buddhist Art, promised gift to the Victoria and Albert Museum, London.

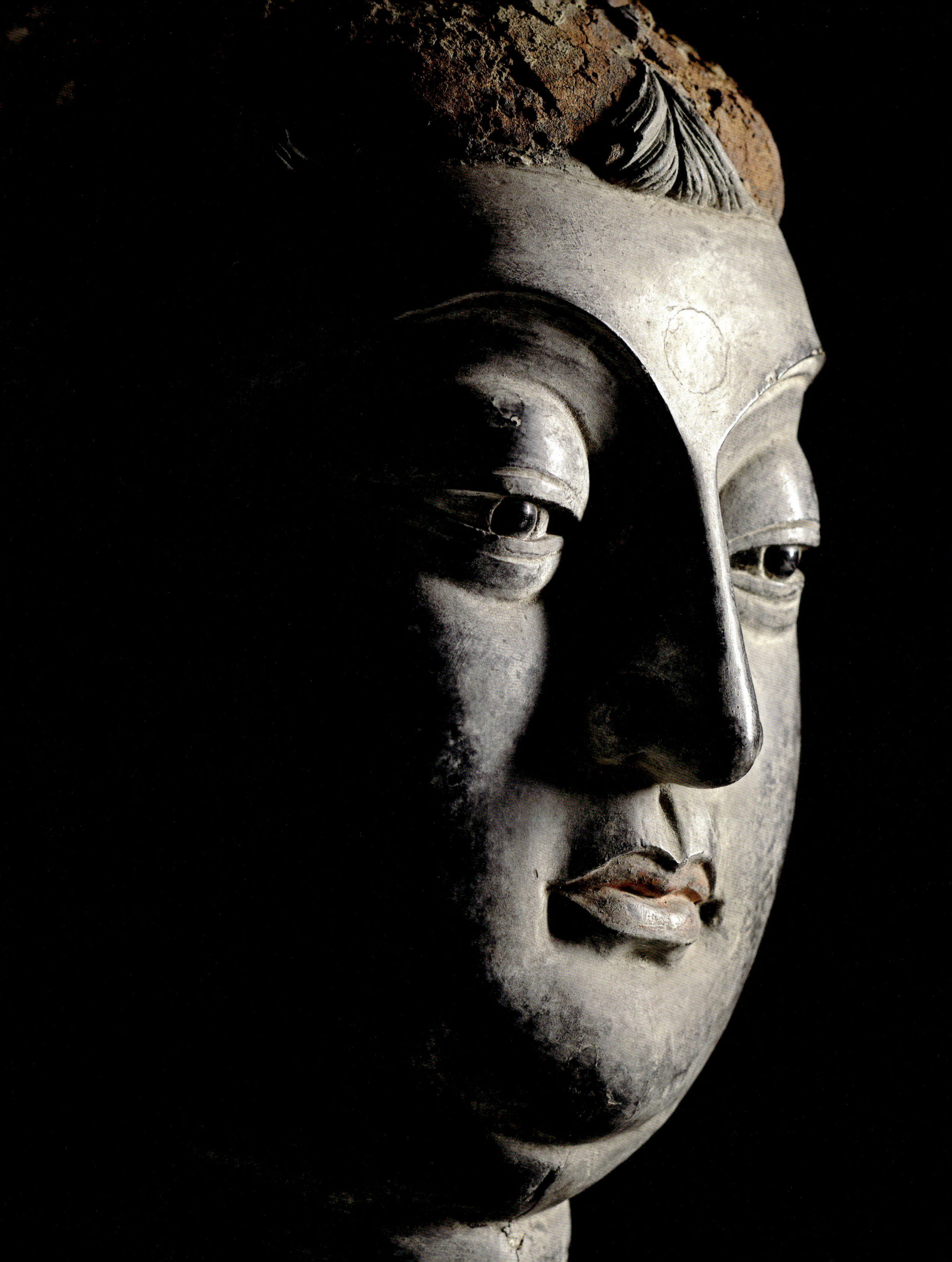

Approaching the Buddha
TRANSMISSION AND TRANSFORMATION

by Hao Sheng

Buddha images aren't static icons but visual dialogues between timeless dharma and present circumstances. When we see how the serene face of the Buddha has been reimagined across centuries and continents, we witness Buddhism's remarkable conversation with changing human needs.
— Buddhist scholar Janet Gyatso

This monumental Buddha head (fig. 1) from eighth-century China, with its somber expression and penetrating stare, offers a way to understand how Buddhist sculptures were meant to function. Through painstaking construction with a difficult medium, solidified tree resin or lacquer, the sculptor achieved something remarkable: a seated figure that would have been over seven feet tall when complete, yet light enough for a couple of people to carry.[1] Such technical achievement was not merely artistic prowess; it enabled sacred images to move between worlds, creating possibilities for encounter.

Chinese texts from the period describe festive processions of Buddhist icons on days of celebration, such as the Buddha's birthday on the eighth day of the fourth month and the emperor's birthday.[2] Sacred images like this one would have been carried from their temples into the crowded avenues, accompanied by performing acrobats and musicians. Meanwhile, throngs of people would line the streets, burning incense, offering flowers, and showing reverence. They vied with each other to catch a glimpse of the sacred icon, but even more important, they sought to be seen by the Buddha to confirm his blessing. This reciprocal vision — seeing and being seen — was central to Buddhist devotional practice.[3] This Buddha's eyes, made of two solid glass spheres that catch and reflect the light, were instruments of this mutual engagement. Even in its current state, separated from its body and original ritual context, this head embodies fundamental aspects of Buddhist art: the reciprocal nature of viewing, the relationship between materiality and meaning, the possibility of a genuine encounter with the sacred.

This Buddha fragment opens up questions: How were Buddhist sculptures meant to be approached? What happens in the space between seeing and being seen? How might understanding the original contexts and functions of such sculptures deepen our engagement with them today?

The collector of the Xuzhou Collection is a lifelong student of Buddhism and meditation. Although he did not acquire these Buddhist sculptures for ritual use, his spiritual practices informed his choice. He was particularly drawn to forms that pull a viewer into meaningful encounters. This sensitivity to the transformative potential of Buddhist images distinguishes the collection from those driven primarily by art historical values and informs the ways in which the images may be approached today.

Though limited in number, the Xuzhou Collection includes representative works from most major Buddhist cultures across Asia, providing valuable insights into how Buddhist artistic traditions continued to evolve across different regions from ancient Gandhara to Kamakura, Japan. The many faces of Buddhist art represented in the collection are as diverse as the Asian cultures that created them, yet the Buddha remains instantly recognizable. This coherence within multiplicity is accomplished through visual conventions that convey the Buddha's physical traits, his biography, his teachings, and his ineffable state of equanimity and bliss.

At the most immediate, the Buddha carries on his body the "marks of a great being" (*mahapurushalakshana*) — physical manifestations of his inner perfection. The *ushnisha* (cranial protuberance) signifies his expanded wisdom and elevated consciousness; the radiant *urna* between his eyebrows illuminates reality beyond ordinary perceptions; his golden complexion is the manifestation of inner radiance. Aided by sacred texts, Indian artists imagined the Buddha by combining the most powerful and beautiful elements from nature — the tapered torso of a lion, supple arms likened to an elephant's trunk, webs

Fig. 1

Buddha Head, China, Tang dynasty, 8th century, hollow-core dry lacquer (cat. 21).

between fingers, and eyelids curved like lotus petals —
to create an awe-inspiring form both human and
transcendent.

Beyond the signs of physical perfection, Buddha
images are coded with references to the Buddha's biography, allowing viewers to contemplate his life's journey.
His elongated earlobes, stretched by heavy jewelry, are the
remaining trace of a royal upbringing. Siddhartha Gautama,
the Buddha-to-be, was born and raised a prince in a kingdom on the border of Nepal and India in the fifth century
BCE. Fearing that Siddhartha would pursue a spiritual
path as had been foretold at birth, his father shielded him
from life's sufferings. Only at age twenty-nine did Prince
Siddhartha step outside the palace walls, and for the first
time he witnessed old age, sickness, death, and a holy man
(known in Buddhist traditions as the "Four Encounters").
Troubled by the inevitable sufferings of samsara, the endless
cycle of birth and rebirth, Siddhartha left home and went
on a spiritual quest (cat. 3). He traded his sumptuous silk
attire for the humble robe of a mendicant seeker, indicating
his "Great Renunciation" of a princely life in search of ways
to end suffering for all. The characteristic "snail shell"
hair represents what remained after he cut off his royal
topknot, a decisive gesture symbolizing his break with
worldly attachment and status.

Formalized hand gestures, or mudras, signify key
moments of the Buddha's journey from seeker to enlightenment to teacher. Open palms stacked in the lap is the mudra
of meditation (cat. 4); the right hand reaching forward and
touching the earth signifies the event of Buddha's enlightenment (cat. 2); two raised hands gesturing together, as
if turning an imaginary wheel of dharma, is the mudra of
teaching (cat. 7). These coded gestures allow the initiated
viewer to recognize which stage in the Buddha's life is
being depicted, and what teachings that moment entails.

For six years after leaving his father's palace,
Siddhartha wandered in the wilderness as an ascetic.
He followed various teachers and underwent punishing
measures of self-denial, depriving his body of nourishment
and rest (fig. 2). Ultimately feeling dissatisfied with these
efforts, he reached a moment of insight. He realized
progress would come through neither the ascetic's depriva-
tion nor princely indulgence, but through the Middle Way
(*Madhyama-pratipada*), a balanced approach to life and
spiritual practice toward enlightenment. Scripture reports
that when he left his fellow ascetics and accepted a bowl
of milk rice from a village maiden named Sujata, his severely
emaciated body immediately regained all its fullness and
splendor, a state of well-being that prepared for his subsequent enlightenment. Thus, in the familiar form of a
Buddha, the beautiful figure can be understood as an
embodied expression of the Middle Way.

Buddhist sculptures do not merely commemorate
the Buddha's journey; they also invite viewers to recognize
their own possibility of awakening. The finest Buddhist
sculptures convey an inspiring state of being. For instance,
the Indian terracotta Buddha (cat. 1) displays a robust
life force tempered through introspection, balancing rigor
with wisdom. The Chinese stone triad (cat. 20) radiates
compassion from the Buddha's warm, inward smile, suggesting boundless empathy for all sentient beings. The
Indian bronze Buddha (cat. 2) emanates the triumphant
power from the one who has conquered samsara. The
meditating Sri Lankan bronze Buddha (cat. 8) embodies
perfect equanimity, a mind undisturbed by worldly concerns
yet fully aware. These spiritual attainments of a fully
enlightened being — neither purely physical nor merely
symbolic — manifest directly through the Buddha's bodily
presence. Here lies a profound paradox of Buddhist art:
While Buddha's teaching offers release from the self,
Buddha images employ his physical body to guide us toward
that very transcendence. This paradox contains a radical
promise — that our own body, with all its limitations, holds
in common the seed for spiritual transformation. The

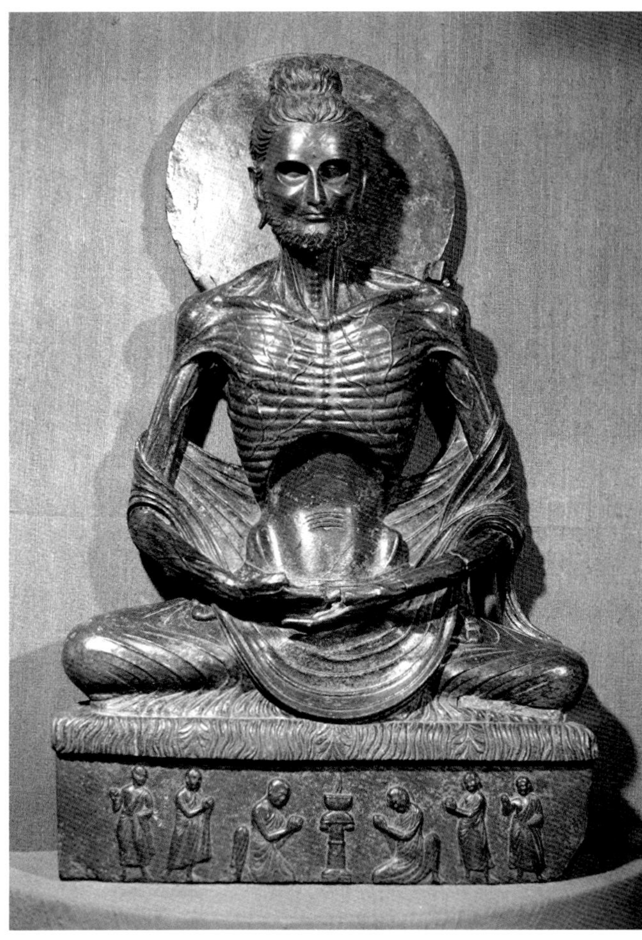

Fasting Siddhartha, Sikri (Gandhara region), Khaibar Pakhtun Khuwa, Pakistan, 4th–mid-6th century, schist, Lahore Museum, Lahore, Pakistan.

Buddha's journey from a prince to the "Awakened One" exemplifies a path potentially open to all.

Buddhist sculptures further expand in meaning and power when understood not as isolated objects but in the context of vast networks of transmission. As Buddhism spread across Asia, images were transmitted between cultures while undergoing transformation in response to local traditions. Particular groups of images gained status and recognition through their lineage, often anchored in origin stories associated with the Buddha. This connection to founding narratives — whether the first image of Buddha created during his lifetime (as represented in the *Standing Buddha* image, cat. 24) or the icon of the Dali kingdom depicting the bodhisattva in the guise of a monk (cat. 22) — established sacred authority that devotees maintained even as forms continued to evolve.[4] Multiple Xuzhou Collection images of Buddha making the earth-touching mudra exemplify this phenomenon, allowing us to trace the founding narrative of a sacred icon, to imagine the means and purpose of its transmission from northern India to the far corners of Asia, and to appreciate the transformation that took place along the way.[5]

On the eve of his enlightenment, vowing not to rise until finding the cause of suffering, the Buddha-to-be sat down under the bodhi tree. The sacred spot is known as *vajrasana*, the diamond seat, the only place where all Buddhas, from the past, present, and future, attain enlightenment. There, he was visited by Mara, lord of death and desire. This confrontation comes alive in a terracotta panel from eastern India (cat. 1). Under the leafy branches of the bodhi tree, Siddhartha sits cross-legged in deep concentration, his eyes half-closed, with one palm open (half of a meditation mudra) and resting in his lap. Mara stands on the left with a long bow, urging his alluring daughters and fearsome soldiers in attempts to distract. Remaining unperturbed, however, Siddhartha reaches his right hand forward to touch the ground, inviting the earth goddess to witness his rightful claim to enlightenment.

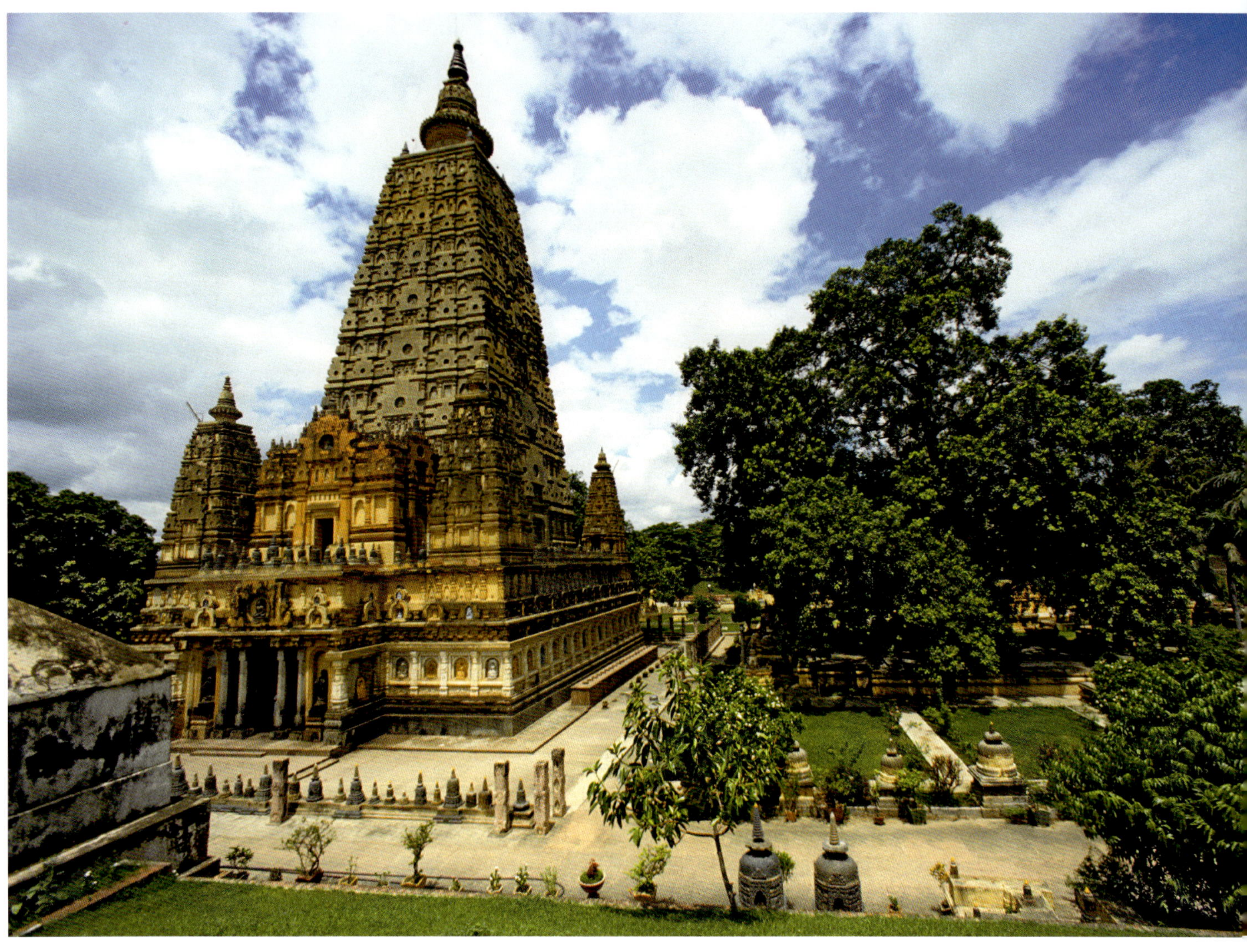

That evening, through his enlightenment beneath the bodhi tree, the Buddha discovered that the root cause of suffering lies in our attachments to impermanent things. In a formulation of cause and effect known as the Four Noble Truths, he taught that suffering exists, that it stems from ignorance and desire, that it can be overcome, and that the means to its cessation is the Eightfold Path, an ethical life dedicated to the cultivation of wisdom and compassion. This fundamental insight from his moment of awakening is summarized in an often-repeated verse form, called the Buddhist creed: "All things arise from a cause, the Tathagata [Buddha] has explained the cause. This cause of things has finally been destroyed. Such is the teaching of the great Shramana [Buddha]."[6]

Bodh Gaya, the place of Buddha's enlightenment, became the holy land in Buddhist culture.[7] It has remained a pilgrimage destination, a place where historical distances collapse — pilgrims could stand where the Buddha achieved enlightenment, connecting directly to that transformative moment across time. The materiality of the site — the rectangular stone slab that marks the vajrasana under the bodhi tree — provides a tangible connection to Buddhism's foundational insight. By the sixth century, the Mahabodhi Temple, a towering stone structure east of the bodhi tree, became the focal point of pilgrimage to Bodh Gaya (fig. 3).[8] The temple once housed a sanctuary that contained the sacred icon of a seated Buddha making the earth-touching mudra (fig. 4).[9] That iconic Vajrasana Buddha, as it is known in India, became the model for faithful replications throughout Buddhist Asia.

The original Vajrasana Buddha in the Mahabodhi Temple has been lost to time. The most informative eyewitness account comes from the Chinese monk Xuanzang (602–664). A scholar and translator of great consequence to

Mahabodhi Temple, Bodh Gaya, India. Photo by John C. Huntington, courtesy of the John C. and Susan L. Huntington Photographic Archive of Buddhist and Asian Art.

East Asian Buddhism, Xuanzang traveled in India and Central Asia over seventeen years and brought home to Tang dynasty China authoritative Buddhist teaching, scriptures, and images.[10] His travelogue, *Records of the Western Regions*, with its rich and accurate details, is still the primary source of seventh-century Buddhist culture and geography in India and Central Asia.[11] Among his descriptions of prominent Buddhist monasteries, universities, and sacred sites, Bodh Gaya and its Vajrasana Buddha occupy a central place. Not only did Xuanzang record the sacred icon's creation story, emphasizing that the Buddha image was made not by human hands but by the future Buddha Maitreya, he also described the Vajrasana Buddha in reverent details, with special attention given to dimensional measurements clearly meant for the image's future replication: "[The Buddha] sits in the lotus position with right foot on top, his left hand resting and right hand reaching down. He sits facing east, dignified as if present. The throne is 4 feet 2 inches in height, and 12 feet 5 inches in width. The figure is 11 feet 5 inches in height. The two knees are 8 feet 8 inches apart, and the width of the two shoulders is 6 feet 2 inches."[12]

In addition to written descriptions, Xuanzang likely brought back visual models to facilitate accurate replications in China. Although his original models no longer exist, the century after his homecoming in 645 saw widespread replications of the Vajrasana Buddha.[13] Scholars have identified nearly forty Chinese paintings and sculptures from the seventh and eighth centuries that pay homage to the Bodh Gaya original. Ranging widely in format and material across great geographic distances, they include massive stone sculptures from Tang dynasty capitals and cave temples in the Western province of Sichuan, as well as painted images on wall murals and silk scrolls preserved in Dunhuang, a frontier garrison on the Silk Road. The most splendid iteration of the Vajrasana Buddha in East Asia is probably the eighth-century Seokguram Buddha in South

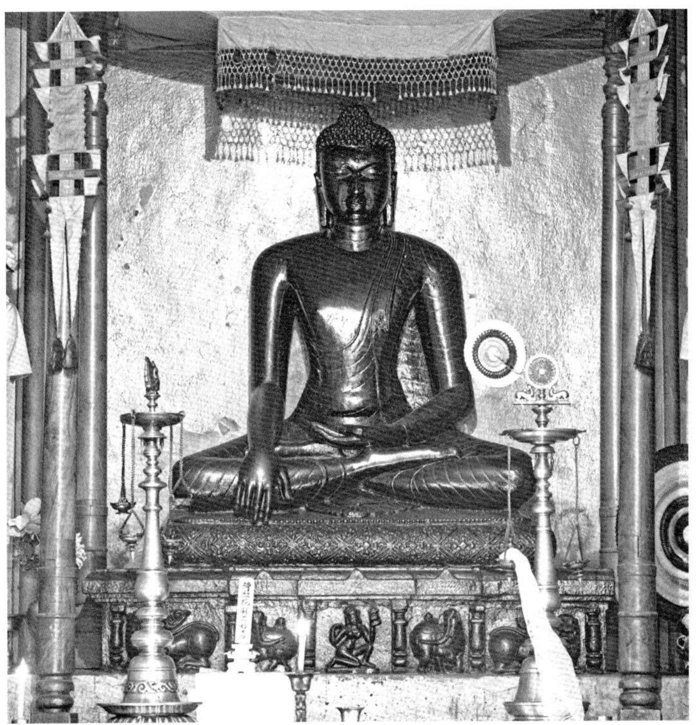

The Vajrasana Buddha in the main shrine of the Mahabodhi Temple, Bodh Gaya, India, c. 11th century, stone. Photographed by John C. Huntington, courtesy of the John C. and Susan L. Huntington Photographic Archive of Buddhist and Asian Art.

Korea. Measuring just over eleven feet tall, the carved granite earth-touching Buddha matches Xuanzang's specifications perfectly, not only in height but also in the exact widths between the knees and the shoulders (fig. 5).[14]

The most revealing material evidence of this transmission process is the mold-pressed clay tablets associated with Buddhist sites in both China and India. Those excavated at temple foundations established by Xuanzang (fig. 6) in China bear striking resemblance to tablets created at Bodh Gaya as commemorative souvenirs for pilgrims (fig. 7). Although surviving examples from Bodh Gaya date to the ninth through tenth centuries, after Xuanzang's era, both tablet varieties likely derived from an earlier Bodh Gaya prototype, as suggested by their design uniformity. In addition to their shared details of beaded border and treatment of the Buddha's diaphanous robe, barely visible except for hemlines across the chest and at the ankles, what remains constant across these tablets is a meaningful combination of three elements: the earth-touching Buddha, the distinctive towers of the Mahabodhi Temple with branches of the bodhi tree, and the Buddhist creed inscription ("All things arise from a cause . . .") in Sanskrit and in Chinese translation. This three-part formula encapsulates the original experience of Bodh Gaya — Buddha, place, and Dharma — collapsing the distance between the sculpture pilgrims saw, the historical Buddha on the night of enlightenment, and the profound insight achieved there.

This understanding deepens our appreciation of the bronze earth-touching Buddha in the Xuzhou Collection (cat. 2). The Buddha is fully realized in the sculptural idioms of its time. The high forehead and full cheeks, the stylized folds that contour the body, and the superb casting and silver inlay make the image one of the finest from tenth-century India. Stylistically, it must have been distinct from the Vajrasana Buddha of centuries earlier. Nonetheless, created in Bihar, home to Bodh Gaya, this bronze would have derived special power from its proximity

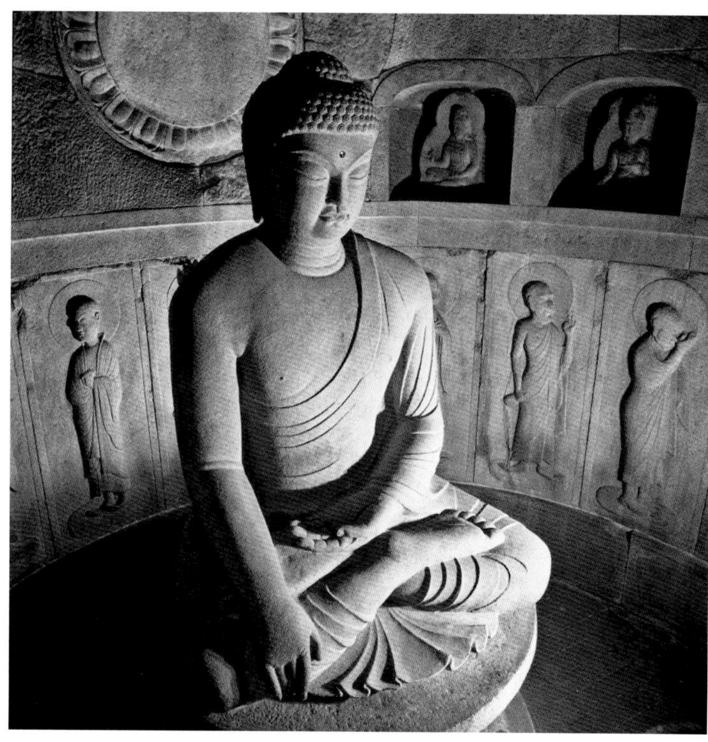

Fig. 5

Statue of Buddha inside the main chamber, Seokguram, Kyongju, South Korea, c. 8th century, granite.

to the holy site — a significance that would have followed it as it traveled far from its source, likely to Southeast Asia as suggested by the later embellishment of its eyes.[15] For devotees distant from the holy site, such bronzes offered a tangible connection to Buddha's enlightenment in Bodh Gaya.

Tibet also participated in the tradition of faithful replications of the Vajrasana Buddha from Bodh Gaya from the tenth through thirteenth centuries, an important era for the transmission of Buddhism and the founding of Buddhist institutions. A specific group of sculptures emerged as direct replicas of the Vajrasana Buddha, transmitted by pilgrims and monks traveling between India and Tibet.[16] However, the three Tibetan examples in the Xuzhou Collection have only a tenuous relation to the Bodh Gaya original, demonstrating how this iconography continued to evolve within local traditions. In Tibetan Buddhist art, the

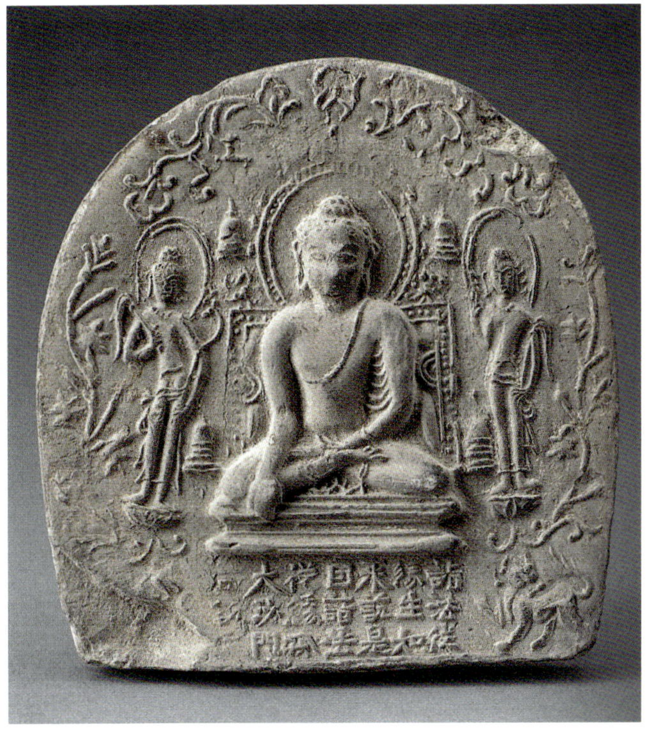

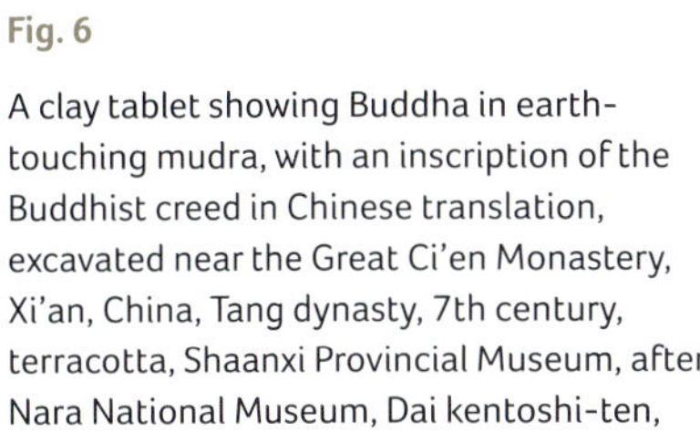

Fig. 6

A clay tablet showing Buddha in earth-touching mudra, with an inscription of the Buddhist creed in Chinese translation, excavated near the Great Ci'en Monastery, Xi'an, China, Tang dynasty, 7th century, terracotta, Shaanxi Provincial Museum, after Nara National Museum, *Dai kentoshi-ten*, pl. 106 right.

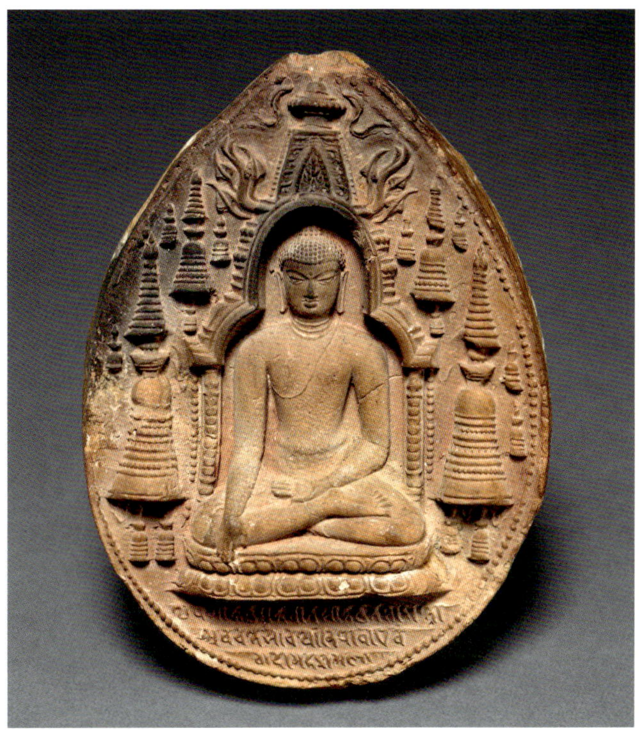

Fig. 7

A clay tablet showing Buddha in earth-touching mudra, the temple at Bodh Gaya, and stupas, c. 800s, terracotta, Cleveland Museum of Art, gift of Michael De Havenon 1985.219.

earth-touching mudra is not exclusively the identifying gesture of the historical Buddha. It is also associated with the Akshobhya Buddha, one of the Five Wisdom Buddhas representing different aspects of enlightened consciousness. The Xuzhou Collection includes a small Buddha figure with copper and silver inlay that could be either the historical Buddha or Akshobhya (cat. 15); a thirteenth-century gilt bronze displaying the mudra in mirror image — with the left hand reaching forward instead of the right (cat. 16); and a standing figure identifiable as Akshobhya based on its now-missing original hands making the earth-touching mudra (cat. 14). Unlike the faithful replications that meant to carry the power and meaning of the original Bodh Gaya icon, these examples represent a significant departure, serving new devotional purposes in their local context.

Looking at these Buddhist sculptures today is like gazing at stars in the night sky — we see distinct points of light and try to trace the constellations that connect them, knowing we are glimpsing only fragments of a vast universe. The terracotta panel, Pala bronze, and Tibetan adaptations shine like individual stars, each brilliant in its own right, yet each suggesting patterns of connection far beyond what we can fully map. It is not possible to comprehend the universe of meaning that these objects once inhabited; however, understanding that the images did exist and function within complex networks — of pilgrimage, of replication, of ritual use, of spiritual teaching — sharpens how we see them.

Approaching Buddhist images today, despite the absence of the sanctuaries where they once resided or the ritual practices that animated them, the awareness of these works as convergence points within vast webs of spiritual transmission invites us into a more profound engagement with their meaning and power. Each sculpture functions as a multilayered vessel, embodying spiritual practices through

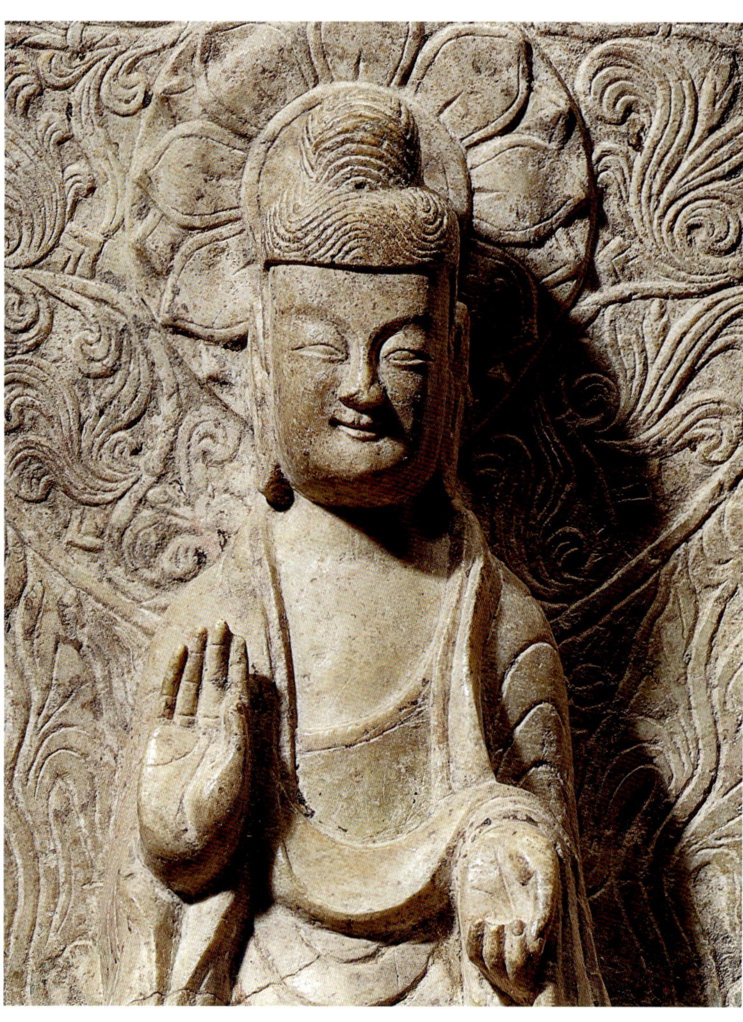

their forms, containing direct expressions of Buddhist
wisdom, and preserving the devotional lineages through
which they traveled. As such, they invite viewers to engage
with them not merely as art objects but as portals to
reflection and insight. The Northern Wei *Buddhist Triad*
(fig. 8) speaks with unexpected relevance to our current
moment. The Buddha's gentle smile accompanies his
eloquent gestures: one hand raised in *abhaya* mudra,
meaning "fear not," while the other extends downward in
varada mudra, granting blessings. In our era of environmental and political challenges, this pair of hands brackets the
distance between fear and denial, encouraging individual

action tempered with equanimity. Though this interpretation brings contemporary concerns to an ancient work,
it demonstrates how Buddhist sculptures continue to
function as teaching vehicles responsive to the questions
we bring, helping us discover our own Middle Way. Like the
lacquer Buddha head with which we began — its glass
eyes both seeing and being seen — these sculptures invite
a reciprocal gaze across time. In this mutual encounter,
these forms remain vibrant conduits of meaning, offering
insight into and reassurance for our present circumstances, just as they did for those who stood before them
centuries ago.

Notes

The author wishes to thank Professor Susan L. Huntington and Professor Karen Hwang for reading drafts of this essay, and for their erudite and insightful advice. The remaining errors are my own.

1. For the lacquer construction of the Buddha head, see Donna Strahan's essay "Technical Case Study: A Tang Dynasty Hollow-Core Lacquer Buddha Head" in this volume (pages 112–17).

2. Zhang Zhetan, "A Study on Origin and Localization of Moving Buddha Image in Middle Age, Zhonggu fojiao xingxiang yishi de xingqi ji bentuhua," *Buddhist Studies* (2020): 158–71.

3. For further discussion of ritual viewing in Buddhist context, see Susan L. Huntington's essay "Creating Merit: Art in Buddhist Practice" in this volume (pages 22–27). See also Diana Eck, *Darsan: Seeing the Divine Image in India* (Columbia University Press, 1998).

4. For stories on the origin and subsequent travels of the "Udayana image," see Donald S. Lopez, "Chapter Three: Art," in *Buddhism: A Journey Through History* (Yale University Press, 2024), 112–23.

5. The *bhumisparsha* mudra, commonly known as the earth-touching mudra, is a hand gesture assumed by the Buddha Shakyamuni, who at his defeat of Mara called upon the earth goddess to witness his enlightenment. A seated Buddha image holding the earth-touching mudra is known as Buddha Calling the Earth to Witness, or Maravijaya, meaning triumph over Mara.

6. Daniel Boucher, "The Pratityasamutpadagatha and Its Role in the Medieval Cult of the Relics," *Journal of the International Association of Buddhist Studies* 14 (1991): 1–27.

7. Janice Leoshko, "The Significance of Bodh Gaya," in Adriana Proser, ed., *Pilgrimage and Buddhist Art* (Asia Society Museum, Yale University Press, 2010), 10–13.

8. John Guy, "The Mahabodhi Temple: Pilgrim Souvenirs of Buddhist India," *Burlington Magazine* 133, no. 1059 (June 1991): 356–67. John C. Huntington, "Sowing the Seeds of the Lotus: A Journey to the Great Pilgrimage Sites of Buddhism, Part I," *Orientations* (November 1985): 46–61.

9. Janice Leoshko, "Time and Time Again: Finding Perspective for Bodhgaya Buddha Imagery," *Ars Orientalis* 50 (Miraculous Images in Asian Traditions) (2020): 6–32.

10. Max Deeg, "The Historical Turn: How Chinese Buddhist Travelogues Changed Western Perception of Buddhism," *Hualin International Journal of Buddhist Studies* 1, no. 1 (2018): 43–75.

11. Xuanzang with Bianji, *Da Tang Xiyu Ji*, first printed in 646.

12. Translation based on Samuel Beal, trans., *Buddhist Records of the Western World*, reprint edition (San Francisco, 1976).

13. On the topic of replication of Vajrasana Buddha in Tang dynasty China, see Li Yumin, "Shilun Tangdai xiangmo chengdao shi zhuangshi fo," in *Gugong xueshu jikan, The National Palace Museum Research Quarterly* 23, no. 3 (2006): 39–157. Sun-ah Choi, "Zhenrong to Ruixiang: The Medieval Chinese Reception of the Mahabodhi Buddha Statue," *Art Bulletin* 97, no. 4 (December 2015): 364–87. Dorothy Wong, "The Light-Emitting Image of Magadha in Tang Buddhist Art," *Ars Orientalis* 50 (Miraculous Images in Asian Traditions) (2020): 33–54.

14. U-bang Kang, *Korean Buddhist Sculpture: Art and Truth*, trans. Cho Yoonjung (Art Media Resources, Youlhwadang Publisher, 2005), 97–124.

15. Suggested by Jane Casey, see page 42.

16. Jane Casey Singer, "Tibetan Homage to Bodh Gaya," *Orientations* 32, no. 10 (2001): 44–51.

Creating Merit

ART IN BUDDHIST PRACTICE

by Susan L. Huntington

Buddhism may be understood as a set of teachings that fosters the spiritual advancement of the devotee. Critical to this progress is earning what is called *punya*, or merit, and negating *papa*, the unvirtuous acts that cause suffering to oneself and others. The goal is to improve one's karma. Predicated on the concept of causality — that all events are caused by preceding events — karma is the fruition of all of one's thoughts, words, and actions, both good and bad, in this life and in past lives. In this way, Buddhism attributes full agency to all living beings and therefore the power to determine one's own karma. Simply, creating good karma is the focus of a Buddhist life. Merit toward one's karma can be accrued in a variety of ways, both informal and formal. A spontaneous act of kindness in daily life can increase one's merit, as can undertaking rigorous practices designed specifically for that purpose. The residents of a Buddhist monastery, for example, spend their days engaged in structured activities that are intended to increase merit, such as meditation and the study of Buddhist texts. Buddhists, both lay and monastic, may also observe guidelines for daily life that include strict dietary practices and physical austerities to add to their store of merit.

Although not usually recognized as such, works of art play an integral role in Buddhist merit-creating. Images are encountered everywhere in Buddhism — in monasteries, shrines, and homes. Although many works are breathtaking in their beauty and technical virtuosity, they do not serve merely as decoration. Instead, they are fully functional participants in Buddhist practice. Endowed with agency through consecration rituals, Buddhist images are actively invoked and are fully expected to respond to the devotee's supplications. Images can also be the focus of deep concentration for advanced practitioners, can instruct devotees in the Buddhist teachings, and can illustrate inspirational stories of meritorious behavior. Along with proffering merit to those who use images in their Buddhist practice, images also confer merit on the patrons and artists who created them.[1]

MERIT FOR DEVOTEES

One of the most important ways that devotees engage with Buddhist images is through a process of visual communion known as darshan, or seeing.[2] The physical act of seeing is itself meritorious, and even an accidental glance at an image can be beneficial. Buddhists particularly wish to see the Buddha of our era, Shakyamuni, who lived in India in the fifth century BCE. Since he is no longer available in this world for his followers to see, his images serve as his surrogates.

A Buddha is a being who has completed the meritorious path to perfection and who therefore serves as an exemplar. Reaching this perfection, called bodhi (enlightenment or awakening), is unimaginably difficult and occurs over the course of many lifetimes in the cycle of rebirths known as samsara. What determines one's status in each life is the cumulative karma one has accrued. Good karma is rewarded with a higher rebirth, either from a lower animal form to human or to higher status as a human, and the retribution for bad karma is a lower rebirth. The ultimate purpose of perfecting one's karma in Buddhism is to attain nirvana, and thereby escape from samsara and its suffering.

Upon his enlightenment, Shakyamuni was able to recall the slow and arduous process by which he accrued good karma and thereby was able to reach bodhi and nirvana. In each lifetime, whether he was an animal or a human, he performed meritorious acts that increased his cumulative karma. To ease the path for all other living beings, Shakyamuni chose to share his knowledge about how to achieve this hard-won state. His teachings, called the Dharma, impart the methods for attaining both bodhi and nirvana. Passed down through the centuries for more than two thousand years, the teachings describe how merit can be accumulated by following the Noble Eightfold Path.

Images of Shakyamuni Buddha abound throughout the Buddhist world. The Xuzhou Collection includes a number of examples such as those illustrated here (figs. 1–3), representing many of the most important artistic styles that developed as Buddhism spread from its homeland in India to Central Asia, China, Japan, the Himalayas, and Southeast Asia.[3] In each of these regions, artists adapted the form of the figure, the clothing, and even the facial features to suit their own cultural tastes. For example, a seated Buddha figure from the ancient greater Gandhara region shows the Buddha wearing a heavy garment with prominent folds that covers both shoulders (fig. 1). The drapery, along with the wavy hairstyle and articulated musculature of the torso, reveals artistic connections between western Asia and the Mediterranean world. A metal image from Thailand bears facial features reflecting the appearance of the local populace (fig. 2). And a sculpture from Tibet shows further distinctions in garment, body type, and physiognomy (fig. 3).

Despite these stylistic and regional variations, the essential iconographic features of a Buddha image are standardized. Another Buddha image and a masterpiece in the Xuzhou Collection displays these easily recognizable characteristics. Created in eastern India during the tenth century, this metal sculpture shows the Buddha seated on a lotus pedestal that symbolizes his transcendence (fig. 4). Although Shakyamuni was born as a prince, he renounced the jewelry, luxurious garments, and long tresses of hair befitting his royal station when he decided to pursue the path to spiritual perfection. His stretched earlobes are a reminder that he had forsaken the heavy earrings he wore as a youth, and the tight curls on his head became standard components of Buddha imagery. He wears a simple monk's robe, reflecting the life of renunciation he had adopted. When he was born, though not yet an enlightened being, Shakyamuni already had thirty-two auspicious marks on his body that signified both the good karma he had accrued

over the course of his past lives and his destiny to achieve greatness. Among these marks, several are commonly shown in artistic portrayals, such as the small dot between his eyes in his forehead (*urna*) and the protuberance at the top of his head (*ushnisha*). Together, these and other physical features go beyond making the Buddha image recognizable; for the devotee, they serve as points of contemplation and instruction.

The eyes are commonly a particular focal point in the image, enabling the devotee and the Buddha to gaze at one another in mutual darshan. The eyes, commonly "opened" and thus awakening the image at the time it is consecrated, can be highlighted through painting, inlay, carving, or other means. Here, the treatment of the eyes may be a later restoration, but even the original was likely to have been inlaid with silver, with drilled pupils, as was typical during this phase of art.

Other standardized features of Buddha images, especially the hand gestures and leg positions, inform and inspire the viewer. The legs in this image are crossed in the *vajrasana* pose commonly used during Buddhist meditation for bodily stability and stillness. The Buddha's left hand rests in his lap, palm upward, in a gesture of meditation. The right hand reaches downward in the "earth-touching" gesture, which signifies that the Buddha is calling the earth goddess to witness the certainty of his attainment of perfect knowledge (bodhi).

Stories about the final life of the Buddha and his previous lives are common themes in Buddhist art, both inspiring and instructing the viewer. One relief sculpture in the Xuzhou Collection depicts an event in the life of the prince who became Shakyamuni Buddha (fig. 5). The scene shows the youth, then known as Siddhartha, in the harem of his father's palace. Overcome by a sense of the vulgarity of the women while they slept, the prince renounced all earthly desires and attachments and decided to pursue the path that led to his eventual enlightenment and nirvana. This

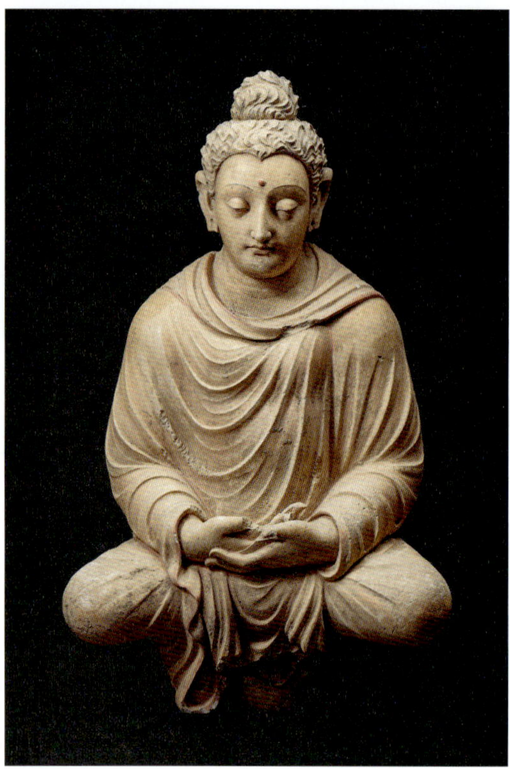

Fig. 1

Buddha in Meditation, ancient region of Gandhara, Pakistan or Afghanistan, c. 5th century, polychrome stucco (cat. 4).

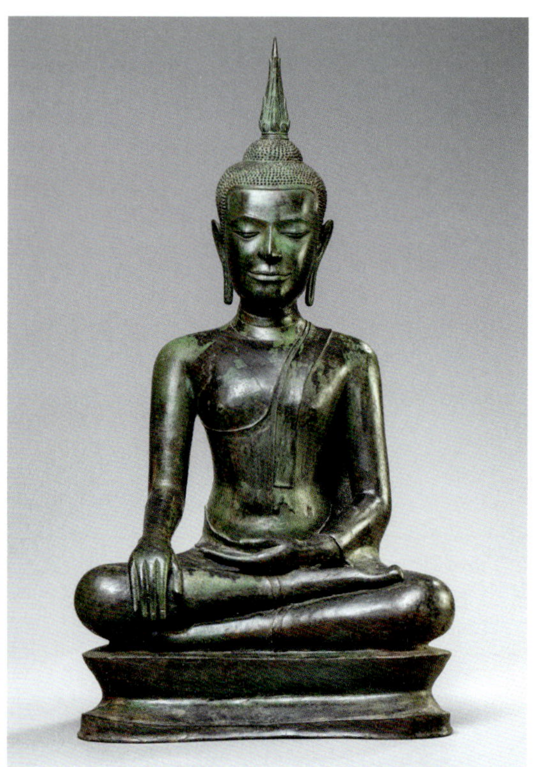

Fig. 2

Buddha Maravijaya, Calling the Earth to Witness, Thailand, U-Thong style, c. 14th century, copper alloy (cat. 11).

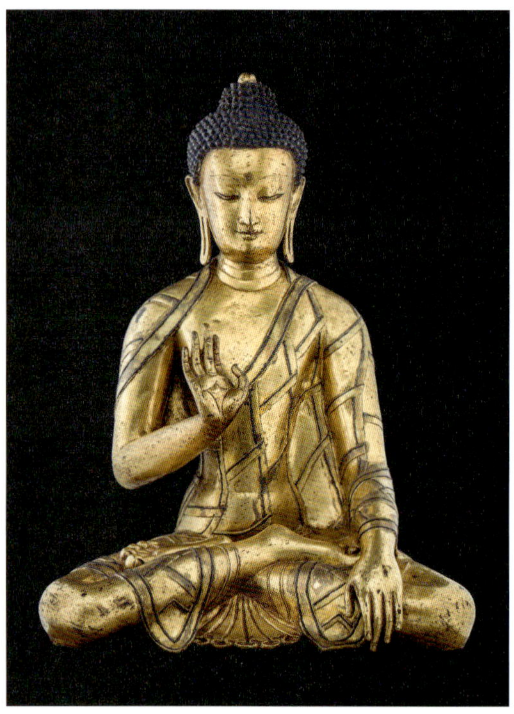

Fig. 3

Buddha Shakyamuni, Tibet, c. 13th century, gilt copper with silver inlay, pigment (cat. 16).

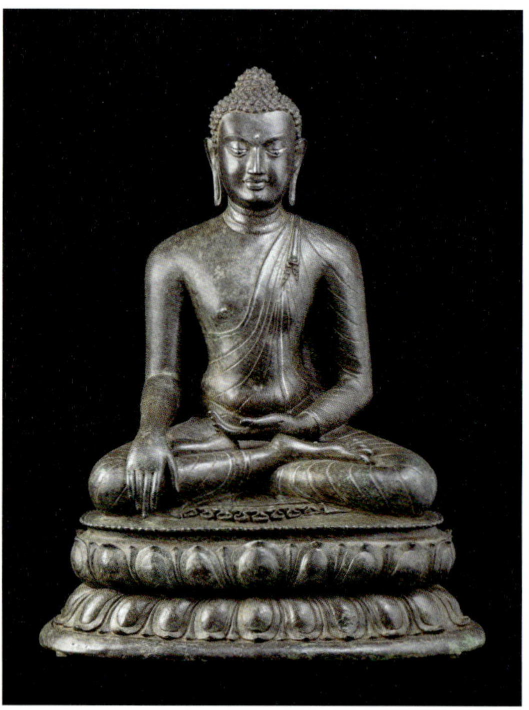

Fig. 4

Buddha Maravijaya, Calling the Earth to Witness, India, Bihar, c. 10th century, copper alloy and silver inlay (cat. 2).

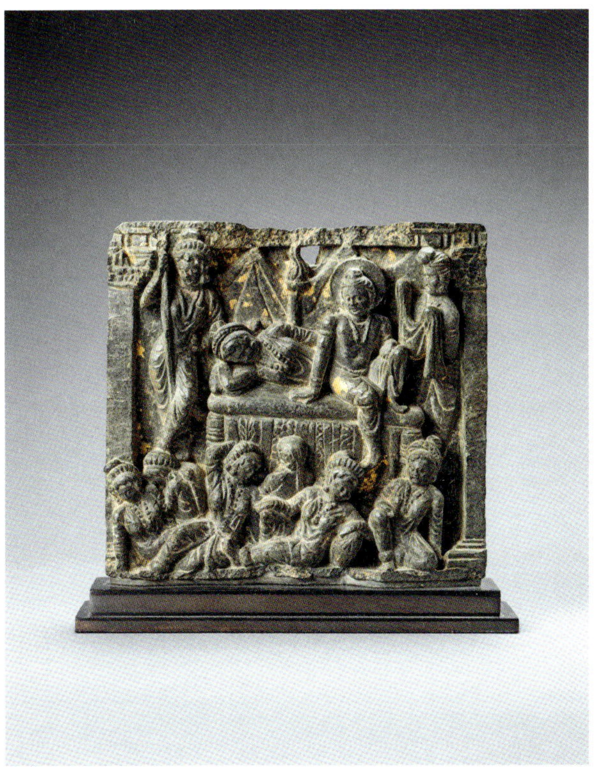

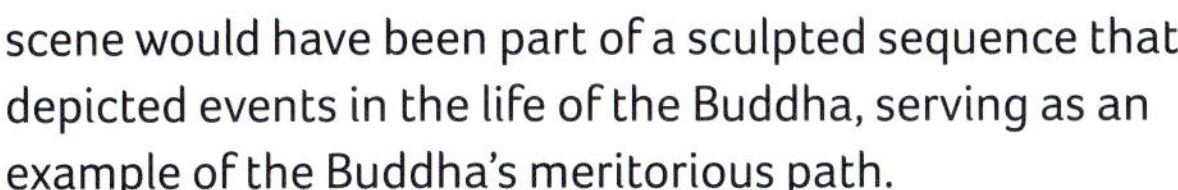

Fig. 5

The Renunciation of Prince Siddhartha, ancient region of Gandhara, Pakistan or Afghanistan, c. 2nd–3rd century, schist stone and traces of gold (cat. 3).

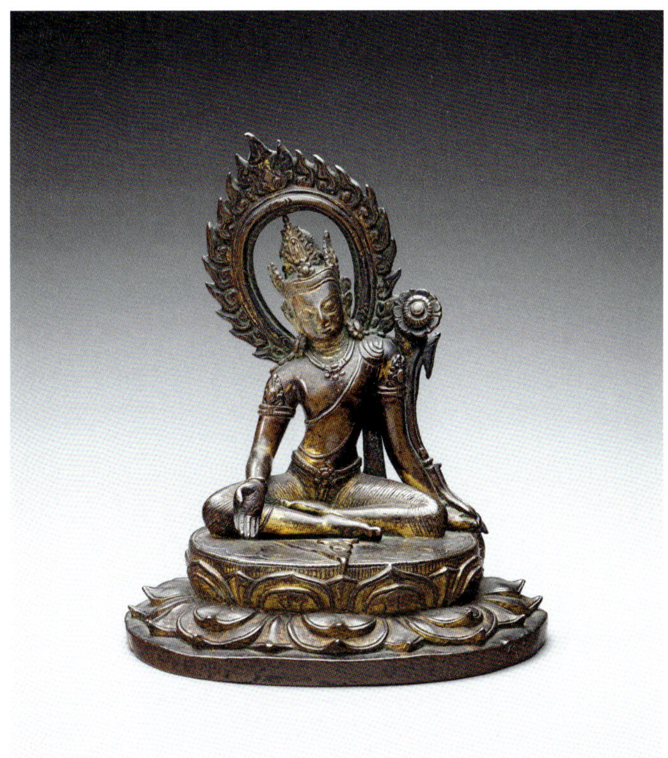

Fig. 6

Padmapani, Lotus-Bearing Avalokiteshvara, Nepal, c. 10th century, gilt copper and pigment (cat. 12).

scene would have been part of a sculpted sequence that depicted events in the life of the Buddha, serving as an example of the Buddha's meritorious path.

Along with their emphasis on Shakyamuni, Buddhists take darshan of other inspiring beings, particularly bodhisattvas. A bodhisattva is a being who has resolved to become a Buddha — even a beginner on the Buddhist path can be called a bodhisattva. However, artistic representations usually depict the *mahasattva*, or Great Being, bodhisattvas. Among these exalted beings is Avalokiteshvara, the Bodhisattva of Compassion. Although he is fully enlightened and therefore qualified to attain nirvana, Avalokiteshvara has vowed to remain active in the world to help others until all sentient beings have been liberated from suffering in the cycle of samsara. Unsurprisingly, Avalokiteshvara is one of the most popular figures in Buddhism and a focus of devotion and practice throughout the Buddhist world.

A Nepali sculpture in the Xuzhou Collection shows Avalokiteshvara seated gracefully on a circular lotus (fig. 6). He sits in a relaxed posture that makes him appear approachable to his devotees. His generosity and compassion are expressed by his right hand, which points downward, with the palm open toward to the viewer in the gift-giving gesture (*varada* mudra). The left hand holds the stem of his emblematic lotus flower, which rises and blossoms above his left shoulder. A halo around his head indicates his transcendent nature.

Another important mahasattva bodhisattva is Vajrapani, "bearer of the *vajra*." A small, silver sculpture from Indonesia in the Xuzhou Collection portrays him seated in a relaxed posture (fig. 7). His identifying feature, a vajra, appears atop the flower stalk he holds in his left hand. As a symbol of indestructible power, the vajra signifies Vajrapani's unwavering dedication to helping devotees defeat obstacles on their path.

Beyond the beings discussed here, the Buddhist universe is populated by a plethora of other exalted figures. Although encountering this vast array of personages can seem overwhelming, all of them help reify the basic principles of Buddhism and the nature of the universe as conceived by Buddhists. By giving concrete, visual form to concepts that

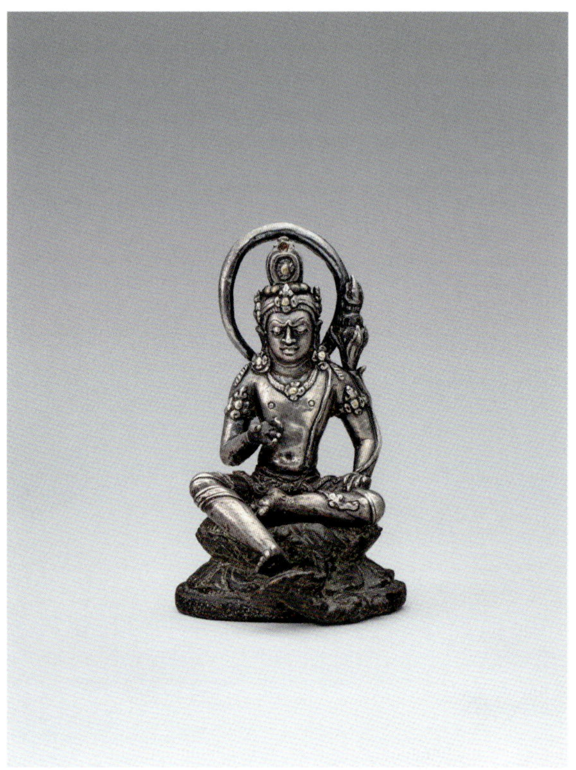

Bodhisattva Vajrapani, Java, Indonesia,
c. 9th–10th century, silver with gold inlay
and copper-alloy base (cat. 10).

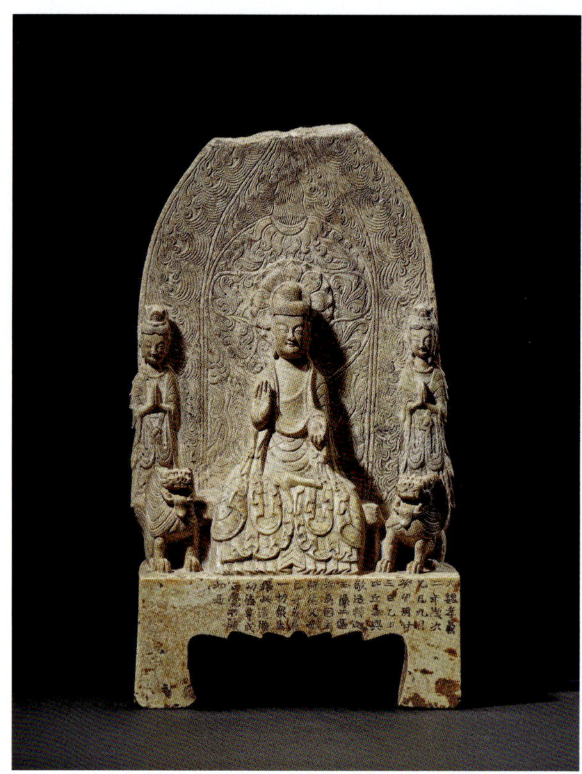

Buddhist Triad, China, Northern Wei dynasty,
dated 526 CE, limestone (cat. 20).

might otherwise seem abstract and unfathomable, Buddhist art is one of the most powerful instruments available to devotees on their path to attainment.

MERIT FOR PATRONS AND ARTISTS

The seventh-century Chinese monk Yijing, known for his record of his travels to Buddhist pilgrimage sites, voiced the widespread belief regarding the merit that accrues from the creation of images, noting that if "a man makes an image even as small as a grain of barley . . . he will obtain special good causes as limitless as the seven seas, and his good rewards will last as long as four rebirths."[4] Image-making merit is also extolled in numerous Buddhist texts and is well known in dedicatory inscriptions on many works of art. Both the patrons who commissioned the works and the artists who created them are beneficiaries of the merit earned.

Inscriptions on two Chinese sculptures in the Xuzhou Collection express the merit-increasing objectives of their patrons.[5] The first is inscribed with a dedication by the Monk Faxing (fig. 8). This stone sculpture depicts Shakyamuni Buddha flanked by a pair of attendants with their hands clasped in a gesture of reverence. The epigraph, located on the front of the base, begins with a date for the gift, which is equivalent to 526 CE, and then identifies the subject of this and a second image, not in the Xuzhou Collection, both representing the Buddha Shakyamuni. Rather than requesting the merit from this gift for himself, Faxing asks that it benefit the emperor, teachers and disciples, parents and relations, and all sentient beings. Expressing the epitome of generosity and compassion, this request to transfer merit (*parinamana*) from oneself to others is a widespread practice in many forms of Buddhism.[6]

A slightly earlier image of Shakyamuni in the Xuzhou Collection, a gilt bronze, also bears a donative inscription (cat. 19).[7] Along with the name of the donor, Qiu Jinu, the epigraph records the date, equivalent to 471 CE, and requests that the merit be transferred to the donor's mother and father. The specific request asks that they be reborn in a paradise, where they would be able to meet all Buddhas, or, if they are reborn in this world, that they be dukes, kings, or elders. Both the desire that merit be transferred to all sentient beings and the request to transfer merit to one's parents are the most common aspirations for merit transfer in Buddhism.

The names of patrons are widely recorded in Buddhist epigraphs wherever Buddhism traveled. In contrast, we know the identities of only a few of the artists who created the images that filled the shrines, monasteries, and homes of Buddhist devotees over the millennia. The loss of these names over time, however, does not diminish the crucial role that artists have played in Buddhism. Patronized by emperors and kings, monks and nuns, and laypeople alike, artists have brought their skills, talent, and imagination to bear on the endeavor to provide objects of meditation, ritual, and devotion and to give form to concepts that might otherwise be difficult to visualize. Together, patrons and artists create one of the most important tools to facilitate progress on the Buddhist path for devotees.

CONCLUDING COMMENTS

Modern audiences are accustomed to seeing sculptures, paintings, and other works of art in museums, but museums are not the natural habitat for Buddhist works of art. Rather, Buddhist art is intended to function in the daily life of Buddhist adherents. The pervasiveness of images and imagery in Buddhism, as well as the vast resources and effort that have been devoted to their creation over millennia, is testament to the fact that art serves a critical role in merit-creating activities. The superbly crafted and aesthetically exquisite works in the Xuzhou Collection demonstrate that works of art dedicated to Buddhist ends can surpass a mere didactic or functional purpose to stand alongside some of the world's greatest artistic achievements. By serving as custodians of these precious works and allowing them to be put on display, collectors of Buddhist art also offer a meritorious gift to the museum-going public, including both those who have already embraced Buddhism and those for whom it opens a new world of understanding and appreciation.

Notes

1. For an outstanding overview of the role of images in Buddhism, see Robert M. Sharf, "Prolegomenon to the Study of Japanese Buddhist Icons," in Robert M. Sharf and Elizabeth Horton Sharf, *Living Images: Japanese Buddhist Icons in Practice* (Stanford University Press, 2001), especially 1–7.
2. For discussion of darshan as well as other ways in which devotees interact with Buddhist images, see Susan L. Huntington, "The Agency of Images," in *The Oxford Handbook of Buddhist Practice*, ed. Paula Arai and Kevin Trainor (Oxford University Press, 2022), chapter 9, 148–75.
3. Full discussion of these and the other images illustrated in this essay can be found in the corresponding catalogue entries.
4. Sramana Yijing, *A Record of the Inner Law Sent Home from the South Seas*, trans. Li Rongxi (Numata Center for Buddhist Translation and Research, 2000), 138.
5. I am grateful to Hao Sheng for providing me with his translations of both of these inscriptions.
6. Although the transfer of merit is commonly thought to be characteristic of Mahayana (Great Vehicle) Buddhism in particular, it is in fact found throughout the Buddhist world.
7. A gilt-bronze image of Avalokiteshvara of about the same size in the British Museum was also dedicated by Qiu Jinu.

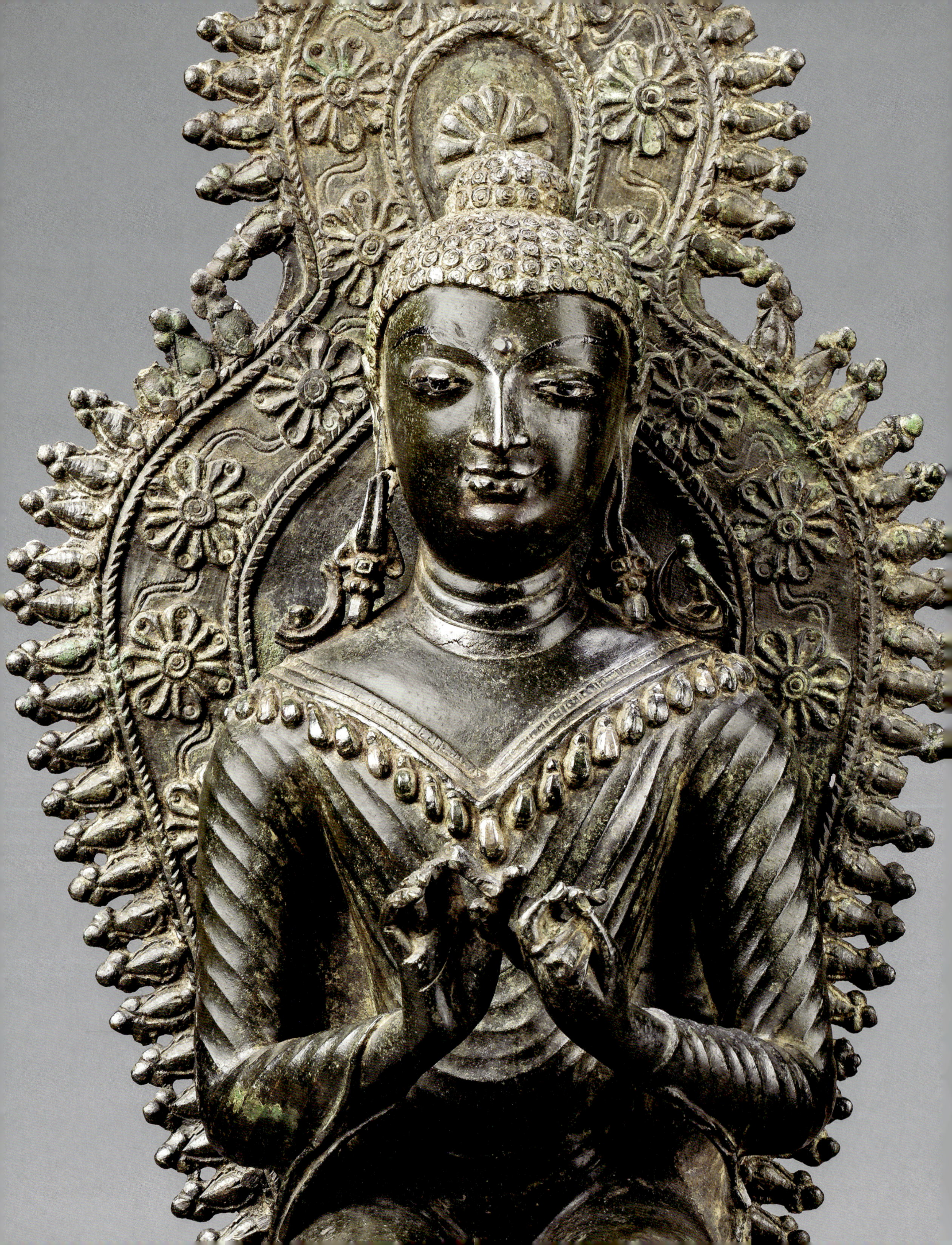

Maitreya

by Donald S. Lopez

Buddhist scriptures speak of the Buddhas of the past, the present, and the future. The Buddha of the Future will appear in our world when the teachings of the previous Buddha, our Buddha, Shakyamuni Buddha, have disappeared into oblivion. Although his advent is millions of years away, we know his name and location. This image, likely produced in the eighth or ninth century in the Swat Valley, now part of Pakistan, is said to represent him (fig. 1).[1] His name is Maitreya ("kindness" in Sanskrit). Here, he is seated on a throne, already with the crown protrusion atop his head, one of the thirty-two "marks of a great being" that adorn the body of a Buddha. He resides in a heaven called Tushita (Joyous) located in the skies above Mount Meru, the center of the Buddhist cosmos.

Maitreya is mentioned only once in the Pali canon, the scriptures of the Theravada, the Buddhist tradition of Sri Lanka and Southeast Asia. However, he descends to earth in a number of important sutras of the Mahayana tradition of Tibet and East Asia, sometimes as a member of the Buddha's audience, other times as an important interlocutor, as in the Lotus Sutra, the Vimalakirti Sutra, and the Gandavyuha Sutra. As the Buddha of the present moved further and further into the past, the Buddha of the Future became more and more important.

The Buddha is said to have set forth forty different topics of meditation from which monks and nuns could choose. One of the most popular is called "recollection of the Buddha" (*buddhanusmrti*), in which one calls to mind the magnificence of the Buddha by contemplating this sentence: "The Blessed One is accomplished, fully enlightened, endowed with clear vision and virtuous conduct, sublime, the knower of worlds, the incomparable leader of humans to be tamed, the teacher of gods and humans, enlightened and blessed."

It is important to recall that images of the Buddha in the form that he is known today did not begin to appear in India until the early second century of the Common Era, some five centuries after he passed into nirvana. With the creation of those images, the practice of "recollection of the Buddha" would come to include visualization of the Buddha. Texts instruct meditators to sit before an image of the Buddha, staring at it until they are able to visualize the Buddha in perfect detail in their mind. Also in the second century of Common Era, monks in what is today Kashmir began to make Maitreya the focus of their practice of "recollection of the Buddha." Some sought to receive his teachings; others sought to be reborn in Tushita and to join his retinue when he descends to restore Buddhism to our world. This statue, produced centuries later, may have been used for that purpose.

The most famous story of meeting Maitreya involves the fourth-century Indian monk Asanga (fig. 2); indeed, the story is so famous that it is often told in the presence of an image of Maitreya, like this one. Asanga was one of the most important figures in the history of Buddhism. He was the founding philosopher of the Mind Only School and the author of an important text on meditation, in which he set forth the practice of visualizing the Buddha. He was born in the city of Purushapura in Gandhara, today the city of Peshawar in Pakistan. Because Asanga knew so much, when he had a question, no one could give him the answer. Therefore, he decided to take his questions to the future Buddha.

In order to meet him, Asanga left his monastery and went to meditate in a cave, where he prayed for Maitreya to appear. After three years, he still had no success. About to give up, he saw a man rubbing an iron spike with a piece of cloth. When Asanga asked him what he was doing, the man said that he was a tailor and made his own sewing needles. Asanga was incredulous until the man opened a small box and showed him the needles he had already made. Inspired by the tailor's persistence, Asanga returned to the cave to entreat Maitreya once again. Another three years passed without success. He gave up, but was then inspired

Buddha Enthroned (detail), greater Kashmir region, India or Pakistan, c. 8th–9th century, copper alloy with silver inlay, body halo not original to sculpture (cat. 7).

Unknown artist, *Indian Teacher – Asanga*, Tibet, 1800–1899, ground mineral pigment on cotton, Rubin Museum of Art, P1996.20.6. In this Tibetan composition, the centrally seated Asanga is surrounded with images from his biography: Asanga meditating in a cave in the upper right corner, caring for the dog in the lower left, and receiving teaching from Maitreya in the upper left.

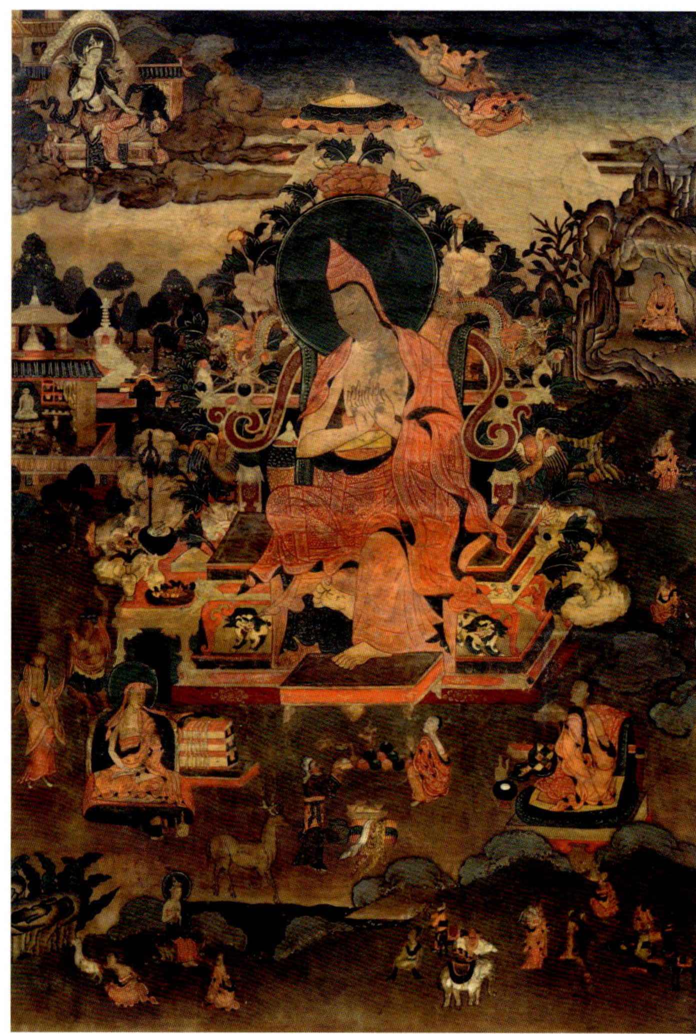

to try again. Then another three years passed; despair was followed by recommitment. Ultimately, he spent twelve years meditating in the cave, with no sign of Maitreya. As Asanga gathered his robes and begging bowl to return to his monastery, he saw a dog lying outside the cave. She had a gaping wound that was filled with maggots.

Asanga took pity on the dog and knelt down to clean the wound. Picking up a stick, he was about to scrape the maggots away when he remembered that the maggots were sentient beings as well, equally deserving of his pity. If he removed them, he would deprive them of their food. Yet he had to save the dog. When a passerby approached, Asanga traded his monk's staff for the man's knife and cut a piece of flesh from his own thigh. He placed it next to the dog and was about to transfer the maggots when he realized that if he used the stick, or even his own fingers, he would kill some of the maggots. The only safe means of transfer was his own tongue. To avoid becoming nauseous, he covered his eyes with his hand, stuck out his tongue, and lowered his head to begin moving the maggots. Yet instead of touching the warm flesh of the infected wound, his tongue touched the cold stone of the cave floor. Uncovering his eyes, he raised his head to see that the dog was gone. Maitreya was standing before him in all his glory.

Understandably confused and somewhat disgruntled, he told the future Buddha that he had been praying to him for twelve years. Maitreya explained that he had been with Asanga all that time, he just could not see him. When Asanga doubted him, Maitreya pointed to the crumbs of food and dried saliva encrusted on his resplendent raiment; he had been so close to Asanga each day that his robes had become soiled when the monk ate his daily meal. Asanga had been unable to see Maitreya because of obstacles in own mind, obstacles that were not removed by twelve years of prayer and meditation; they were removed by a moment of kindness. Asanga still did not believe him, and so, in one of the stranger scenes in Buddhist literature, Maitreya

instructed Asanga to pick him up and carry him into town. No one saw Maitreya. An old woman saw a monk carrying a dog. Maitreya told Asanga to put him down and grab hold of his robe. He then flew up to Tushita heaven, where Asanga spent one celestial morning, the equivalent of fifty human years, returning to earth with what are called the "five books of Maitreya," some of the most influential treatises of Mahayana Buddhism.

Eventually, Maitreya will appear in our world for a longer stay. In Buddhism, the world — a world that is the product of our collective karma — passes through various cosmic stages. The current stage, called the Stage of Abiding, also passes through cycles, in which the lifespan of humans rises and falls. At present, the cycle is on a downward slope, with the human lifespan decreasing, eventually dropping to ten years, after which it will rise again until it reaches eighty thousand years. During this period of decline, not only will the conditions of the world deteriorate but also the dharma will disappear.

This decline is attributed to what are called the "five degradations": the degradation of the lifespan, because the human lifespan decreases; the degradation of views, because wrong views become rampant; the degradation of afflictions, because negative emotions like desire and hatred become stronger; the degradation of sentient beings, because both their physical and mental powers weaken; and the degradation of the eon, because the physical environment deteriorates over time. As these degradations grow, the ability to follow the path to enlightenment declines to the point that enlightenment becomes impossible. But when does that period begin? And, more importantly, has it already begun? Various calculations have been made over the centuries. In Japan, it was concluded that the period of the decline of the dharma began in 1052. Especially in East Asia, the faithful have therefore decided not to wait for Maitreya but to seek to be reborn in a different universe, the western paradise called Sukhavati, the Land of Bliss, the abode of the Buddha of infinite light and infinite life called Amitabha. Its happy denizens need never be reborn in our world again. All are destined to achieve Buddhahood from his pure land.

The future Buddha will decide the appropriate period in the fluctuating human lifespan to enter the world. In the Theravada account of the birth of the Buddha of our age, he fears that if the lifespan was thousands of years, it would take too long for the sufferings of aging and death to become apparent. If the lifespan was under one hundred years, it would be too short for his disciples to progress on the path. He therefore concluded that a Buddha should appear in the world when the lifespan was one hundred years.

Maitreya must have come to a different conclusion, because it is said that he will not descend from his heaven until the human lifespan has reached its maximum length of eighty thousand years, something that will not occur for almost six billion years. Thus, the leaders of millenarian movements who have declared themselves to be Maitreya over the past centuries have been pretenders. Still, the long wait for Maitreya should not be a reason for despair; the long temporal distance from his advent is mitigated by his physical proximity. Maitreya is not in a pure land; he remains in samsara, in our realm, called the Realm of Desire, because we are so attached to the pleasures of the senses. He is now in a heaven above Mount Meru, a place where we can be reborn. It is not so far away.

In this beautiful piece, Maitreya's hands show that he is teaching the dharma, perhaps to Asanga. But his seat is also significant. It is said that he sits on a throne instead of in the lotus posture so that he can quickly rise when it is time for him to enter our world to bring back Buddhism. Yet, as the story of Asanga suggests, until that day, whenever we practice kindness, Maitreya stands before us. This is how to see a Buddha.

Note

1. Buddhas from the Kashmir region, seated with legs pendant and with their hands in the teaching mudra, have been traditionally identified by art historians as Maitreya, including this image. Recent scholarship has called this into question. The object entry for cat. 7 reflects this uncertainty.

Found in Translation

EARLY CHINESE BUDDHIST SCULPTURE (FIRST CENTURY–849 CE)

by Michael Knight

As with the spoken and written languages, the differences between the artistic languages employed in Buddhist cultures and those native to China were enormous at the time of the introduction of Buddhism. As the religion spread, the translation and adaptation of the visual language of Buddhist art presented serious issues for indigenous artisans. The tensions between the desire to be authentic to the arts of northeast India, Pakistan, and Central Asia, which were the primary early sources of Buddhism, and to find means of expression that fit Chinese cultural tastes led to translations in visual representation and changes in technologies in traditional media.

Among the issues faced by Chinese artisans at the introduction of Buddhism was the depiction of the human figure. Early Chinese religion focused on ancestor worship, which called for the interment of massive numbers of objects in bronze, jade, and other precious materials in tombs.[1] While the human figure did appear with some frequency, prior to the arrival of Buddhism it played a secondary role; the ultimate deities were not anthropomorphic; and ancestors were not represented in sculptural form.[2] The primary focus for artistic creation was vessels and tools used in rituals dedicated to the ancestors and to symbols of power and the means to maintain that power, ranging from weapons and chariot fittings to objects of personal adornment. In contrast, deities in human form are the primary focus of Buddhist art. Each deity has a complex iconography with different manifestations, identified by hairstyle, personal adornment, hand gesture (mudra), body position, and other elements.

Chinese artisans also had attitudes and approaches to media different than those of their counterparts to the west, a prime example being bronze. As K. C. Chang has pointed out, during China's Bronze Age, bronze was symbolic of religious power, wealth, and political control.[3] Vessels and other objects cast in gold or other metals were rare, in part because these metals did not have higher religious or cultural prestige than bronze; their use did not enhance the actual or symbolic value of objects. To the cultures along the Silk Road and in Gandhara that served as the inspiration for the earliest Buddhist works created in China, however, gold was highly symbolic and carried deep religious connotations. In these cultures, bronze was primarily functional and lacked the prestige of gold or the symbolic value it had in China. The rarity and expense of gold made casting large-scale sculptures from the metal unattainable. Therefore, the surfaces of bronze sculptures in these areas were frequently gilded, in effect hiding or disguising the bronze rather than celebrating it.

Differences in attitudes toward bronze were compounded by differences in casting technologies. Up to the fourth century CE, the Chinese employed a piece-mold system for most objects cast in bronze.[4] This system proved ideal for the largely compact shapes and contained decoration of the objects that made up the required repertoire. However, piece-mold technology has limitations. It requires large amounts of bronze, since the walls of the vessels tend to be relatively thick. Also, due to the need to remove the mold slabs from the model, creating three-dimensional decoration with multiple layers or penetrations of space is not possible.[5]

In contrast, Buddhist cultures to the west of China primarily cast bronze using the lost-wax technique.[6] Although Chinese artisans working in bronze were aware of this technology as early as the sixth century BCE, they rarely employed it prior to the arrival of Buddhism. The arrival of Buddhism brought about a significant change, and by no later than the beginning of the sixth century CE, lost-wax casting had become primary among the technologies employed in creating Buddhist sculpture in China.

The chaos around the fall of the Han dynasty in 220 CE and the centuries that followed laid the groundwork for the introduction of Buddhism into China and allowed it to flourish as a formal religion and as an alternative to

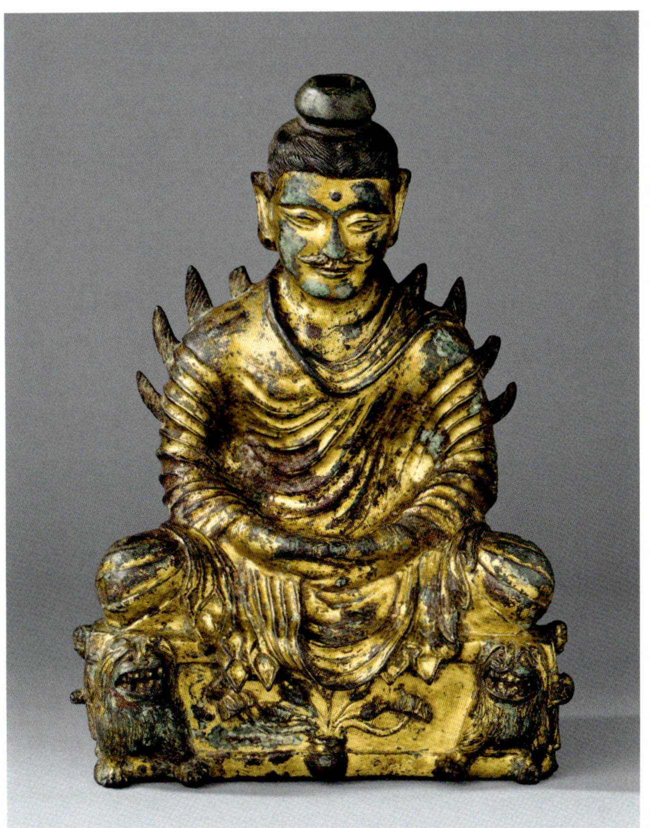

Fig. 1

Seated Buddha Shakyamuni in Meditation with Hands in Dhyana-Mudra and with Flaming Shoulders, gilt bronze, Fogg Museum, Harvard University, 1943.53.80.A.

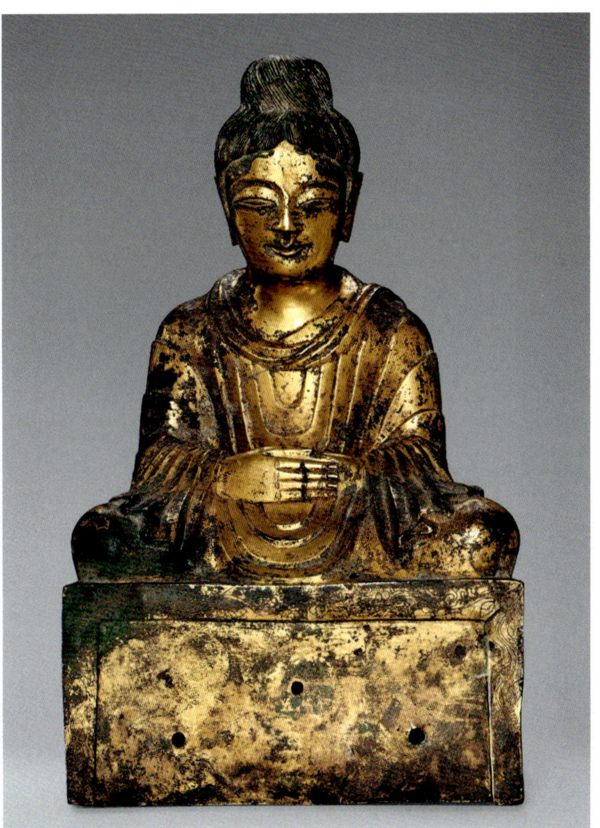

Fig. 2

Seated Buddha, Later Zhao kingdom (319–351), dated 338, Hebei Province, China, bronze with gilding, the Asian Art Museum of San Francisco, The Avery Brundage Collection, B60B1034.

native systems of belief.[7] Images were invaluable in Buddhist religious practice and for the dispersal of the religion. While very few drawings and paintings have survived from the fall of the Han dynasty to the consolidation of north China by the Northern Wei (385–535) in 439, sculptures exist in some numbers. The translation of Buddhist artistic language into something acceptable to a Chinese population followed lines like those found in the translation of Buddhist texts. As Annette Juliano points out, "At first, spiritual leaders, often of Parthian origin called *acaryas*, translated [Buddhist texts] by reading aloud to Chinese monks who served as scribes. By the fourth century, translators developed the concept of *geyi*, a method of matching meanings by searching through Chinese literature, mainly Daoist, for terminology that would better explain Buddhist teachings, a process that gave this foreign religion greater legitimacy."[8] In a similar fashion, the earliest Buddhist images in China relied upon the visual translations of actual sculptures or descriptions

of desired images provided by Buddhist monks from South and Central Asia.

A well-studied source of models for these works was images from Central Asia, Gandhara, and other Buddhist sites carried by monks when they visited China. Even though it is cast using the piece-mold rather than lost-wax technique, an early sculpture in the Fogg Museum at Harvard University is an example of a work that is visually very close to Gandharan images, suggesting models or precise descriptions were available (fig. 1). Some significant sculptures featuring a seated meditating (*dhyana*) Buddha dating to the fourth and early fifth century appear to be translations of artistic language based on descriptions provided by early promulgators of Buddhism combined with elements from existing Chinese religion, an artistic version of geyi seen in textual translations of the same period.[9] The best-known example of this group is a gilt-bronze seated Buddha in the collection of the Asian Art Museum of San Francisco that is inscribed with a date equivalent to

338 (fig. 2).[10] A study by Donna Strahan indicates that this piece and those in the related group were cast in the piece-mold technique, providing evidence that these early Buddhist sculptures were cast by Chinese metalworkers employing traditional Chinese techniques; it also indicates that at this early date there was limited direct contact between specialists in bronze casting from sites in Gandhara or other parts of the Buddhist world and those in China.[11]

An intact example from this group in the Hebei Provincial Museum shows the seated meditating Buddha with two attendants on a square base under a round parasol. A pair of lions and a lotus bud are presented on the lower front.[12] The circle and the square represented heaven and earth in Chinese religion; their combination appears in mirrors, bronze chariots, and other objects related to funerary practices dating to the Han dynasty and later. The parasol also plays an important role in Buddhist iconography, as do the lions and the lotus. The hand gesture seen in this group is not consistent with Buddhist sources and has been interpreted as a Chinese greeting.[13] These sculptures serve as evidence that, similar to the way concepts from Daoism and other native religions gave legitimacy to textual translations, the adaptation of elements from existing traditions to represent Buddhist concepts played a vital role in the early acceptance of Buddhist imagery.

The two bronze figures dated in accordance with 470 and 471 in the Xuzhou Collection (cats. 18 and 19) herald a wave of more direct contact between artisans in China and those from Buddhist cultures. The Tuoba rulers of the Northern Wei dynasty (385–535) were not Chinese; Buddhism was their state religion. By 439, they controlled much of northern China.[14] The stability brought by their rule, combined with economic reforms, allowed the imperial family to patronize Buddhism on an enormous scale.[15] They relocated artisans and monks from the lands they had conquered to their capital at Pingcheng (modern Datong,

Shanxi Province); as a result, direct contact between Chinese artisans and those from Central Asia and from points farther west increased dramatically. This allowed for a greater familiarity with artistic styles, iconography, and technologies from the sources of origin of Buddhism. It was during this period that lost-wax replaced piece-mold as the preferred technology for casting bronze Buddhist sculpture.

Translations of the Lotus Sutra (Sanskrit: Saddharma Pundarika Sutra) made available in the early fifth century played a pivotal role in addressing the tastes and practices of the Chinese population. In part told in parables like Confucian moral writings, the Lotus Sutra was easily grasped by a Chinese audience.[16] In the central miracle of the Lotus Sutra, Shakyamuni, the Buddha of the Present, and Prabhutaratna, a Buddha from the immensely remote past, reveal themselves seated side by side within a magically disclosed stupa.[17] In China, Chapter 25, dedicated to the bodhisattva Avalokiteshvara (Chinese: Guanyin, literally "One Who Hears the Cries of the World"), had the greatest impact. Avalokiteshvara was seen as the bodhisattva of compassion and became the most beloved bodhisattva, the one to whom devotees turn in moments of crisis and suffering. The sculpture in the Xuzhou Collection dated 470 (cat. 18) is among the earliest Chinese stand-alone representations of Avalokiteshvara.

As part of an overall program of Sinicization, the Northern Wei moved their capital south to the ancient Chinese city of Luoyang (in modern Henan Province) in 492. Large numbers of temples were built within the city, many converted from residences donated by members of the local gentry.[18] A dramatic increase in the market for freestanding sculptures was one result. While most freestanding sculptures predating this move were made of bronze, stone competed successfully for these new markets.

The inscription on the stone triad dated 526 (cat. 20) describes the stone as jade (*yu*).[19] Chinese culture endowed jade with symbolic qualities associated with immortality and virtue. Beginning in the Neolithic period, jade objects played an important role in the ritual and funerary practices of China's elite. By the time of Confucius (probably 551–479 BCE), it was associated with the qualities of a true gentleman.[20] Jade is most often found as pebbles, rendering it impractical for large-scale sculpture. In response, the definition of yu was broadened to include marble and other fine stones. Since jade was the stone of highest prestige in China, the use of yu in this inscription and elsewhere to describe certain types of marble and other fine stones was a clear attempt to attach that prestige to the object. The artisans and their patrons knew the difference and had specific terms for the stones they used; describing them as jade was good marketing in the competition with bronze and other media.

The eighth-century Tang dynasty dry-lacquer Buddha head in the Xuzhou Collection (cat. 21) offers another example of a Buddhist sculpture created in a medium traditionally given high value in China. Lacquer had been a favored medium for nearly four thousand years by the time it was created. The earliest surviving examples come from Neolithic sites, while excavated texts indicate that, by the early second century BCE, objects made with lacquer had higher monetary value than comparable pieces in bronze. Unlike jade, lacquer was not associated with positive human virtues.

Collected from a tree of the *Toxicodendron* family, lacquer in its raw stage is volatile, spoils easily, and can cause severe dermatitis. It is hard to collect, difficult to transport while raw, must go through a purification process before use, accepts a limited range of pigments, and requires very specific environmental conditions to cure. However, once cured it is a natural polymer, with many of the characteristics of modern plastics.[21] In most cases, lacquer is applied to a core, usually made of wood. The lacquer is in effect a paint.[22] Dry lacquer is a rare subset in which lacquer is combined with fabric, much like modern fiberglass. While cores are used to support the sculpture until the lacquer cures, they are then removed, resulting in a work that is light in weight and therefore ideal for use in the Buddhist processions that proliferated in the Tang dynasty. Due to the complexity of the technique, the fragility of sculptures created by it, and the use of those sculptures in processions, few, if any, dry lacquer examples from before the seventh century CE remain.[23] Only a small number from the Tang dynasty have survived, making this Buddha head all the more remarkable.[24] This head displays a new synthesis reached during the Tang dynasty, incorporating elements from Central Asia, South Asia, and native Chinese traditions to create a cosmopolitan aesthetic that would in turn inspire Buddhist art across East Asia.

From the first arrival of Buddhism into China, there was a dynamic interplay between the desire to be true to its sources while providing legitimacy and comprehensibility to the textual and artistic language present in existing Chinese religion and cultural identity. In sculpture as in text, early efforts at translation involved incorporating elements found in existing religions with those from sources in South and Central Asia to form new vocabularies. Over the centuries that followed, Chinese traditional styles, formats, and media, along with contemporary fashion and taste, joined with sources from foreign contact to inspire the development of uniquely Chinese forms of Buddhism. This was not a passive acceptance of influences from foreign sources but rather an active search for textual and artistic inspiration that best suited the taste of the time and location. The results of this search in turn served as sources of inspiration for the surrounding cultures, which selected elements from Chinese Buddhism that best suited their own cultural context.

Notes

1. As an example, approximately ten metric tons of bronze were discovered in the tomb of the Marquis Yi of the minor state of Zeng, who died in 433 BCE. One purpose of the dedication of this massive amount of wealth to the ancestors was to ensure they were properly equipped in the afterlife. Another was more self-serving: The spirits of the ancestors were considered a conduit for communicating with *Tian*. It was believed that a burial furnished with the appropriate or an exaggeration of the appropriate furniture might influence Tian and impact the standing of the donors.

2. Examples of human figures in art of the late Bronze Age and early imperial period include the large and detailed representations serving as part of the stand for the set of sixty-five bells found in the tomb of the Marquis Yi of the state of Zeng in Leigudun, Hubei Province, which dates to 433 BCE. There are equally detailed representations in lamps and candle stands dating from the Warring States period (c. 475–221 BCE). A pair of sculptures associated with the Jincun site in a private collection tentatively identified as Leizu and Shen Nong are early sculptural representations of deities. These pieces must predate 256 BCE, when Jincun was destroyed by the armies of Qin. Xiwang Mu, Dongwang Gong, Fu Xi, Nu Wa, Shen Nong, the Buddha, and other spiritual beings are commonly found as denizens of immortal paradises on Han dynasty mirrors, money trees, incense burners, and related objects in bronze and ceramic. There are numerous examples of human figures in bronze associated with chariots dating to the Eastern Han dynasty. These represented funerary processions and were part of ancestor worship. Archaeological evidence indicates that by the fifth century BCE there was an increased desire to replicate an idealized version of a palace in the tomb environment. This contributed to a tradition of interring representations of warriors, servants, and others in the tomb environment and can be linked to the belief in paradises of the immortals. The best-known example is the army found in pits around the tomb of the First Emperor. These were not objects of worship and were often created in low-fired clay, a medium lacking cultural prestige. These figures are true to a type — the desire was to capture the essence of martial figures, such as a foot soldier, an archer, or a general, and other figures, such as servants, dancers, and foreign grooms; no attempt was made to make them powerful in a spiritual sense. Human figures are also a common subject in paintings in tombs of the Han dynasty and later; common themes for these paintings are rituals and ceremonies, along with parables demonstrating Confucian values. This focus on narrative content inspired an interest in Jataka tales, which are among the earliest Buddhist themes explored by Chinese artists. See Wu Hung, "Buddhist Elements in Early Chinese Art (2nd and 3rd Centuries A.D.)," *Artibus Asiae* 47, no. 3/4 (1986); Marilyn Rhie, *Early Buddhist Art of China and Central Asia*, part 4, vol. 12 (*Handbook of Oriental Studies*) (Brill, 2002), and Michael Knight, "The 338 Buddha Revisited," *Lotus Leaves* 15, no. 2 (Spring 2013): 1–10.

3. Chang states, "The nine ding stories suggest strongly that the possession of such sacred vessels served to legitimize the King's rule. These vessels were clear and powerful symbols: they were symbols of wealth because they were wealth and possessed the aura of wealth; they were symbols of the all-important ritual that gave their owners access to the ancestors; and they were symbols of the control of metal, which meant control of exclusive access to the ancestors and to political authority." K. C. Chang, *Art, Myth, and Ritual: The Path to Political Authority in Ancient China* (Harvard University Press, 1983), 97.

4. The first step in this process involves making a model of the intended object in clay. After allowing this to dry, soft clay slabs are pressed against it, taking an impression of the model and any surface decoration. Once removed, these slabs become the outside sections of a mold; the model is carved down to become the core. The clay slabs with the impressions of the model are then assembled over the core with bronze spacers, called chaplets, strategically placed to separate them. The ensemble is heated, and molten bronze poured into it. Because they are in contact with both the core and the outer sections of the mold, chaplets do not completely melt and fuse with the molten bronze. They are often visible in the finished piece or can be detected through X-rays. Their presence is evidence of the use of the piece-mold technique. For a discussion of the use of lost-wax casting in early Chinese Buddhist sculpture, see Donna Strahan, *Piece-Mold Casting: A Chinese Tradition for Fourth- and Fifth-Century Bronze Buddha Images* (Metropolitan Museum of Art; Yale University Press, 2010).

5. Appendages such as loop handles that could not be created in the mold were cast separately. In some cases, they were cast first and inserted into the mold or (more rarely) a mold for them was attached to the cast object and they were cast on. Parts were cast separately and joined with solder where multiple layers were dictated by function, as in certain chariot ornaments.

6. In lost-wax casting, a model of the desired object is first made in wax; in most examples, the wax model is built over a core or a supporting armature. Clay or some other material is then packed around the model. Bronze pins are used to keep the sections of the mold in place during casting. The ensemble is heated, and the wax melts away, leaving a void for the molten bronze. Since an impression of the model does not need to be taken to make the mold, lost-wax casting allows for objects with thin walls, deep undercutting, and with multiple layers of decoration. A detailed analysis of a sculpture cast in the lost-wax technique is found in John Twilley's essay in this catalogue.

7. A significant source of support came from the non-Chinese rulers who controlled north China during this period and declared Buddhism as their state religion. The first to do so was Shi Le (274–333) of the state of Later Zhao (311–351). He selected Buddhism as the state religion under the tutelage of Fotudeng (Fotu Cheng, traditional dates 232–348 CE), one of the great early promulgators of the religion. See Michael Knight, "The 338 Buddha Revisited," *Lotus Leaves* 15, no. 2 (Spring 2013): 1–10.

8. Annette L. Juliano, "Buddhist Art in Northwest China," in Annette L. Juliano and Judith A. Learner, eds., *Monks and Merchants: Silk Road Treasures from Northwest China, Gansu and Ningxia, 4th to 7th Century* (Harry N. Abrams, Asia Society, 2001), 119–25.

9. It has been suggested that Fotudeng (Fotucheng, 232–348) was a major source. Born in the Central Asian state of Kucha likely to Indian parents, Fotudeng trained in Kashmir and Dunhuang before traveling to Luoyang. He arrived there in 310, just as that city was falling to foreign invaders. Fotudeng was instrumental in converting the non-Chinese rulers of the Later Zhao (319–351) to Buddhism. The primary religions practiced in China at the time were Daoism and Confucianism, which did not offer the right to rule to a non-Chinese. Buddhism was a foreign religion and had no such limitations. The conversion of the Later Zhao rulers marked the beginning of Buddhism as a state religion by non-Chinese rulers in northern China, which was to continue for nearly three hundred years. By the end of his very long life, Fotudeng reportedly had over 10,000 disciples and had established 893 Buddhist temples. His disciples played important roles in the spread of Buddhism throughout much of China and in building the foundations for the flourishing of Buddhism during the fifth century. Among them were Dao'an (312–385), who was a translator and impacted the early cult of Maitreya in China, and Huiyuan, who is credited as the founder of Pure Land Buddhism. Dao'an was a source of inspiration to Kumarajiva (343/344–413, arrived in China in 401), the great Buddhist translator of the early Northern Wei. See Arthur Frederick Wright, "Fo-Tu-Teng, A Biography," *Harvard Journal of Asiatic Studies* 11 (December 1948), and Knight, "The 338 Buddha Revisited."

10. In her essay "Buddhist Art in Northwest China," Annette Juliano states of this group, "Although the robe and disproportionately large head, bent slightly forward, along with the high *ushnisha*, display Gandharan origins, the strong overall pattern of the abstract drapery folds, coupled with the insistent symmetry of the entire image, reflects Chinese adaptation." See Juliano and Learner, eds., *Monks and Merchants*, 119–25.

11. See Strahan, *Piece-Mold Casting*.

12. See Yang Renkai, ed., *Zhongguo Meishu Quanji*, vol. 3, *Sculpture* (Wenwu, 1985), plate 35.

13. See Knight, "The 338 Buddha Revisited."

14. Northern Wei consolidated its rule of northern China in 439 with the conquest of the Liu Song dynasty and the state of Liangzhou, which controlled the Gansu corridor. According to Albert Dien, when they captured the capital of Liangzhou, it is reported to have had a population of 200,000. As Dien points out, Liangzhou played an important role in the translation of Buddhist texts and art; it was both on the route by which the Silk Road entered China and the first area where there was a substantial Chinese population, allowing Buddhist concepts to be adjusted to the needs of that population. See Albert Dien, "Encounters with Nomads," in Juliano and Learner, eds., *Monks and Merchants*, 61.

15. An example is Yungang, the imperially sponsored Buddhist cave temple complex located near the Northern Wei capital at Pingcheng, modern Datong, Shanzi Province.

16. A significant translation of the Lotus Sutra into Chinese was completed in 286 as the result of efforts led by Dharmasaka, another between 401 and 413 by a team of translators assembled in Chang'an by Kumarajiva.

17. A bronze sculpture dated 472 in the collection of the Asian Art Museum of San Francisco, B60B1035, is an example.

18. See W. F. J. Jenner, *Memories of Loyang: Yang Hsüan-chih and the Lost Capital (493–534)* (Oxford University Press, 1981) for a contemporary description of this trend. As with other arts of the time, the translation of residential architecture into forms appropriate for Buddhist practice resulted in a merging of elements from both. See Nancy S. Steinhardt, *Chinese Traditional Architecture* (China Institute, 1984), and *Chinese Architecture in an Age of Turmoil, 200–600* (University of Hawaii Press, 2014).

19. See cat. 20 in this catalogue for a translation and discussion.

20. For a description of the qualities associated with jade by Chinese culture, see He Li, "Chinese Jade Art in the Ming and Qing Dynasties," in *Later Chinese Jades, Ming Dynasty to Early Twentieth Century* (Asian Art Museum of San Francisco, 2007), 15–17. The artisan who incised the inscription on the sculpture in the Xuzhou Collection certainly knew this stone was not jade; rather, the use of the term jade (yu) was an attempt to attach the cultural prestige associated with jade to the stone from which this piece was created. This broader use of the term is also indicated by the context in which the character appears in texts, such as the description of the palace of Shi Hu of the Later Zhao, who died in 350, and in several instances in Yang Xuanzhi's "Memories of Old Luoyang," where jade could not have been the stone mentioned. The use of yu in inscriptions on sculptures such as the example in the Xuzhou Collection and those in the white marble from Dingxian in the Taihang mountains of Hebei Province dating to the Northern Qi dynasty (550–577) are in accordance with what is seen in those texts.

21. See essay by Donna Strahan in this catalogue for a complete discussion of the technical qualities of lacquer.

22. In later Chinese lacquers, multiple layers were applied, creating a surface thick enough to be carved.

23. Surviving wooden sculptures with lacquer decoration appear in the archaeological record as early as the fifth through fourth century BCE. These sculptures were created for use in tombs.

24. Regina Krahl identifies a total of seven. See Regina Krahl, "Divine Features in Lacquer," Sotheby's Hong Kong, sale HK049, lot 120.

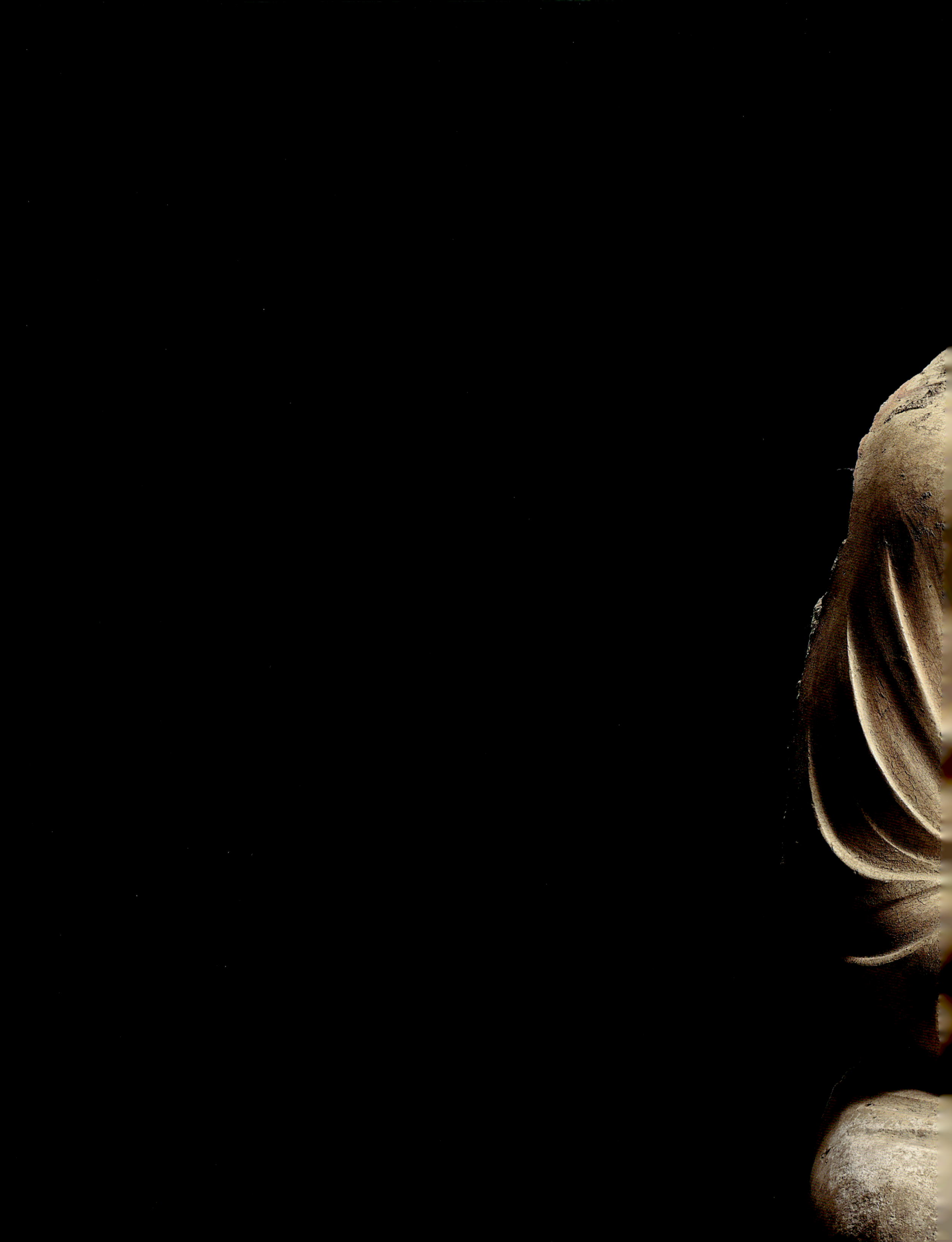

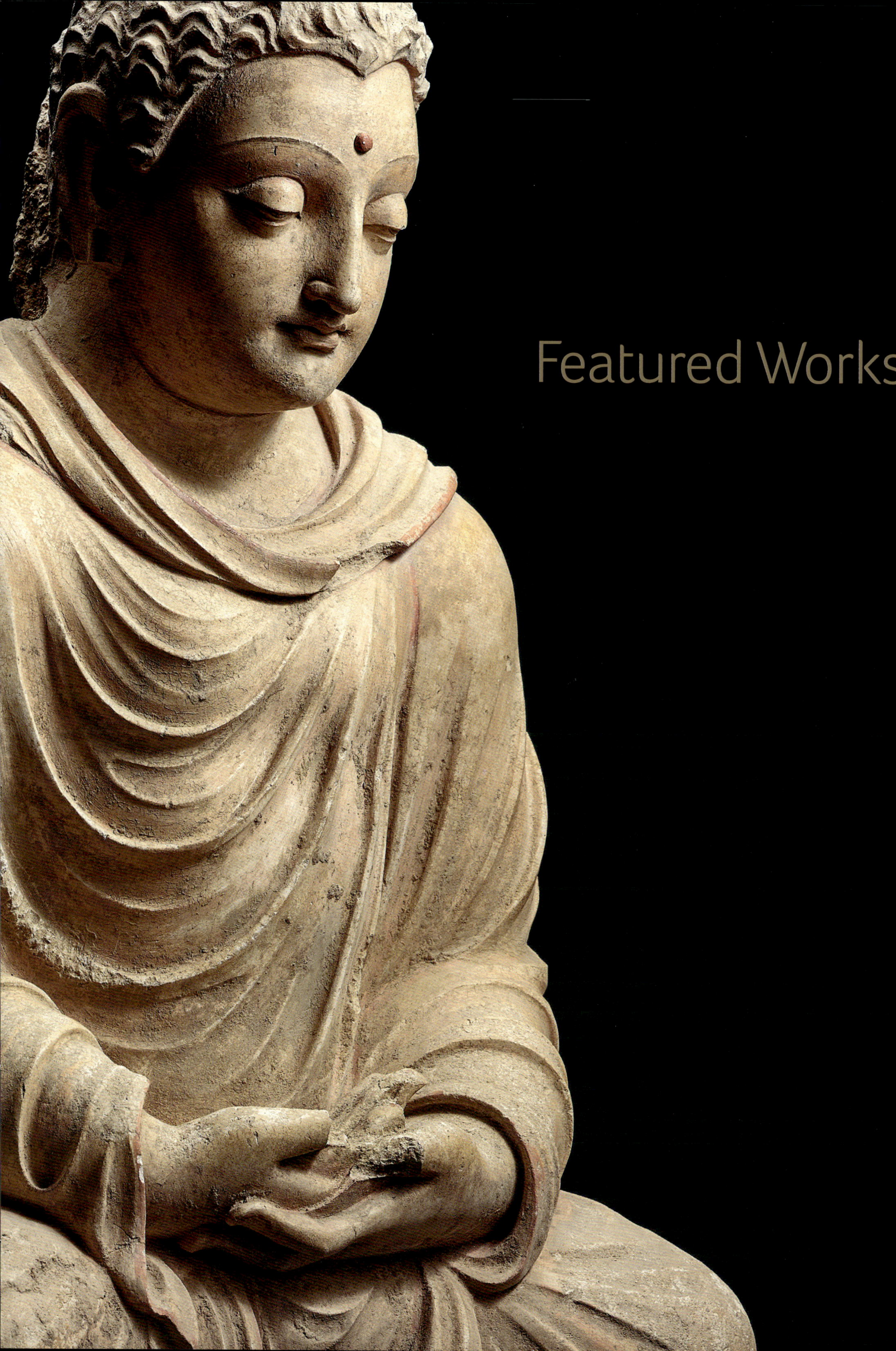
Featured Works

Buddha Maravijaya, Triumphing over Mara

Eastern India or Bangladesh, c. 6th–7th century

Terracotta
34 ¹³⁄₁₆ × 20 ¾ × 7 in. (88.4 × 52.7 × 17.8 cm)

This superb sculpture depicts the historical Buddha Shakyamuni on the threshold of enlightenment. Having vowed to remain in meditation until he had penetrated the mysteries of existence, Siddhartha was visited by Mara, the deity of death and desire, who challenged his lofty goal of enlightenment and freedom from rebirth. Amid the furious assaults of Mara's demons and the alluring distractions of his beautiful daughters, Siddhartha maintains his meditative equipoise. Mara, armed with bow and arrow, watches the drama unfold as he stands to the Buddha's right. Aided by spirits who reminded him of the countless compassionate efforts he had made on behalf of sentient beings throughout his many animal and human incarnations, Siddhartha recognized that it was his destiny to be poised on the threshold of enlightenment. According to tradition, he touched the earth with his right hand (*bhumisparsha* mudra), calling the earth to bear witness to his enlightenment, an iconographic form known in the Indian tradition as Maravijaya, or Victory over Mara. Following established iconography, the earth goddess Prithvi emerges from below (seen from the back, now headless).

One of the greatest phases of Indian art flourished under the Gupta (c. 320–550 CE) and Vakataka (c. 250–500 CE) kingdoms and their tributaries. Indian artists of the Gupta period rendered the human form according to principles of proportion and ideals of beauty that came to define Indian classical norms. Perfected around the last quarter of the fifth century at major centers like Sarnath and Mathura, the Gupta Buddha, in the form of an idealized spiritual youth, became a model for Buddhist art throughout the Indian subcontinent and much of South and Southeast Asia.[1]

Gupta-period sculpture is rare, with most surviving examples rendered in stone. A preaching Buddha from Sarnath, dated about 475 and now in the Sarnath Museum, is one of the most celebrated Gupta stone sculptures to survive.[2] Another important stone sculpture of a seated Buddha, now in the British Museum, was also likely carved at Sarnath in the same period.[3] A few remarkable bronzes, notably those in the Asia Society Museum in New York, demonstrate the transcendent calm for which this school of Indian art is famed.[4] Gupta-period terracotta sculptures are also rare, with a few splendid examples in public collections, notably a Ganesha plaque fragment in the Kimbell Art Museum and a Rama and Lakshmana sculpture in the Asia Society Museum in New York, and a few unpublished examples in private collections.[5] Religious institutions in North India at this time were often made of brick, with sculptural adornment rendered in terracotta or stucco, conceived as panels inserted into niches.[6]

In Bangladesh, where Gupta imperial power lingered longest and where this terracotta sculpture was reportedly found, important Gupta-period objects have been uncovered.[7] The Bangladesh region possesses no stone quarries. Clay, however, is abundant due to the rich and ample silt deposits left by its many ever-shifting waterways, including the Ganges (Padma) and Brahmaputra (Jamuna) rivers and their tributaries. Terracotta was therefore the preferred artistic medium. This important Maravijaya sculpture exhibits many of the same classical refinements associated with the finest examples of Gupta sculpture from Sarnath and other celebrated centers in North India. **JC**

Notes

1. See John M. Rosenfield, "On the Dated Carvings of Sarnath," *Artibus Asiae* 26 (1963): 10–26.

2. Published in Karl Khandalavala, ed., *The Golden Age: Gupta Art — Empire, Province and Influence* (South Asia Books, 1991), 40.

3. Published in Wladimir Zwalf, *Buddhism: Art and Faith* (British Museum, 1985), 97.

4. Published in Jane Casey, Naman Ahuja, and David Weldon, *Divine Presence: Arts of India and the Himalayas* (5 Continents, 2003), 66–67; Pramod Chandra, *The Sculpture of India: 3000 BC–1300 AD* (National Gallery of Art, 1985), 92–93.

5. See Pratapaditya Pal, *The Ideal Image: The Gupta Sculptural Tradition and Its Influence* (Asia Society Galleries, 1978); Amy G. Poster, *From Indian Earth: 4,000 Years of Terracotta Art* (Brooklyn Museum of Art, 1986); J. F. Jarrige et al., *L'Age d'or de l'Inde classique: L'Empire des Gupta* (Éditions de la Reunion des musées nationaux, 2007), 85–91.

6. See the Gupta-period brick temple at Bhitargaon in Uttar Pradesh, published in Joanna Williams, *The Art of Gupta India: Empire and Province* (Princeton University Press, 1982), pls. 107–9; and at Deogarh, in ibid., plates 201–10.

7. For a summary of Gupta hegemony in this region, see ibid., 147–48; Vincent Lefèvre and Marie-Francoise Boussac, eds., *Art of the Ganges Delta: Masterpieces from Bangladeshi Museums*, trans. John Adamson (Éditions de la Reunion des musées nationaux, 2008), 126–31.

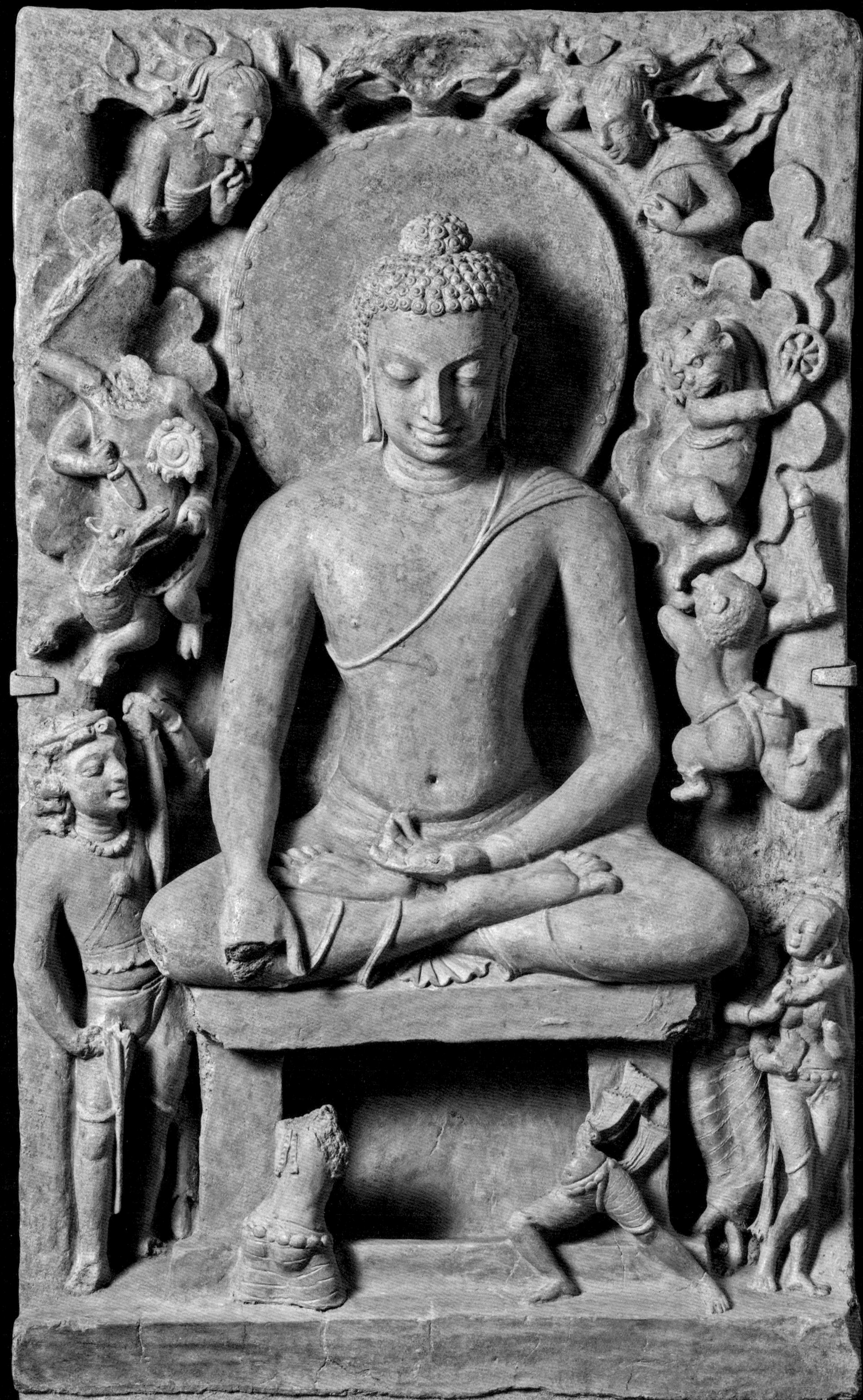

Buddha Maravijaya, Calling the Earth to Witness

Bihar, India, c. 10th century

Copper alloy and silver inlay
20 ½ × 16 × 10 ½ in. (52.1 × 40.6 × 26.7 cm)

Of all the iconographic forms devised to represent the historical Buddha Shakyamuni, the earth-touching Buddha has particular appeal because it captures the moment he triumphed over his final obstacle to liberation. This iconographic form is known in India as the Vajrasana or "Diamond Seat" Buddha.[1] It pays homage not only to the Buddha's enlightenment but also to Bodh Gaya, the site where it took place. Indian legends are full of references to Bodh Gaya as *vajrasana*, the diamond seat, the only place where all Buddhas, past, present, and future did, do, or will attain enlightenment.

This iconographic form became popular in the Buddhist home-land, particularly in Bihar, the district of eastern India that encompasses Bodh Gaya and other sites sacred to the Buddha's biography. The modeling of the sculpture supports an attribution to this region, as it epitomizes the regional style that developed under the Pala (c. 750–1160 CE) and Sena (c. 1070–1230 CE) rulers. The strong shoulders and the somewhat elongated torso, the physiognomy, and the superb casting all indicate an origin in Bihar. Pala sculpture sometimes included inset gems, as described by medieval pilgrims and as found in some surviving works from this region.[2] Silver inlay in the eyes, between the brows, along the hem of the robes, in the soles of the feet, and in the palms of the hands enhances the beauty of the work and further reflects traditions of the eastern Indian medieval school of sculpture.[3] Similarly accomplished copper-alloy sculptures from the Buddhist centers of Nalanda and Kurkihar, some bearing inscriptions with the dates of their manufacture, help to establish a date for this work of about the tenth century.[4] Indeed, a significant number of eastern Indian medieval sculptures bear inscriptions that include the regnal dates of local kings, making it possible to construct a fairly reliable chronology.[5] Pala sculptors sometimes used a dark, pitch-like substance to delineate the pupils, making them more lifelike, contrasted with the whites of the eyes, denoted by silver inlay. The eyes of this figure were previously inset with a dark stone, which conservation analysis indicated was a modern feature, and it was therefore removed.[6] Similar treatment of eyes can be found in Cambodian and Thai sculpture of the ninth century and later.[7] Pala sculptures have been found in Southeast Asia, and it could be that this work was once worshipped in Southeast Asia, where the eyes were adapted to local taste.

The considerable size of the image is also reflective of the school, which produced thousands of sculptures in dimensions ranging from a few inches to several feet in height. Medieval pilgrim accounts describe two ten-foot-high silver statues of Avalokiteshvara and Maitreya in niches flanking the entrance to the Mahabodhi Temple at Bodh Gaya.[8] Recent excavations in Bangladesh have revealed large copper-alloy and gilt-copper Buddhist sculptures, at least one of which would have been at least eight feet in height when cast.[9] **JC**

Notes

1. Janice Leoshko, "The Vajrasana Buddha," in Janice Leoshko, ed., *Bodhgaya: The Site of Enlightenment* (Marg Publications, 1988), 30.
2. Ulrich von Schroeder, *Indo-Tibetan Bronzes* (Visual Dharma Publications, 1981), 238; David Weldon and Jane Casey Singer, *The Sculptural Heritage of Tibet: Buddhist Art in the Nyingjei Lam Collection* (Laurence King Publishing, 1999), 56–57.
3. This school often used gold, silver, and copper inlay in its copper-alloy sculptures. Von Schroeder, *Indo-Tibetan Bronzes*, 238.
4. See comparable examples published in Nihar Ranjan Ray, Karl Khandalavala, and Sadashiv Gorakshka, *Eastern Indian Bronzes* (Lalit Kala Adademi, 1986), nos. 84, 99, 101, 104, 135, 143, 168b, 169b, 232a, 232b.
5. On Pala chronology, see Stella Kramrisch, "A Note" [Appended to K.P. Jayaswal's "Metal Images of Kurkihar Monastery"], *Journal of the Indian Society of Oriental Art* 2, no. 2 (December 1934): 77–82; Von Schroder, *Indo-Tibetan Bronzes*; Susan L. Huntington, *The "Pala-Sena" Schools of Sculpture* (E. J. Brill, 1984); and Ray, Khandalavala, and Gorakshka, *Eastern Indian Bronzes*.
6. Condition report by Dr. Anna Bennett, December 14, 2017: "The inlaid eyes are restorations. The round pupil itself is a modern stone with significant modern manufacturing marks which had been secured in the eye socket using a modern adhesive."
7. See examples published in Emma C. Bunker and Douglas Latchford, *Khmer Bronzes: New Interpretations of the Past* (Art Media Resources, 2011), 180, 222, 236, and Emmanuel Guillon, *Hindu-Buddhist Art of Vietnam: Treasures from Champa* (River Books, 2006), 103.
8. Hiuen Tsiang [Xuanzang], *Si-Yu-Ki: Buddhist Records of the Western World*, Book 8, reprint ed., trans. Samuel Beal (Chinese Materials Center, 1976), 118–19, 122–23, 133.
9. Vincent Lefèvre and Marie-Francoise Boussac, eds., *Art of the Ganges Delta: Masterpieces from Bangladeshi Museums*, trans. John Adamson (Éditions de la Reunion des musées nationaux, 2008), 190–91.

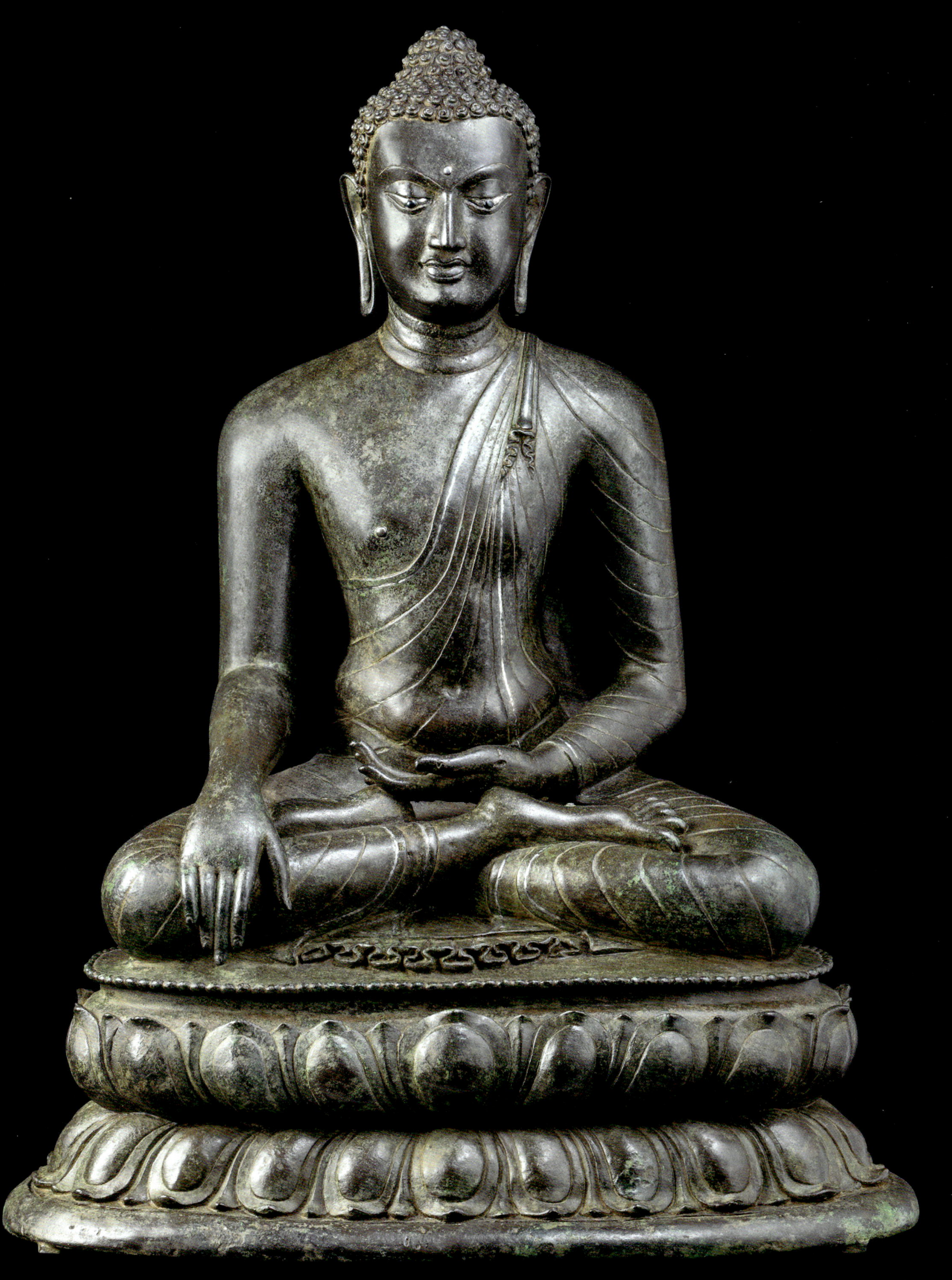

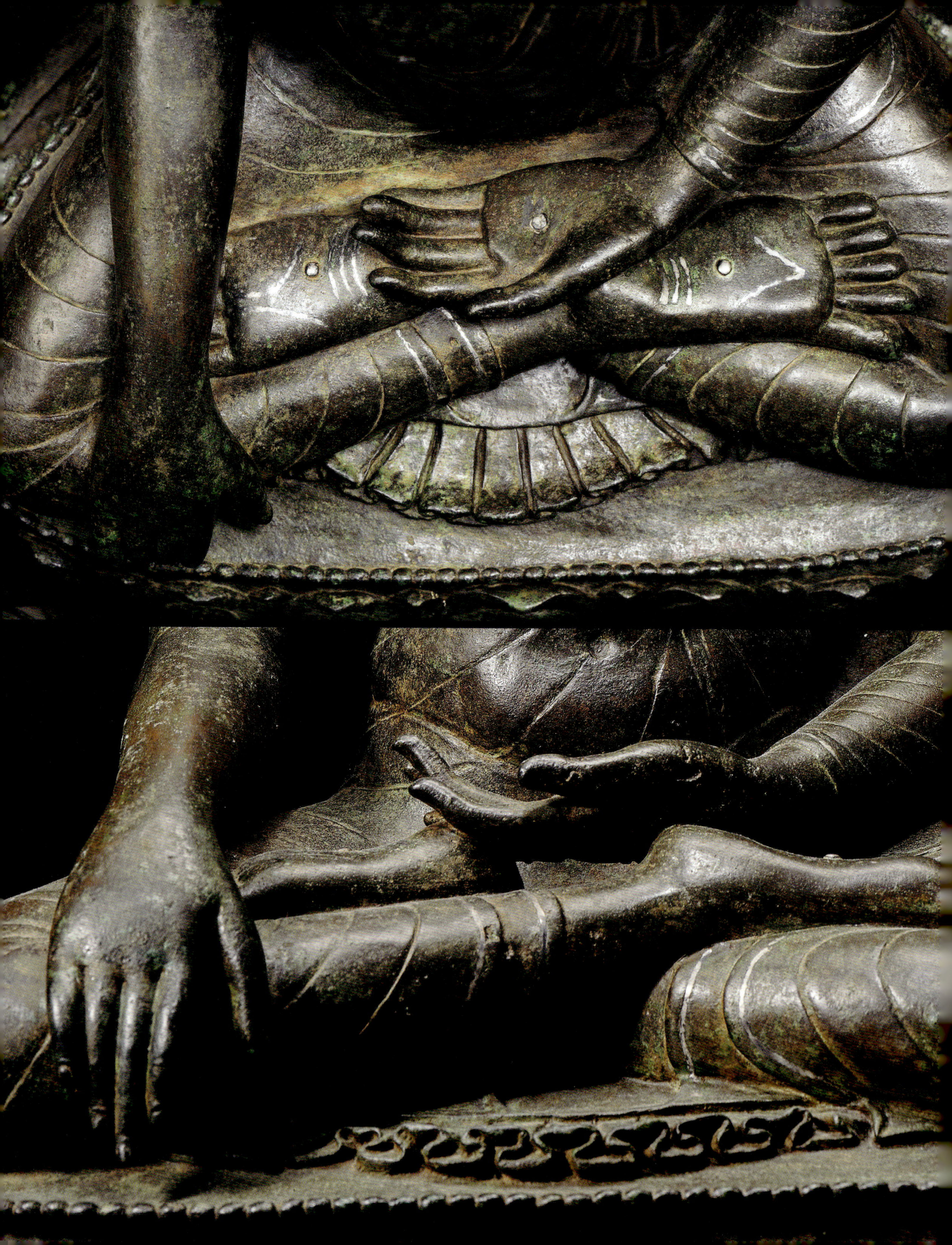

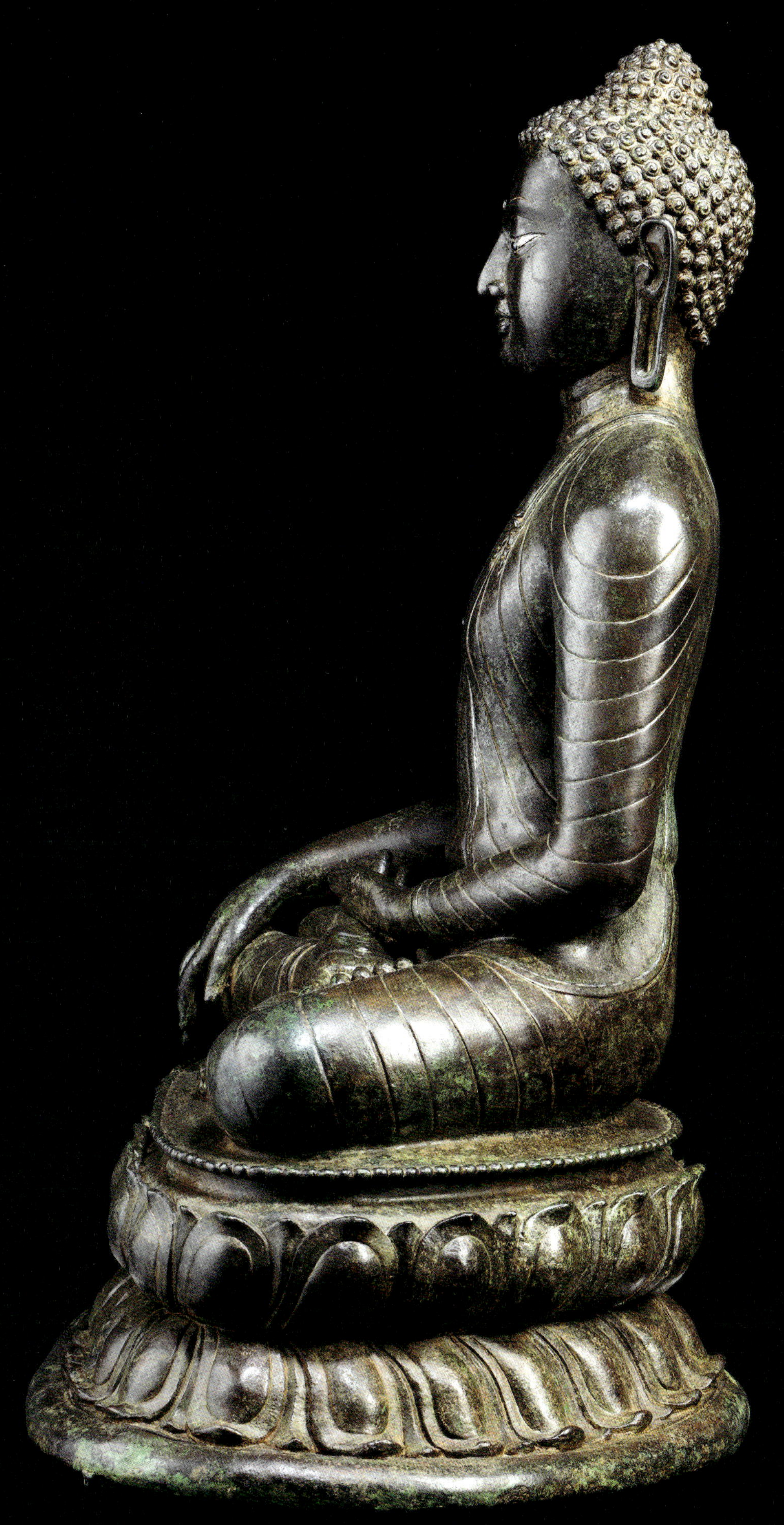

The Renunciation of Prince Siddhartha

Ancient region of Gandhara, Pakistan or Afghanistan, c. 2nd–3rd century

Schist stone and traces of gold
7 ¹¹⁄₁₆ × 8 ⅜ × 2 ½ in. (19.5 × 21.3 × 6.3 cm)

This narrative scene refers to a pivotal moment in the life of the historical Buddha when, in the palace of Kapilavastu, the young prince leaves his marital bed, determined to relinquish his princely life and follow the path of an ascetic practitioner. Glancing at his sleeping wife, Yashodhara, Prince Siddhartha arises in the bedchamber. An attendant holds forth a garment as six female attendants rest below, with another standing female attendant adjacent to the bed.[1] An open flame appears behind, in front of a cloth curtain. Two pillars frame the narrative. The dramatic scene illustrates Siddhartha's profound insight into the nature of impermanence. Recognizing the fleeting nature of the women's beauty, as well as the inevitability of aging and death, he felt compelled to leave the palace and begin his spiritual quest.

Legendary biographies of the historical Buddha were recorded in manuscripts in the early centuries CE and are among the earliest genres of Buddhist literature.[2] Authoritative texts in Sanskrit include the Buddhacarita, the Mahavastu, and the Lalitavistara.[3] Earlier than the earliest surviving textual accounts of the Buddha's life are narrative scenes of his life carved in major Indian Buddhist architectural sites such as Sanchi (c. late second–first century BCE) and Bharhut (c. 125–75 BCE) in Madhya Pradesh, and Nagarjunakona in Andra Pradesh (c. third century CE). The narratives highlight the historical Buddha's legendary journey from a life of privilege and comfort to a more deeply satisfying spiritual life, free from fear, desire, and all manner of mental and emotional afflictions. Born a prince, Siddhartha was shielded from the harsh realities of life by his father, who had been told that the prince's destiny would either be that of a great king or a revered spiritual teacher. King Shuddodana sought to prevent the latter by enveloping his son in a life of luxury and pleasure. Nevertheless, Siddhartha encountered instances of illness, old age, death, and a wandering ascetic during brief excursions outside the palace, which instilled in him a profound desire to understand the true nature of existence. After years of intense austerities and meditation, the Buddha reached a state of tremendous wisdom and freedom, which he shared with his followers and which continues to inspire countless Buddhists today.

In the Gandhara region of Pakistan and Afghanistan arose a school of Indian art in the early centuries CE that was heavily influenced by classical art and architecture. An emphasis on physical realism is sometimes seen in this school, as well as the occasional use of classical costumes and physiognomy.[4] But the iconographic content of this regional school of art is predominantly Buddhist. Large Buddhist reliquaries (stupa) were constructed in the region's local black or gray schist, and later in stucco. These structures were covered with narrative scenes illustrating the life of the Buddha, such as this example, as well as narrative scenes of his previous lives. The great renunciation was one of the most popular narratives in Gandharan Buddhist art, alongside that of the birth of Buddha.[5]

Traces of gold can be seen in sections of the panel. Other Gandharan works with remaining traces of gold include a panel now in the Metropolitan Museum of Art.[6] **JC**

Notes

1. Robert E. Buswell, Jr., and Donald S. Lopez, Jr., note that a whole canto in the Buddhacarita describes in detail a vision of the women sleeping in the palace, just prior to the Buddha's departure, in *The Princeton Dictionary of Buddhism* (Princeton University Press, 2014), 150.

2. Peter Skilling, *Buddhism and Buddhist Literature of South-East Asia* (Ludwig Reichert Verlag, 2010), 161–62.

3. Professor Donald S. Lopez notes that this version of the prince's renunciation is based on the Mulasarvastivada Vinaya (email from Lopez to the author, June 21, 2024). See John Strong, "A Family Quest: The Buddha, Yaśodharā, and Rāhula in the Mūlasarvāstivāda Vinaya," in Juliane Schober, ed., *Sacred Biography in the Buddhist Traditions of South and Southeast Asia* (University of Hawaii Press, 1996).

4. See the Gandharan panel depicting Aquatic Deities in the Metropolitan Museum of Art, where the musculature of the standing male figures is highly accentuated in the classical manner, and the costumes are Hellenistic (for example, acanthus skirts), the scene framed between two Indo-Corinthian columns. See Jane Casey, Naman Ahuja, and David Weldon, *Divine Presence: Arts of India and the Himalayas* (5 Continents Editions, 2003), 52–53.

5. Jessie Pons, "The Figure with a Bow in Gandharan Great Departure Scenes, Some New Readings," *Entangled Religions* 1 (2014): 17, available online at https://er.ceres.rub.de /index.php/ER/issue/view/30. See a Gandharan birth of the Buddha panel in the Metropolitan Museum of Art at https://www.metmuseum. org/art/collection/search/40598.

6. *Dipankara Jataka (The Story of the Ascetic Megha and the Buddha Dipankara)*, c. second century CE, 1998.491: https://www.metmuseum .org/art/collection/search/49809.

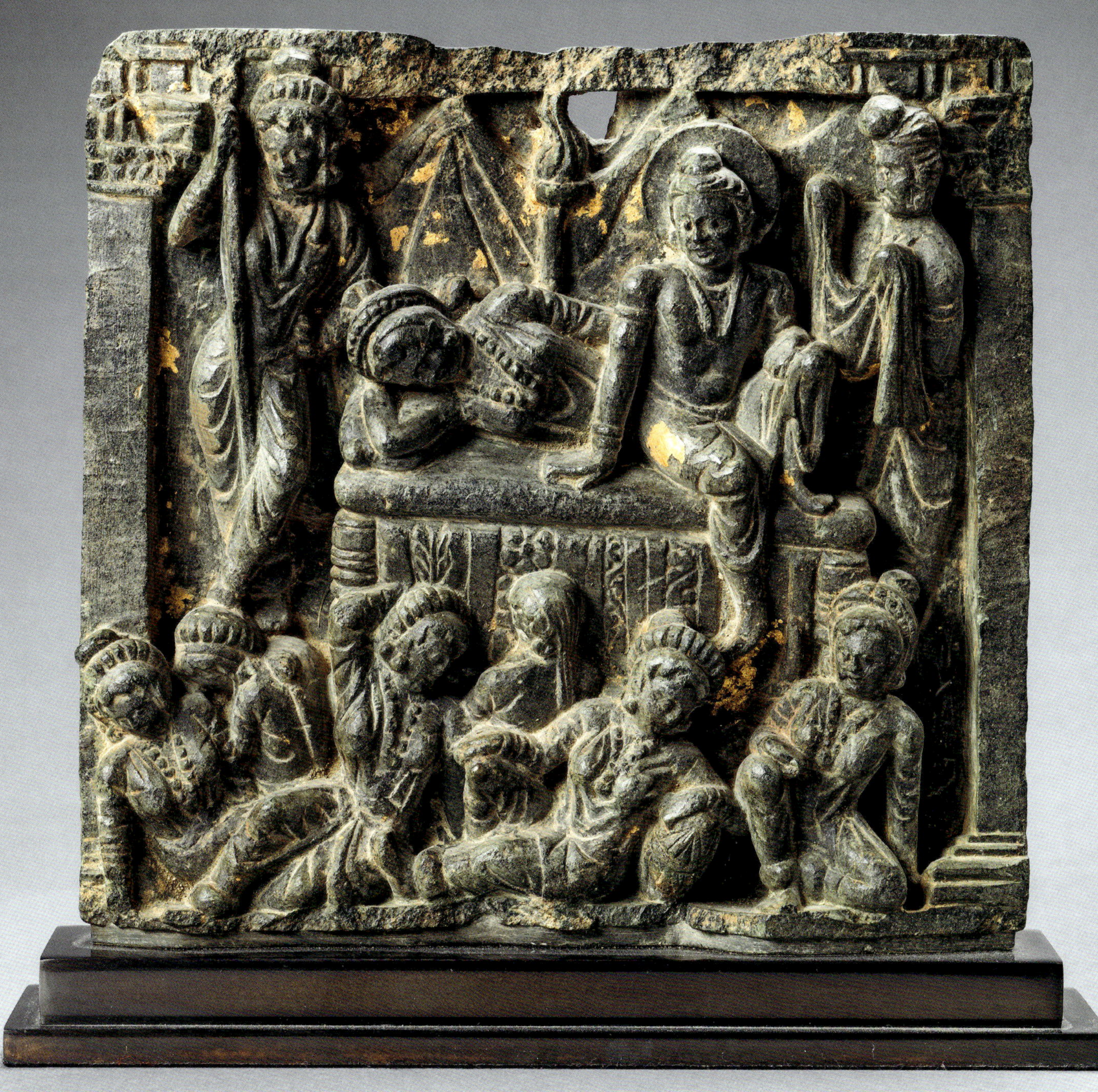

Buddha in Meditation

Ancient region of Gandhara, Pakistan or Afghanistan, c. 5th century

Polychrome stucco
23 ½ × 14 × 6 ¼ in. (59.7 × 35.6 × 15.9 cm)

The finely modeled stucco figure depicts the historical Buddha seated in a contemplative posture (*dhyanasana*) with legs crossed and hands folded in the lap.[1] The sculpture displays specific signs of the enlightened being (*lakshana*), including the cranial protuberance (*ushnisha*), the auspicious mark on the forehead (*urna*), here colored red, three undulations on the neck delineated with concentric red lines, and long webbed fingers. Red pigment also highlights the lips, rims of the eyes, and folds of the robe; black accentuates waves of hair, eyebrows, and irises, with the hooded eyes evoking a meditative state. A stucco head of Buddha in the Metropolitan Museum of Art has similar, well-preserved red and black painted details.[2] The earlobes (now partly missing) are pierced and elongated by heavy earrings, recalling Buddha's royal heritage before his spiritual awakening and rejection of worldly trappings. Notwithstanding damage to the earlobes, fingers, and some folds of the robe, the state of preservation is remarkable for such a delicate medium.

The Buddha wears a simple, voluminous monk's robe made from a single length of cloth draped around the shoulders and falling in deep folds across the body, with the end of the cloth thrown back over the left shoulder. The garment is modeled in the characteristic Greco-Roman sculptural style of the Gandhara region, a legacy of Alexander the Great's invasion of northern India (329–326 BCE) and the region's continued contact with the classical world. The naturalistic flow and deep folds of the Gandhara robe are often compared with the Roman toga in classical sculpture. The robe style remains more or less consistent throughout the Gandhara period, between approximately the first and fifth centuries CE. In the earliest days, Gandhara sculpture was made predominantly from local gray schist, but stucco became increasingly popular, especially in regions where schist was not readily available.[3] By the fourth and fifth centuries, stucco was the more common medium for temple sculpture and interior architectural elements.[4] The medium allows for great attention to detail and very large scale, seen for instance in the remaining foot of a monumental standing figure adjacent to a near life-size seated Buddha at Taxila, Pakistan.[5] Fine stucco sculpture is seen at Hadda in Afghanistan, and particularly elegant stucco heads and feet survived from massive figures of Buddha at Takht-i-Bahi, Pakistan.[6] A stucco head of Buddha found in Swat, Pakistan (now in the British Museum), has remains of hair arranged in similar waves to the Xuzhou Buddha, the same hair type as the renowned stucco Buddha head with painted details in the Victoria and Albert Museum.[7]

Stucco sculpture is made from a lime or gypsum plaster built up over a rough core. The core might be cemented rubble, clay, or even a cast-off part of a broken stucco sculpture, providing a base on which to build the shape of the figure, with a final layer of plaster to define the details. The finished sculpture is left unfired and sets to the relatively durable consistency seen in this fine example. **DW**

Notes

1. Stucco loosely describes the medium but does not strictly conform to the classical definition of the term, as discussed in Wladimir Zwalf, ed., *A Catalogue of the Gandhara Sculpture in the British Museum*, vol. 1 (British Museum Press, 1996), appendix 4, 363. The medium was known in the region by the beginning of the Common Era by way of imported plaster casts of Late Hellenistic and Roman metal plaques; see Michael Jansen and Christian Luczanits, *Gandhara, The Buddhist Heritage of Pakistan: Legends, Monasteries, and Paradise,* English ed. (Verlag Philipp Von Zabern, 2008), 92–93, 318.
2. Kurt A. Behrendt, *The Art of Gandhara in the Metropolitan Museum of Art* (Metropolitan Museum of Art and Yale University Press, 2007), 79, fig. 61.
3. Stanislaw J. Czuma, *Kushan Sculpture: Images from Early India* (Cleveland Museum of Art, 1985), 214.
4. Jansen and Luczanits, *Gandhara, The Buddhist Heritage of Pakistan,* 319.
5. Ibid., 318, fig. 1.
6. Ibid., 319, fig. 3; Behrendt, *The Art of Gandhara in the Metropolitan Museum of Art,* 65, fig. 28.
7. Zwalf, *A Catalogue of the Gandhara Sculpture in the British Museum,* vol. 2, fig. 545; Czuma, *Kushan Sculpture,* cat. no. 120.

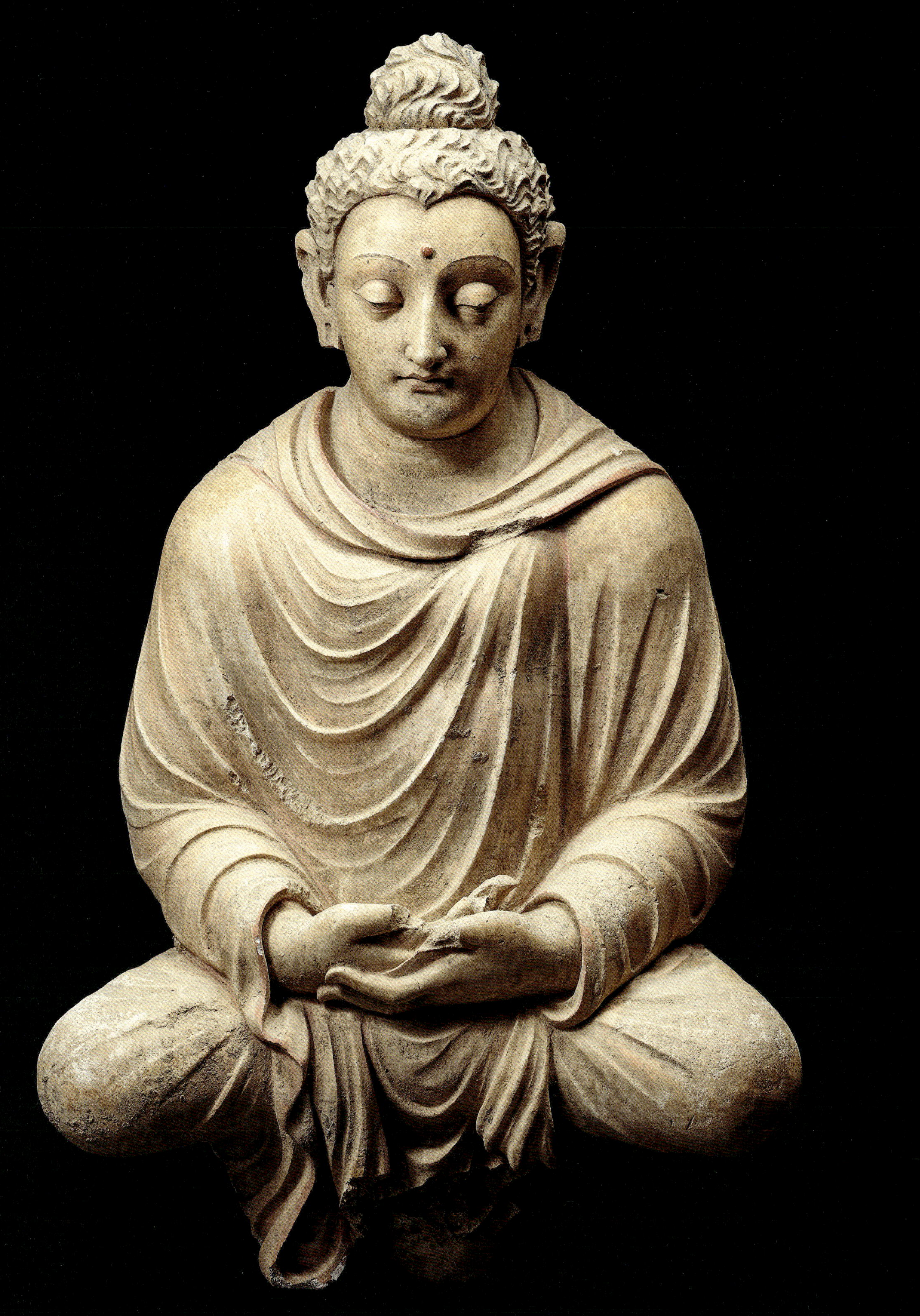

Buddha Shakyamuni

Ancient region of Gandhara, Pakistan or Afghanistan, c. 6th century

Copper alloy
11 ⅛ × 3 ⅞ × 2 ¹⁵⁄₁₆ in. (28.2 × 9.9 × 7.4 cm)

Here, Buddha Shakyamuni stands in a graceful posture (*abhanga*) with subtle movement of the hips and his right knee slightly flexed. The hair is arranged in concentric rings extending from the forehead, in a variant of the wave and snail-shell curl styles associated with the Gandhara Buddha.[1] The Buddha wears a simple monastic robe with the generous drape of the cloth falling in loose folds over the body. An inner garment shows at the ankle. His lowered left hand holds a gathered hem of the robe (the once protruding folds of cloth now missing). The raised right hand is broken off at the wrist but would have made the open-palmed gesture of reassurance (*abhaya* mudra): The style and iconography of late Gandhara copper-alloy standing Buddhas is consistent, and the hand gesture is thus predictable. The figure was cast separately from the pedestal and attached by tangs beneath the feet, and the tall, tapering plinth is chased with a dedicatory inscription in Brahmi characters.[2] The dating of this Buddha is supported by the paleography of the Brahmi inscription.[3] Three copper-alloy statues of Buddha of similar size and overall style were reputedly discovered at the important monastic site of Sahri Bahlol in the north of present-day Pakistan, two with the snail-shell curl hairstyle and one with the concentric ring style of the Xuzhou example.[4] A find of three similar bronzes at one major cultural site suggests that they are likely to have been cast at a local foundry, and closely comparable stylistic elements might indicate a similar provenance for the Xuzhou Buddha. Buddhist images are known to have accompanied traveling monks, pilgrims, and merchants, and in this way the works would have influenced the Buddhist art of surrounding regions and farther afield on the Silk Road in Central Asia and China: The concentric ring hairstyle of Chinese Northern Wei (386–534 CE) Buddhas echoes the earlier Gandhara model.[5] Two similar standing Buddhas, lacking their original pedestals, have been discovered recently in a Tibetan monastery collection,[6] and they are the only examples in the style group — perhaps less than two dozen bronzes in total — that retain an original patina with no surface corrosion as a result of burial. One of these bronzes evidently had similar casting issues seen on the back of the Xuzhou Buddha, with large flaws and substantial contemporary repairs.[7]

The naturalistic flow of the Gandhara robe, reminiscent of the Roman toga in classical sculpture, is quite distinct from the contemporaneous Kushan (first–fourth century CE) and Gupta (fourth–sixth century CE) traditions in which the Buddha's robes are either diaphanous and cling to the body or have folds of cloth falling in a more or less symmetrical pattern.[8] This rare statue of Buddha Shakyamuni represents the final phase of the Greco-Roman sculptural style of the Gandhara region, the legacy of Alexander the Great's invasion of Northern India (329–326 BCE) and subsequent contact with the classical world. **DW**

Notes
1. See for comparison the hairstyle of schist and stucco Buddhas in Wladimir Zwalf, *A Catalogue of the Gandhara Sculpture in the British Museum*, vol. 2 (British Museum Press, 1996), figs. 30, 112, 573–79; ibid., figs. 1, 111.
2. Translated by Dr. F. R. Allchin as "This is the pious gift of the Sakya monk . . . an image of the Buddha, by Yaso-Nandini . . . together with mother and father, most difficult . . . Buddha, by the teacher." See Nick Douglas, *The Enlightened Ones in Sacred Buddhist Art* (Kreitman Gallery, 1980), 16–19, pl. 6.
3. Pratapaditya Pal, *Asian Art at the Norton Simon Museum: Art from the Indian Subcontinent* (Yale University Press in association with the Norton Simon Art Foundation, 2003), 55.
4. Ulrich von Schroeder, *Indo-Tibetan Bronzes* (Visual Dharma Publications, 1981), 81, figs. 4A, B, C.
5. See for comparison the hairstyle of the Northern Wei gilt-bronze Maitreya dated 486 CE in Denise Patry Leidy and Donna Strahan, *Wisdom Embodied: Chinese Buddhist and Daoist Sculpture in the Metropolitan Museum of Art* (Metropolitan Museum of Art and Yale University Press, 2010), cat. no 4.
6. Ulrich von Schroeder, *Buddhist Sculptures in Tibet*, vol. 1 (Visual Dharma Publications, 2001), 30–31, figs. 1A-E.
7. Ibid., pl. 1E.
8. See Stanislaw J. Czuma, *Kushan Sculpture: Images from Early India* (Cleveland Museum of Art in cooperation with Indiana University Press, 1985), pls. 15, 16, and Von Schroeder, *Buddhist Sculptures in Tibet*, 1981, figs. 43B, 45E.

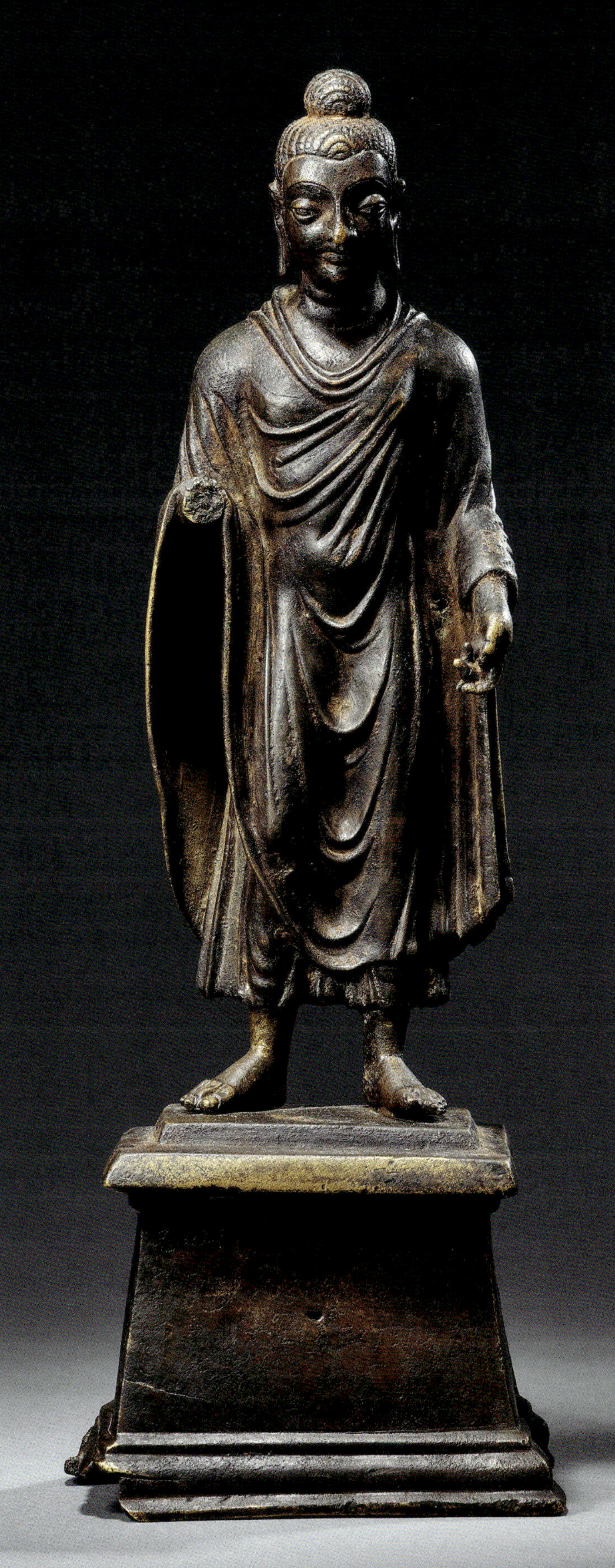

Padmapani, Lotus-Bearing Avalokiteshvara

Swat, Pakistan, c. 7th century

Copper alloy with silver inlay
5 ⁵⁄₁₆ × 3 ¹⁄₁₆ × 2 in. (13.5 × 7.7 × 5.1 cm)

Avalokiteshvara Padmapani is identified by the lotus flower (*padma*) held in the left hand and the effigy of Buddha Amitabha, the bodhisattva's spiritual progenitor, at the center of the crown amid abundant hair curls. The important Buddhist deity is seated in a regal attitude with left leg pendant (*lalitasana*) and the index finger of the right hand extended toward the side of the head, a posture that has led this form of Padmapani to be described as "the pensive bodhisattva." The youthful, robust figure wears a dhoti around his naked torso, with loose cloth draped over the front of the pedestal,[1] and jewelry that includes a large hoop ear plug in the left ear and a small gem-set earring in the right. Similar asymmetric ear adornment is seen on other seventh- and early eighth-century bronzes from the region.[2] It likely reflects contemporary precious metal and gem-set jewelry designs worn by local nobility: A Patola Shahi bronze group dated by inscription to 714 includes the figure of a donor king wearing a tubular ear plug in the left ear and a smaller jeweled earring in the right.[3] In the Greater Kashmir regions, this distinct jewelry fashion appears in sculpture from about the early seventh century into the eighth century.[4] The vogue is also evident in seventh- or eighth-century stone reliefs depicting donor figures at Chabahil, Kathmandu, Nepal,[5] suggesting cultural exchange between the Himalayan kingdoms. Nepalese deities are similarly adorned, such as a seventh-century stone Vajrapani at Dhvaka baha, Kathmandu, and an eighth- or ninth-century Nepalese gilt-copper goddess now in the Potala Palace in Lhasa.[6]

This specific iconographic form of Avalokiteshvara originated during the Kushan period (first–fourth century CE). Stone sculpture from Gandhara and Mathura mostly depict the deity seated at ease on a wicker stool.[7] The wickerwork roundels of a Gandhara example in the Matsuoka Museum are closely comparable to this figure, illustrating Gandhara's stylistic legacy in Swat.[8] The number of seventh- and eighth-century Swat bronzes with this iconography is evidence of the deity's continued popularity in the province.[9] A rare example now in the Potala Palace depicts an eight-armed aspect of the bodhisattva with diminutive donor figures kneeling at his feet, revealing an elaborate cult and devout veneration of the pensive Avalokiteshvara Padmapani in the Swat Valley region.[10]

Chinese pilgrims such as Faxian (337–c. 422 CE) traveled the Silk Road to Gandhara and south to Buddhist centers of the Kushan and Gupta (fourth–sixth century CE) empires, absorbing local cultural and artistic traditions. This distinct sculptural form was introduced to China by at least the Northern Wei period (386–534 CE): A bodhisattva in the pensive attitude is depicted in low relief on the back of the aureole of the Chinese gilt-bronze Buddha from 471 in the Xuzhou Collection (cat. 19). By the seventh century, when this elegant figure of Avalokiteshvara Padmapani was cast in the Swat Valley, the sculptural model had become popular in Korea and Japan, although worshipped there as Maitreya, Buddha of the Future.[11] **DW**

Notes
1. A short inscription incised on the back of the pedestal is read as *vajrasina* in Bonhams, Hong Kong, October 7, 2019, lot 801.
2. Ulrich von Schroeder, *Indo-Tibetan Bronzes* (Visual Dharma Publications, 1981), figs. 6D, 6H.
3. John Siudmak, *The Hindu-Buddhist Sculpture of Ancient Kashmir and Its Influences* (Brill, 2013), pl. 146.
4. A standing Prajnaparamita from Bolor dating to 600–625 seems to be one of the earliest examples with a large tubular ear plug in the left ear, ibid., pl. 141, and the 714 bronze group is perhaps toward the end of the period, ibid., pl. 146.
5. Pratapaditya Pal, *The Arts of Nepal: Part I, Sculpture* (E. J. Brill, 1974), pls. 159, 161.
6. Ibid., pl. 14; Ulrich von Schroeder, *Buddhist Sculptures in Tibet*, vol. 1 (Visual Dharma Publications, 2001), 479, fig. 150C.
7. See Wladimir Zwalf, *A Catalogue of the Gandhara Sculpture in the British Museum* (British Museum Press, 1996), figs. 79, 80, and Stanislaw J. Czuma, *Kushan Sculpture: Images from Early India* (Cleveland Museum of Art in cooperation with Indiana University Press, 1985), 78, cat. no. 19, and 79, figs. 19.1-.2.
8. Michael Jansen and Christian Luczanits, *Gandhara, The Buddhist Heritage of Pakistan: Legends, Monasteries, and Paradise*, English ed. (Verlag Philipp Von Zabern, 2008), 246, fig. 6.
9. Ibid., 43; and Von Schroeder, *Indo-Tibetan Bronzes*, 1981, 85, figs. 6G, 6I.
10. Von Schroeder, *Buddhist Sculptures in Tibet*, vol. 1, 44–45.
11. René-Yvon Lefebvre d'Argencé and Diana Turner, eds., *5000 Years of Korean Art* (Asian Art Museum of San Francisco, 1979), 83, fig. 76; Kyōtarō Nishikawa and Emily J. Sano, *The Great Age of Japanese Buddhist Sculpture AD 600–1300* (Kimbell Art Museum, 1982), 58–59, cat. no. 2.

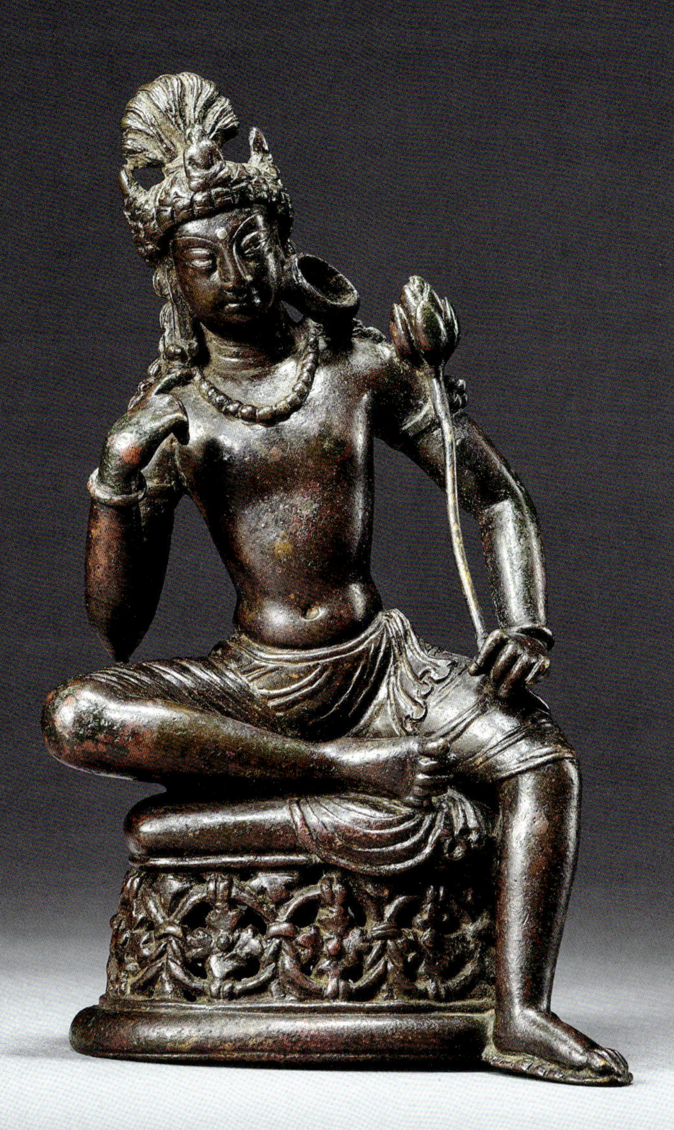

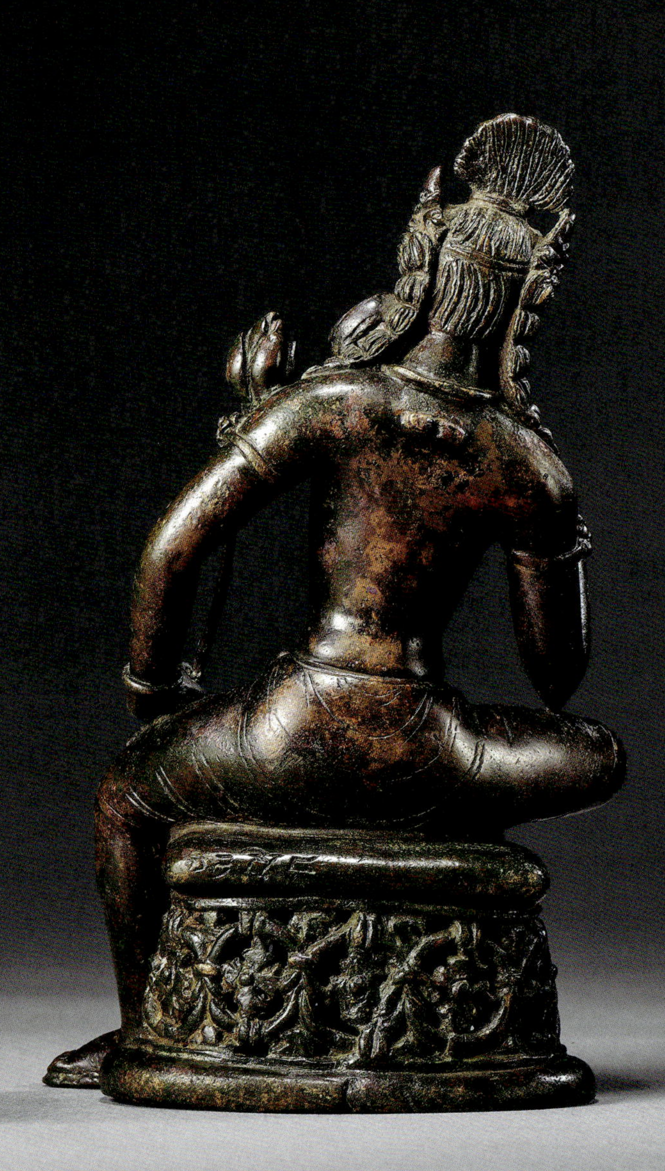

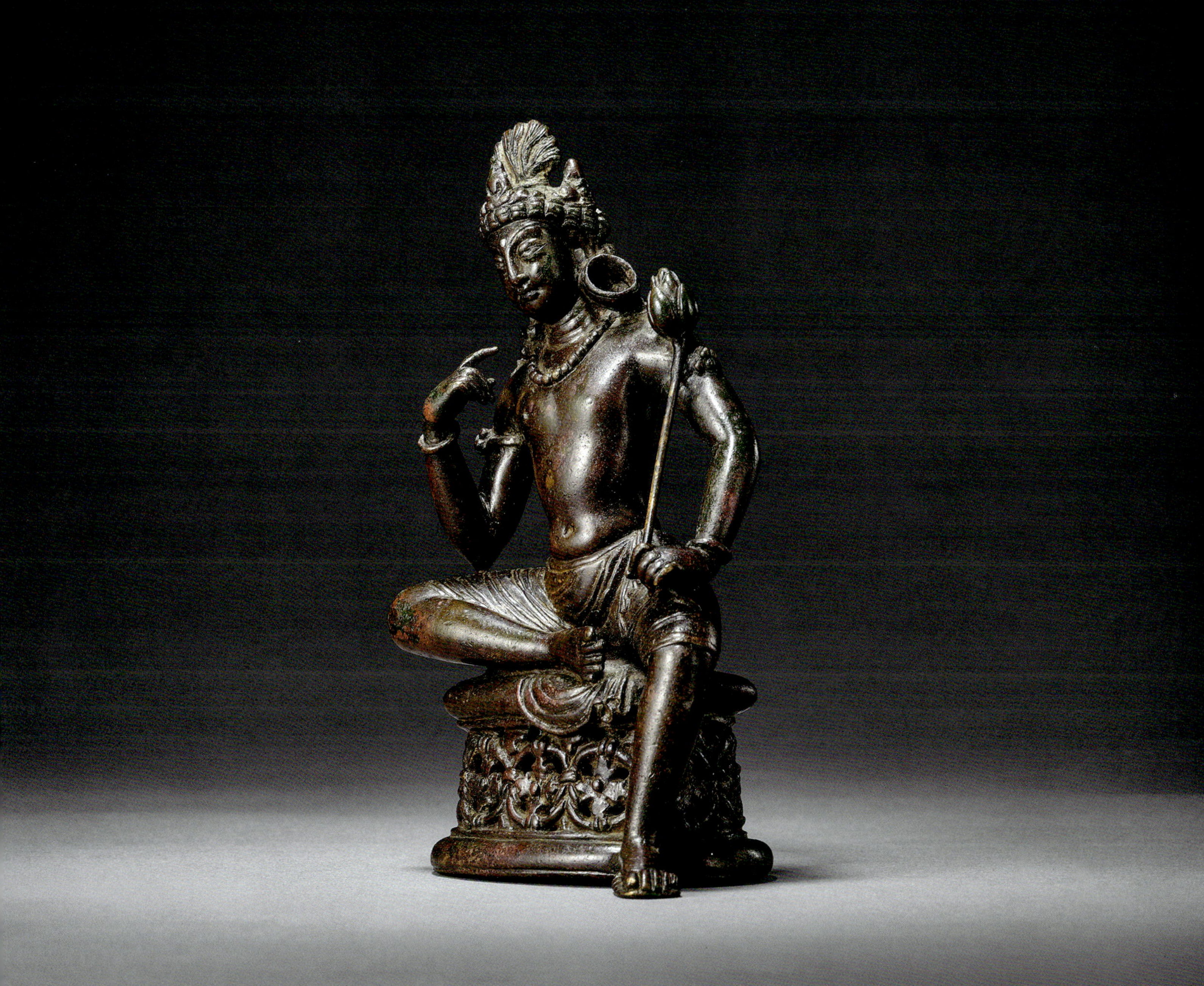

Buddha Enthroned

Greater Kashmir region, India or Pakistan, c. 8th–9th century

Copper alloy with silver inlay
15 ⁹⁄₁₆ × 6 ⁵⁄₁₆ × 4 ½ in. (39.5 × 16 × 11.5 cm)

The Buddha is seated with legs pendant (*bhadrasana*). Both hands make the teaching gesture (*dharmachakra* mudra) while the left holds a gathered hem of the robe. This specific iconographic posture appears in fifth- and sixth-century Gandhara and western Deccan sculptures that depict seated bhadrasana teaching Buddhas flanked by standing figures of the bodhisattvas Maitreya and Avalokiteshvara.[1] Juhyung Rhi suggests that the Buddha in the majority of these sculptures likely represents Shakyamuni, and the inclusion of Avalokiteshvara indicates that many of the triads were dedications by Mahayanists.[2] The iconographic combination of the bhadrasana teaching Buddha, Maitreya, and Avalokiteshvara is maintained in the greater Kashmir region, seen in a Patola Shahi group in the Pritzker Collection dated 714.[3] The Buddha in the Pritzker group wears earrings and a tasseled mantle of Scythian origin, similar to this Xuzhou Buddha.[4] The mantle and earrings are symbols of regal status, but in this context the adornments are likely meant to celebrate the majesty of Buddha's spiritual attainment. The crescent moon and sun disk at each shoulder (now partly broken and missing on this example) represent the radiance of Buddha's divine light.[5] Statues of the Buddha from the Greater Kashmir region that include the combination seen on this figure of mantle, earrings, and sun and moon symbols usually include a necklace and crown. Furthermore, the simple V shape of the mantle differs from the classical tripartite design that extends over the upper arms of such sculptures, as seen in the Pritzker Buddha and the teaching Buddha in the Speelman Collection.[6] The placement of the feet on the edge of the pedestal (rather than on individual lotus flowers) is also unusual for classical sculpture from the region, although it does occur in later examples.[7]

The openwork pedestal is supported by columns at the back with pseudo-Corinthian and acanthus-leaf capitals, a legacy of the Greco-Roman influence in Gandharan sculpture. Two rampant leonine beasts with beaked muzzles appear at the front of the dais. This composite griffin-like mythical animal is depicted in northern Indian sculpture of the Kushan period (first–fourth century CE), seen crouching in the crown of a Mathura stone Avalokiteshvara and in motion on an openwork ivory plaque from Begram.[8] In Kashmir, the rampant form of the creature is seen in the pedestals of late seventh- and early eighth-century works, typically in conjunction with lions and nature spirits (*yaksha*) that are not included in the Xuzhou example.[9] The Buddha's eyes and *urna* are inlaid with silver, and black pitch accentuates the rims of the eyes, pupils, and eyebrows.[10] The almond-shaped eyes, lobed lower lip, grooved eyebrows, peaked hairline, and the evenly spaced rows of hair curls on the head and cranial protuberance (*ushnisha*) are comparable to a Buddha head in the Sri Pratap Singh Museum dating to the second or third quarter of the eighth century.[11] An eighth- or ninth-century date is thus possible for this large Kashmir school bronze, although unorthodox iconographic and stylistic features make a precise provenance and dating uncertain. **DW**

Notes
1. Michael Jansen and Christian Luczanits, *Gandhara, The Buddhist Heritage of Pakistan: Legends, Monasteries, and Paradise*, English ed. (Verlag Philipp Von Zabern, 2008), 246–48, figs. 8, 9.
2. Juhyung Rhi, "Changing Buddhism," in ibid., 246.
3. John Siudmak, *The Hindu-Buddhist Sculpture of Ancient Kashmir and Its Influences* (Brill, 2013), 320, pl. 146.
4. The mantle is discussed in Siudmak, *The Hindu-Buddhist Sculpture of Ancient Kashmir and Its Influences*, 319, and in Rob Linrothe, *Collecting Paradise: Buddhist Art of Kashmir and Its Legacies* (Mary and Leigh Block Museum of Art and Rubin Museum of Art, 2014), 56–57.
5. Linrothe, *Collecting Paradise*, 56.
6. Siudmak, *The Hindu-Buddhist Sculpture of Ancient Kashmir and Its Influences*, 328, pl. 149.
7. Helmut Uhlig, *On the Path to Enlightenment: The Berti Aschmann Foundation of Tibetan Art at the Museum Rietberg Zürich* (Museum Rietberg Zürich, 1995), 81.
8. Martin Lerner, *The Flame and the Lotus: Indian and Southeast Asian Art from the Kronos Collections* (Metropolitan Museum of Art, 1984), 31, 33, cat. no. 7; Jansen and Luczanits, *Gandhara, The Buddhist Heritage of Pakistan*, cat. no. 264.
9. Siudmak, *The Hindu-Buddhist Sculpture of Ancient Kashmir and Its Influences*, pls. 137, 161.
10. The tradition of metal and pitch inlay may have originated in Indian bronzes around the sixth century, with the earliest evidence seemingly the Gupta bronzes found at Phopnar with silver inlaid eyes and pitch-filled grooves denoting eyebrows. Ibid., 71n87.
11. Ibid., pl. 162.

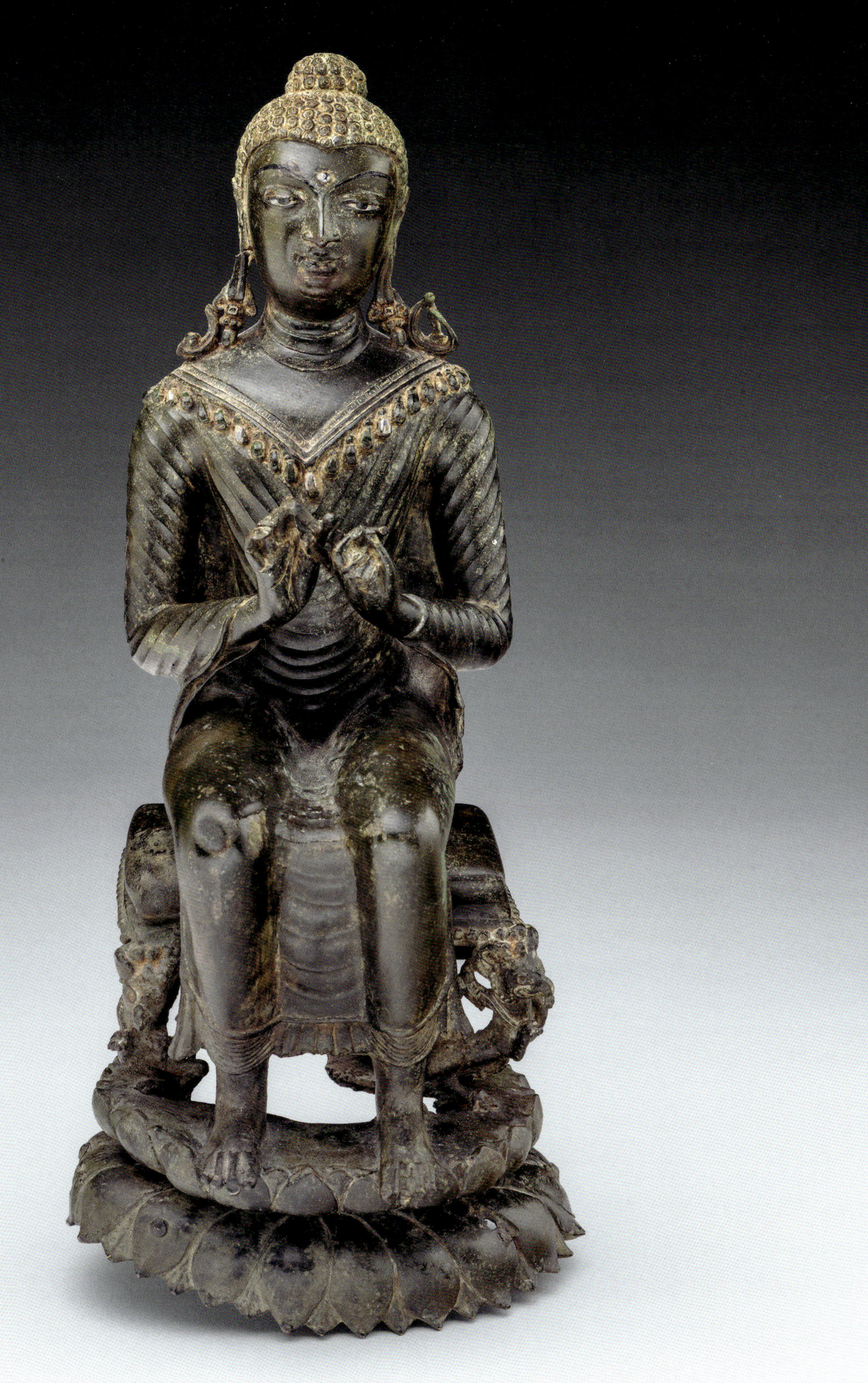

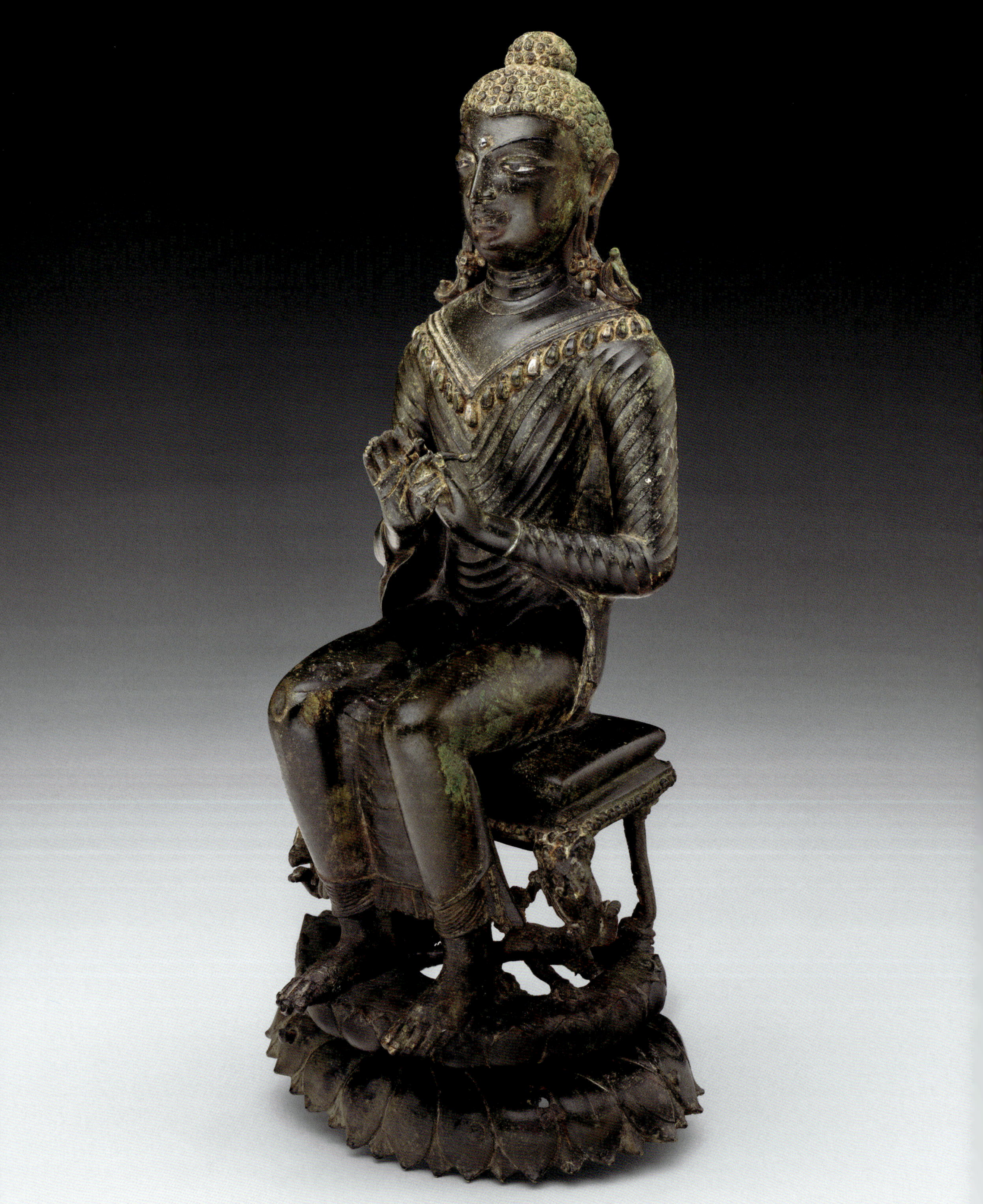

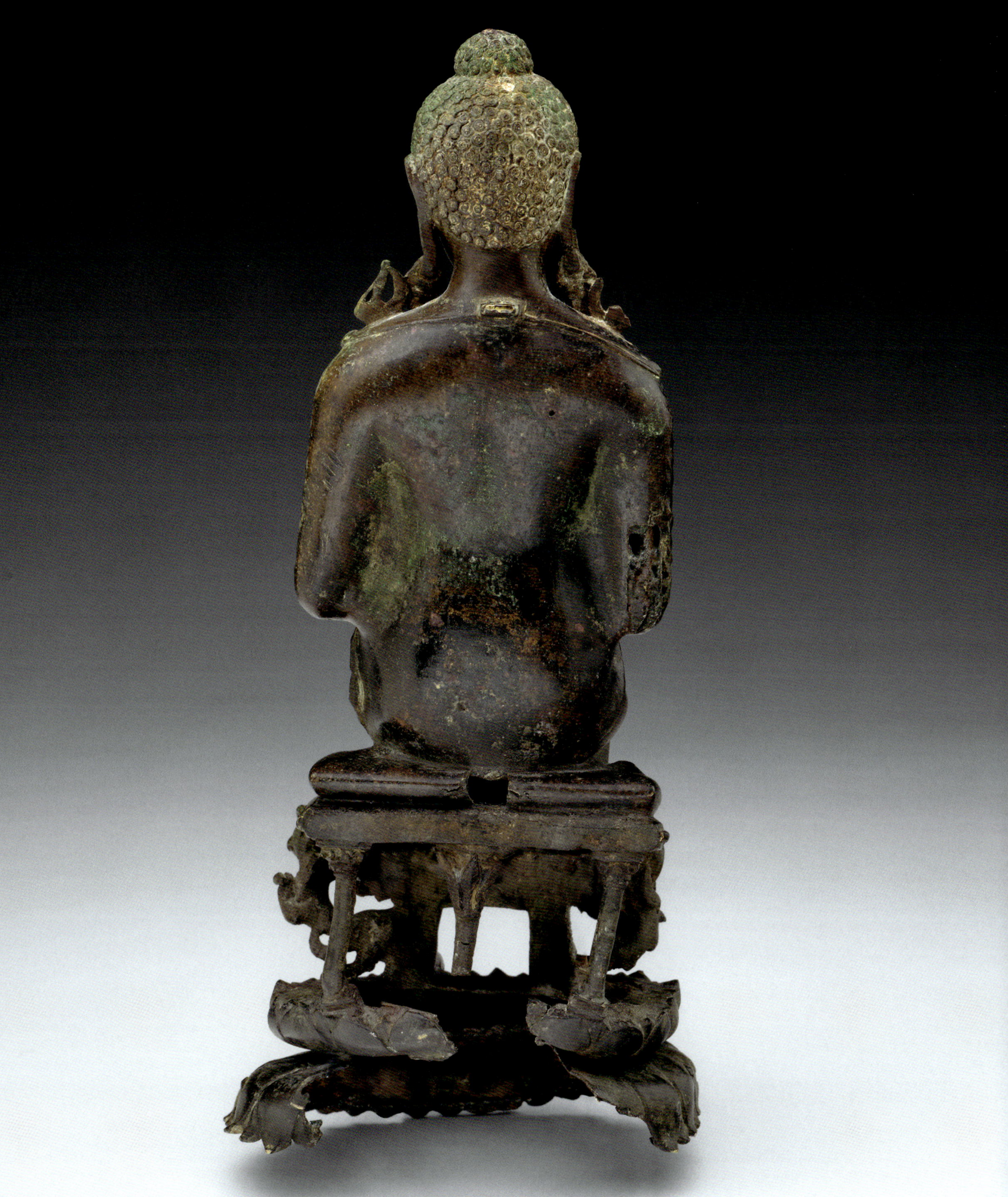

Buddha in Meditation

Sri Lanka, Anuradhapura period, c. 8th–9th century

Copper alloy with inlaid crystal
15 ¾ × 14 × 7 ¼ in. (40 × 35.6 × 18.4 cm)

This impressive work exemplifies the sculptural style of the late Anuradhapura period (c. 300–993 CE) in Sri Lanka.[1] Buddhism was introduced to Sri Lanka in the third century BCE by Indian missionaries. According to legend, Sanghamitta and Mahinda, daughter and son of the Indian ruler Ashoka, planted at Anuradhapura, the ancient capital of Sri Lanka, a sapling from the sacred bodhi tree of Bodh Gaya, under which the historical Buddha sat when he experienced his great enlightenment.

The figure of Buddha sits in meditation, his beautifully rendered hands resting on top of folded legs.[2] The calf of the right leg is placed on the left, with the sole of only the right foot fully visible, a posture known in Buddhist literature as *virasana*, "hero's seat."[3] The hands and feet are rendered naturalistically and with great sensitivity, suggesting the figure is relaxed and in deep repose. The image was once placed on a seat or throne setting, now lost.[4] The eyes are inset with crystal. As noted by Ulrich von Schroeder, the crystal eyes in Sri Lankan sculpture were often inset with a small gem or dark substance corresponding to the pupil of an eye, making the eyes all the more lifelike.[5] The Buddha wears an upper and lower robe, the former falling in regular pleats over the left shoulder, under the right breast, around the back, and over the upper thighs. A folded shawl rests on the left shoulder, ending in an elegant flutter just above the navel. This feature is seen in other contemporary works from Sri Lanka, notably three copper-alloy sculptures in the Archaeological Museum, Anuradhapura.[6] Close stylistic affinities can be found in South Indian sculpture as well.[7] The lower robe covers the hips and falls to the ankle and midcalf. The particular treatment of the fine robe is characteristic of Sri Lankan sculpture, seen in the works noted above and in others, including a masterwork in the Archaeological Museum, Anuradhapura.[8] The facial features, including a protruding full lower lip, an aquiline nose, and a notably rounded chin, are physiognomic features typical of fine works from Sri Lanka of this period.[9] The hair curls and long earlobes are signs (*lakshana*) of the transcendent nature of Buddha and are part of the traditional iconography used for representing the historical Buddha.[10] The back is finished as beautifully as the front of the sculpture, with the robe cascading exquisitely along the body, the folded cloth falling from the left shoulder down the back and ending in a subtly observed flutter. The surface of the sculpture reflects the conditions in which it was kept over the last twelve hundred years, which likely included careful burial. According to Von Schroeder, "In times of war, the treasured possessions of the monastic establishments were either carried away by the monks to their new shelters or buried."[11] Works of outstanding quality such as this sculpture can impart the experience of profound peace that the Buddhist tradition expounds. **JC**

Notes
1. On the periodization of Sri Lankan sculpture based on its respective capitals (Anuradhapura and Polonnaruva), see Ulrich von Schroeder, *The Golden Age of Sculpture in Sri Lanka* (Visual Dharma Publications, 1992), 14.
2. Von Schroeder notes that Sri Lankan and South Indian sculptures of seated Buddhas differ from those of North India, where the soles of both feet are exposed, unlike this example where the right foot lies on top of the left. See ibid., 33.
3. Ibid.
4. See a contemporary sculpture of Buddha seated on a lotus seat in ibid., 44–45.
5. See another example of Sri Lankan sculpture of this period with crystal eyes in ibid., 52–53.
6. Ibid., 46–49.
7. See a standing bronze Buddha in the Rijksmuseum, Amsterdam. The circa seventh-century Rijksmuseum sculpture has been attributed to South India, Sri Lanka, or (less convincingly) Java. See Jan Fontein, *The Sculpture of Indonesia* (Harry N. Abrams, 1990), 178–79.
8. Von Schroeder, *The Golden Age of Sculpture in Sri Lanka*, 44–45.
9. See especially ibid., 52–53.
10. For a succinct description of these marks of transcendence, see Robert E. Buswell, Jr., and Donald S. Lopez, Jr., *The Princeton Dictionary of Buddhism* (Princeton University Press, 2014), 463.
11. Von Schroeder, *The Golden Age of Sculpture in Sri Lanka*, 44. See Xuzhou Collection conservation report on this sculpture by Dr. Anna Bennett, December 12, 2017.

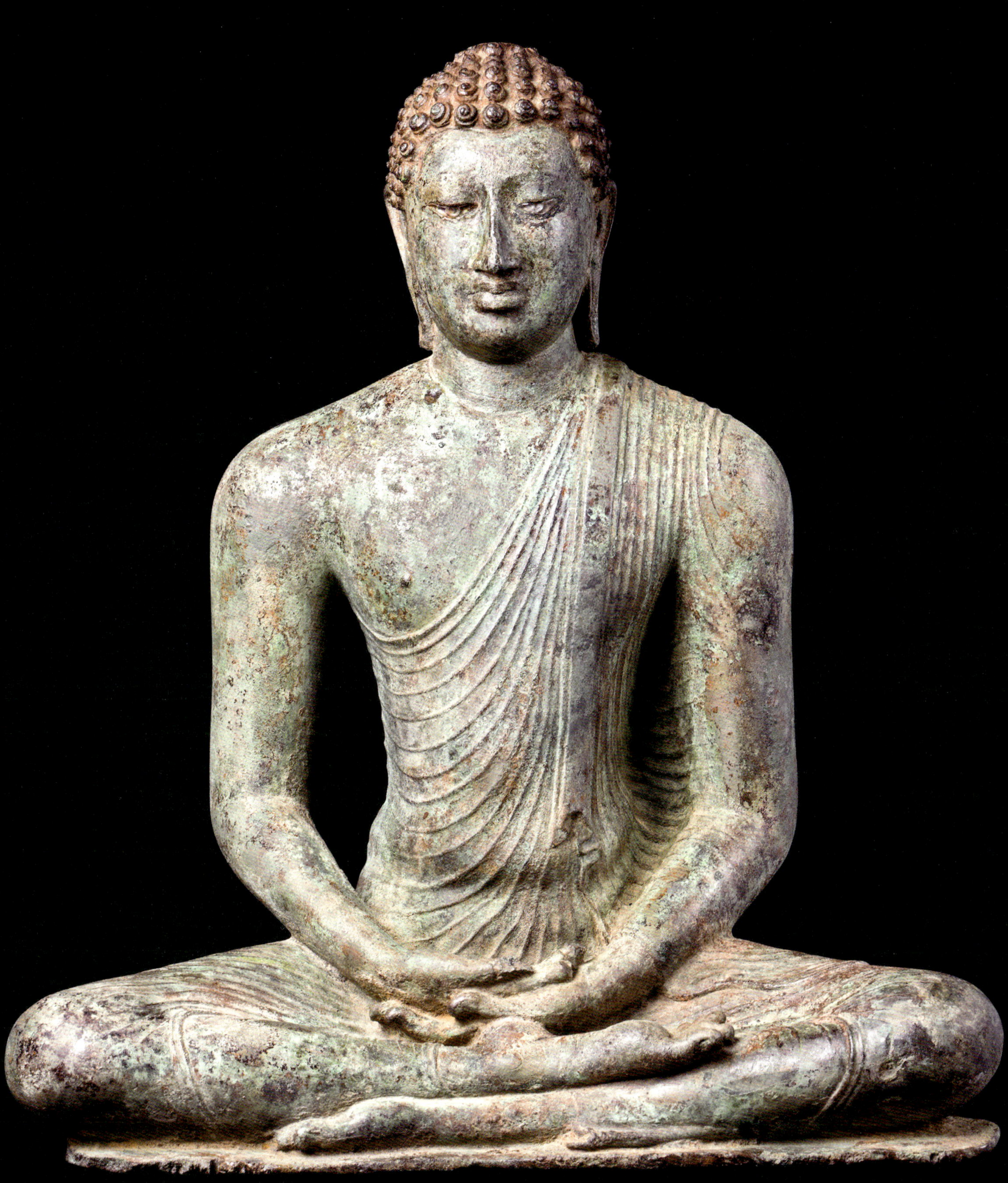

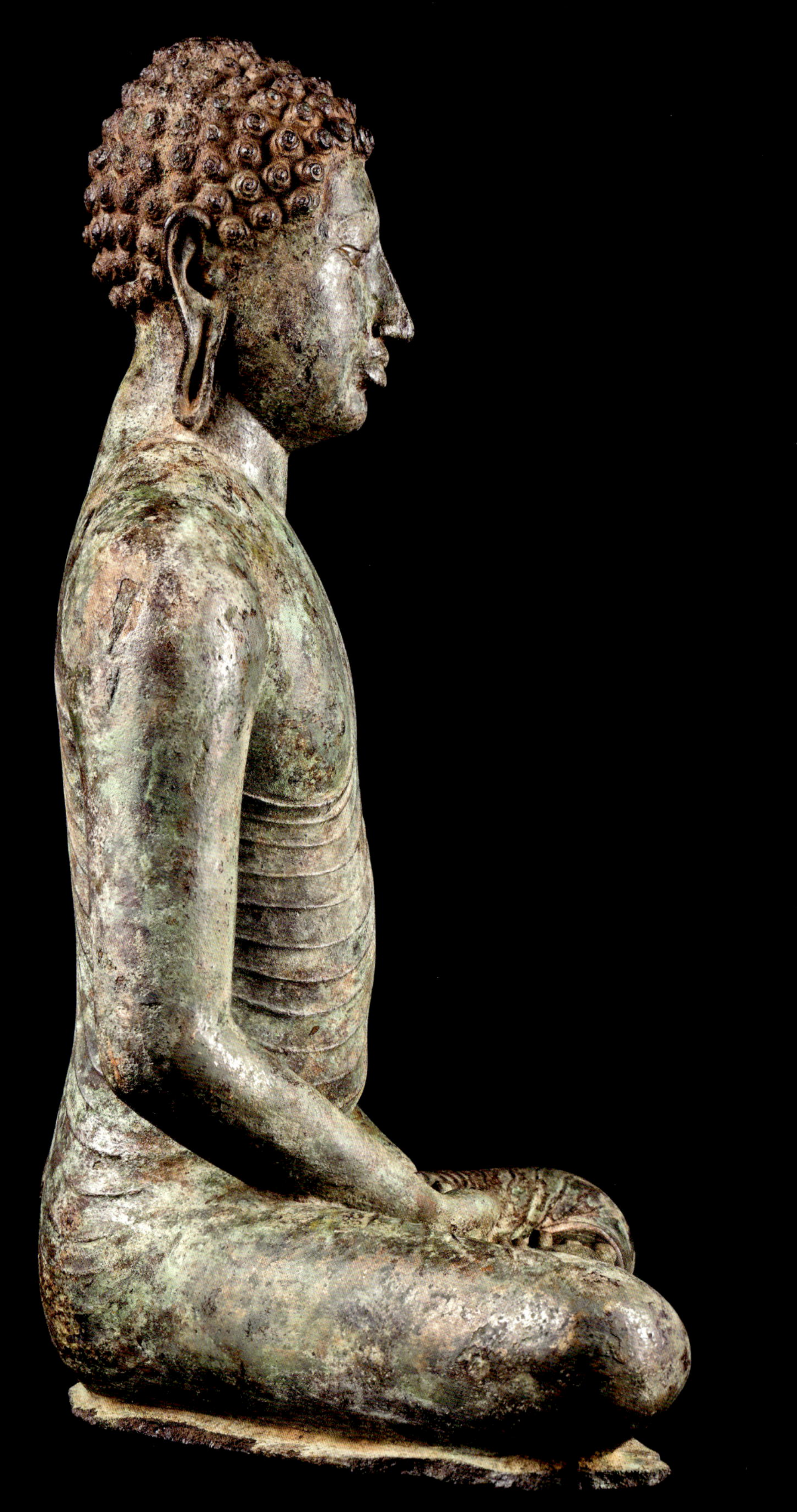

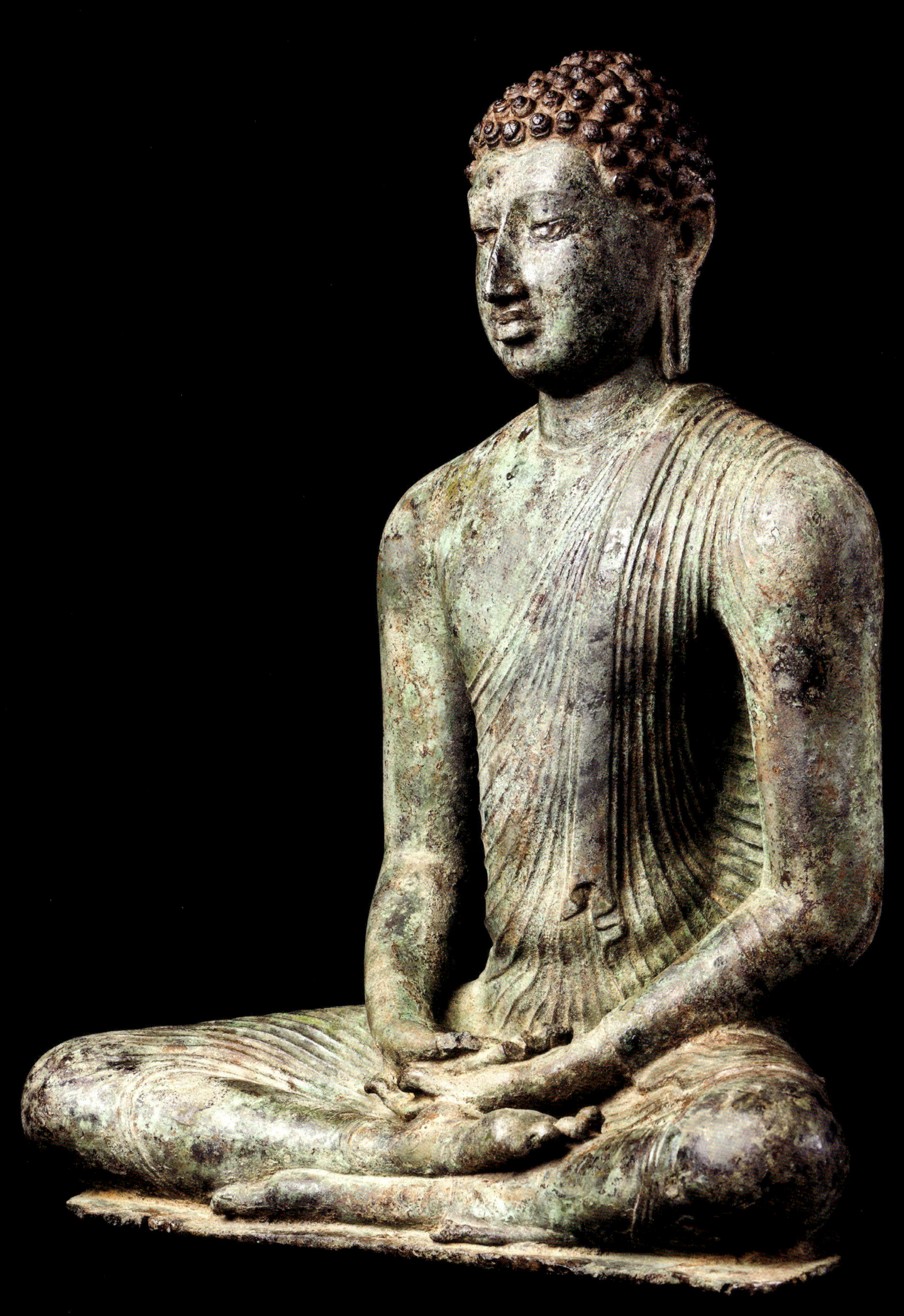

Buddha Amitabha

Indonesia, c. 9th century

Copper alloy
10 ⁷⁄₁₆ × 8 × 6 ½ in. (26.4 × 20.3 × 16.5 cm)

Amitabha, the Buddha of Infinite Light, sits in meditation on top of an opened lotus flower. The posture (legs folded in a relaxed *padmasana*),[1] the hand gesture (back of the right hand resting on the left palm, thumbs touching), and the downward gaze indicate a deep inward focus, befitting the spiritual presence of the Enlightened One. The Buddha wears a monk's robe, the gossamer fabric covering his left shoulder and arm, crossing the chest and covering both legs to the ankles. One end is gathered in a cascade of folds at his left shoulder. His right arm and shoulder are bare. Amitabha Buddha was one of a group of Wisdom Buddhas that became popular in Mahayana Buddhism. He is particularly associated with the Pure Land Sukhavati, where he is said to reside and where his devotees aspire to be reborn. Under patronage from the ruling Shailendra dynasty (c. sixth–ninth centuries), Buddhism flourished in central Java and remains potent in the extraordinary monuments they built during their hegemony.

Although this iconographic form can be found in cultures throughout the Buddhist world, the style of the figure, its physiognomy, the treatment of the hands and feet, and the lotus petals and base indicate that the image was made in central Java, Indonesia, probably in the ninth century. The sculpture is very similar to those in the central Javanese site of Borobudur, which was constructed at about that time. This remarkable stone monument consists of seven ascending tiers adorned with narrative scenes and images that reflect increasingly refined spiritual states. One hundred and eight seated Buddhas appear on four sides, and an additional seventy-two Buddha images are depicted in the uppermost terrace of the structure. An image of Amitabha Buddha at Borobudur, just over a meter (41 ¾ inches) in height and carved from andesite stone, shows the same treatment of the torso, hands, folded legs, long earlobes, and prominent hair curls seen in this figure.[2] Another stone image of Amitabha Buddha from Borobudur that is now in the National Museum, Jakarta, is remarkably similar to this sculpture in its treatment of the arms and hands, with long, full fingers and the tips of the thumbs touching as they rest in the lap.[3] At Borobudur, ninety-two life-size sculptures of Amitabha are arranged on the western side of the monument.

Another close comparison can be found in a copper-alloy Javanese sculpture of Buddha Vairochana in the Metropolitan Museum of Art.[4] The Metropolitan Buddha's torso, lotus petals, and base are particularly like those in this sculpture. The Metropolitan sculpture has a halo encircling the head and two openings at the back of the pedestal, indicating that a larger halo or throne back was once attached to the sculpture. The base at the back of this sculpture has an opening and a brace that once secured a halo of some sort, and what appears to be a broken tang at the back of the Buddha's head would have helped to secure the missing halo.

The notable jade-green patina of the Xuzhou Buddha Amitabha resulted from chemical reactions between the copper alloy and the environmental elements to which it was exposed over many centuries. **JC**

Notes

1. The padmasana or "lotus seat" usually places both feet turned upward on the opposite thigh; here, the left foot rests on the opposite thigh, but the right foot rests on the opposite calf.
2. Denise Patry Leidy, *The Art of Buddhism: An Introduction to Its History and Meaning* (Shambhala, 2008), fig. 8.18, 184.
3. Published in Jan Fontein, *The Sculpture of Indonesia* (Harry N. Abrams, 1990), 134–35.
4. Published in Martin Lerner and Steven Kossak, *The Lotus Transcendent: Indian and Southeast Asian Art from the Samuel Eilenberg Collection* (Metropolitan Museum of Art, 1991), fig. 139, 179. The Metropolitan Museum of Art sculpture is 19 ⅝ in. (19.3 cm) tall.

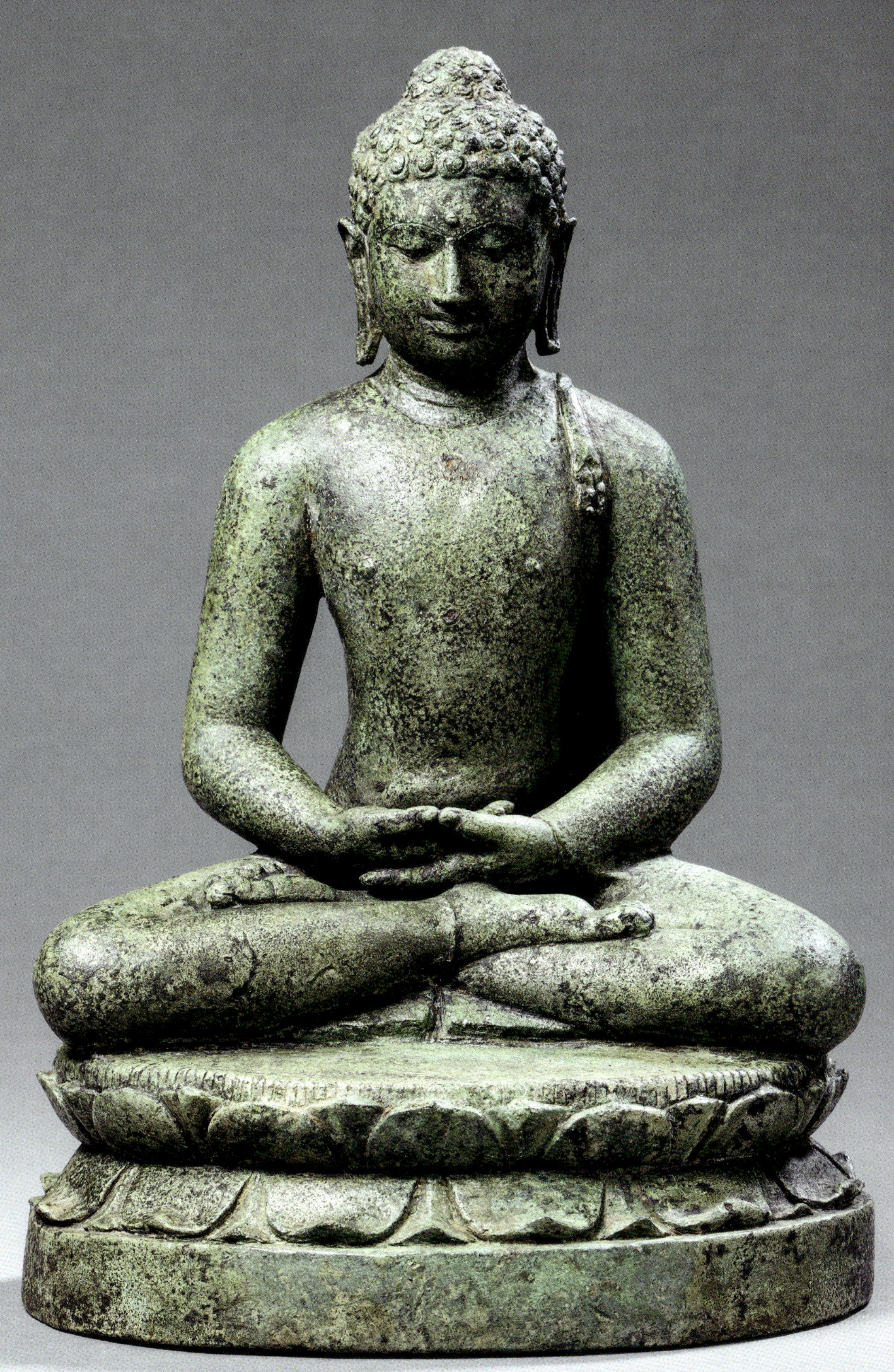

Bodhisattva Vajrapani

Java, Indonesia, c. 9th–10th century

Silver with gold inlay and copper-alloy base
3 ¼ × 1 ¹⁵⁄₁₆ × 2 ⁵⁄₁₆ in. (8.2 × 5 × 5.9 cm)

Vajrapani is a Buddhist deity whose emblem is the thunderbolt scepter (*vajra*), here resting on the lotus above his left shoulder. The vajra is an implement sometimes described as diamond-like and indestructible, thereby imparting a fierce power to Vajrapani. Indeed, he is portrayed in this sculpture as a semi-wrathful deity, with eyebrows furrowed over an intense gaze. Wrathful deities play a significant role in Buddhist practice, for they highlight the necessary transformation of negative emotions (anger, fear) into the enlightened qualities of wisdom and compassion through meditative practices. Buddhist images were sometimes made to be part of large groups, representing Buddhist mandalas. Eighteen contemporary sculptures of similar size were uncovered in Java in 1976.[1] Assemblies of small sculptures formed three-dimensional mandalas, meant as a focus for contemplation and transformation. Such may have been the original intention for this finely cast image.

Particularly similar in style and period is a silver image of Avalokiteshvara in the Rijksmuseum, Amsterdam.[2] Dr. Pauline Lunsingh Scheurleer, a specialist in Indonesian sculpture, has assigned a date of about 870–930 to the Rijksmuseum sculpture and to this work as well, which was familiar to her from an earlier publication.[3] She noted that this sculpture is very similar to the Rijksmuseum sculpture in body shape and facial features, stating, "Both probably originate from the same Central Javanese workshop."[4] Dr. Pratapaditya Pal observed that the bodhisattva's foot does not rest properly on the lotus support arising from the base and, for this reason, argued that the base may not have been made specifically for this image.[5] However, the lotus-petal design of the base is very similar to that in the aforementioned Rijksmuseum sculpture. More likely, wear over more than a thousand years may have shifted the sculpture on its base. Numerous commissions of sculpture in silver, often with copper-alloy bases, can be found in Javanese sculpture of this period.[6] Moreover, artists of this period made spectacular use of gold and silver inlay in copper-alloy sculptures.[7]

During the ninth and tenth centuries, the Indonesian maritime kingdom of Shrivijaya (perhaps based in Sumatra) was a renowned Buddhist center, but there were also important Buddhist centers in central Java, such as the circa ninth-century temple of Borobudur. Less than one hundred yards from Borobudur, archaeologists have recently uncovered fragments of an inscription invoking a wrathful form of Vajrapani.[8] At the nearby ninth-century Javanese temple site of Mendut, a large stone image of the Buddha Avalokiteshvara is flanked by the bodhisattvas Avalokiteshvara and Vajrapani. The Sailendra rulers who built these monuments in central Java also supported the founding of a monastery at Nalanda in eastern India, perhaps the leading monastic university of its day.[9] That monastery likely was intended to house Indonesian students who traveled to India to study there before returning to Indonesia with advanced training in Buddhist literature, art, and practice. **JC**

Notes
1. See Jan Fontein, *The Sculpture of Indonesia* (Harry N. Abrams, 1990), 223–33.
2. Published in Pauline Lunsingh Scheurleer and Marijke J. Klokke, *Ancient Indonesian Bronzes: A Catalogue of the Exhibition in the Rijksmuseum Amsterdam* (E. J. Brill, 1988), 79.
3. Pratapaditya Pal, *The Sensuous Immortals: A Selection of Sculptures from the Pan-Asian Collection* (Los Angeles County Museum of Art, 1977), 192.
4. Scheurleer and Klokke, *Ancient Indonesian Bronzes*, 79.
5. Pal, *The Sensuous Immortals*, 192.
6. See Fontein, *The Sculpture of Indonesia*, nos. 46, 49, 65.
7. Ibid., nos. 39, 44, 45, 51, 52.
8. As noted in William Dalrymple, *The Golden Road: How Ancient India Transformed the World* (Bloomsbury Publishing, 2024), 194, citing Hudaya Kandahjaya, "The Scheme of Borobudur," in Andrea Acri and Peter Sharrock, eds., *The Creative South: Buddhist and Hindu Art in Medieval Maritime Asia*, vol. 2 (ISEAS, 2022), 55–73.
9. Scheurleer and Klokke, *Ancient Indonesian Bronzes*, 4.

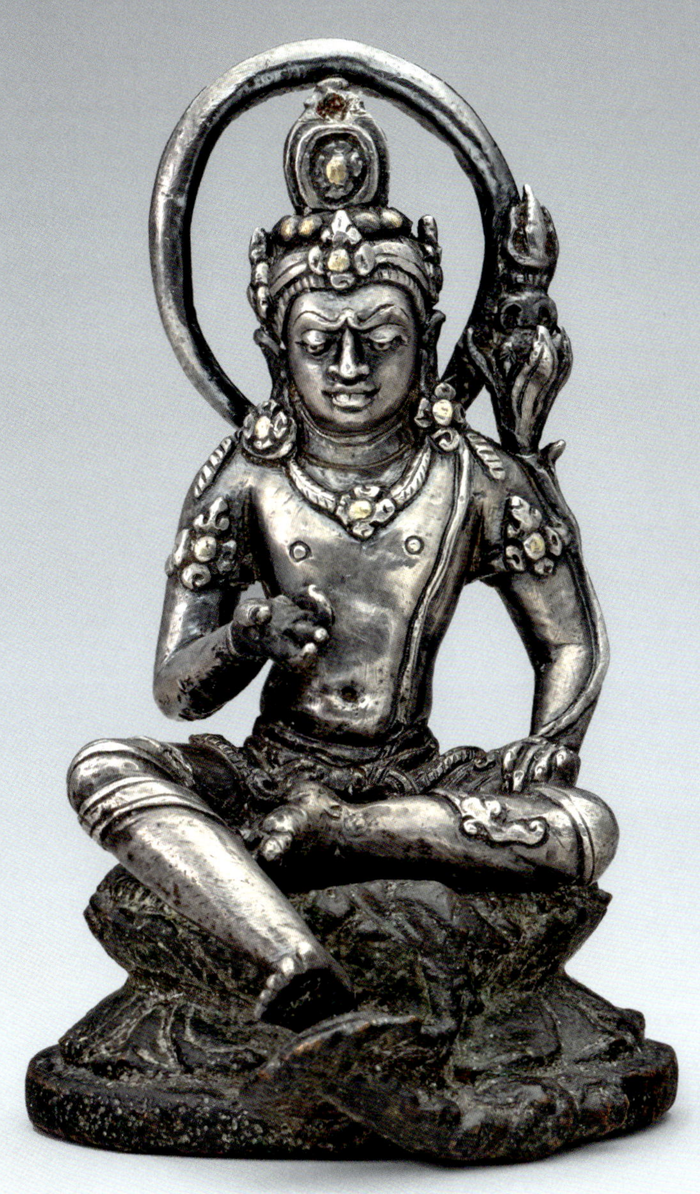

Buddha Maravijaya, Calling the Earth to Witness

Thailand, U-Thong style, c. 14th century

Copper alloy
31 × 17 ½ × 12 ¼ in. (78.7 × 44.5 × 31.1 cm)

This image captures the moment when the Buddha invoked the earth goddess to witness his great spiritual awakening, symbolized by the gesture of his right hand (*bhumisparsha* mudra, "earth-touching" gesture). The sculpture may be attributed to the early phase of the Ayutthaya kingdom, the ancient, southeastern capital of the modern state of Thailand. It became a powerful kingdom in the late fourteenth century, when Thai kings drove out the Cambodian Khmer rulers and governed from Ayutthaya between 1351 and 1767. Described by foreign visitors in the early sixteenth century as one of the three great powers of Asia (together with Cambodia and China), the Ayutthaya kingdom was built upon maritime trade.

Thai Buddhism, like that in the surrounding regions of Sri Lanka, Myanmar, Laos, and Cambodia, is one of the oldest forms of Buddhism, known as Theravada, the "Way of the Elders." It is rooted in the early Buddhist canon that was written in the Pali language.[1] According to the Theravada tradition, the Buddha's teachings were first recorded in texts written in Pali in Sri Lanka near the end of the first century CE.[2]

Earlier Thai Buddha images took inspiration from the artistic styles of eastern India, the Buddhist homeland.[3] However, after the destruction of Buddhist centers in North India in the early thirteenth century, Thai artists relied on local regional styles. The dignified, restrained expression, the narrow brows, incised lips and eyes, and the relatively flat planes of the face are all expressions of a uniquely Thai aesthetic, as is the elongated flaming protrusion on top of the Buddha's head. The U-Thong style, based in the city-state Ayutthaya, flourished between the thirteenth and fifteenth centuries. The name derives from the first ruler of Ayutthaya, who was known prior to the founding of the capital in 1351 as Prince U-Thong.

An emerald-green patina covers much of the surface. The dark brown areas may reflect prior attempts to clean the surface of external corrosion, revealing the dark oxide within the surface.[4] The long earlobes are one of the thirty-two major signs (*lakshana*) of the Buddha's spiritual nature, as is the flaming protrusion on the top of the head, known as *ushnisha* in Sanskrit.[5] In Thai Buddhist sculpture, the ushnisha tends to be especially tall, as in this example. The hair curls, more naturalistic in earlier Buddhist sculpture, here appear as tiny, regular spikes. The figure sits on a raised platform, shaped much like an opened lotus, though notably no lotus petals are delineated. The Buddha's upper and lower robes cling to the body beneath, and a narrow shawl falls from over the left shoulder to just above the navel.[6] The image is beautifully cast, with the back of the figure finished with great care and finesse. **JC**

Notes
1. Robert E. Buswell, Jr., and Donald S. Lopez, Jr., *The Princeton Dictionary of Buddhism* (Princeton University Press, 2014), 904–5.
2. Ibid., 612.
3. See Philip Rawson, *The Art of Southeast Asia* (Thames and Hudson, 1967, reprinted 1995), figs. 123–24.
4. My thanks to Dr. John Twilley for sharing his scientific assessment of the surface of this sculpture.
5. See Buswell and Lopez, *The Princeton Dictionary of Buddhism*, 463, 945.
6. Dr. Hiram Woodward notes similarly fashioned robe ends in Buddha figures; see Kanohansawat Prachoom, *Buddha Images* (Bangkok, 1969), 214–15. Email from Woodward to author, June 22, 2024.

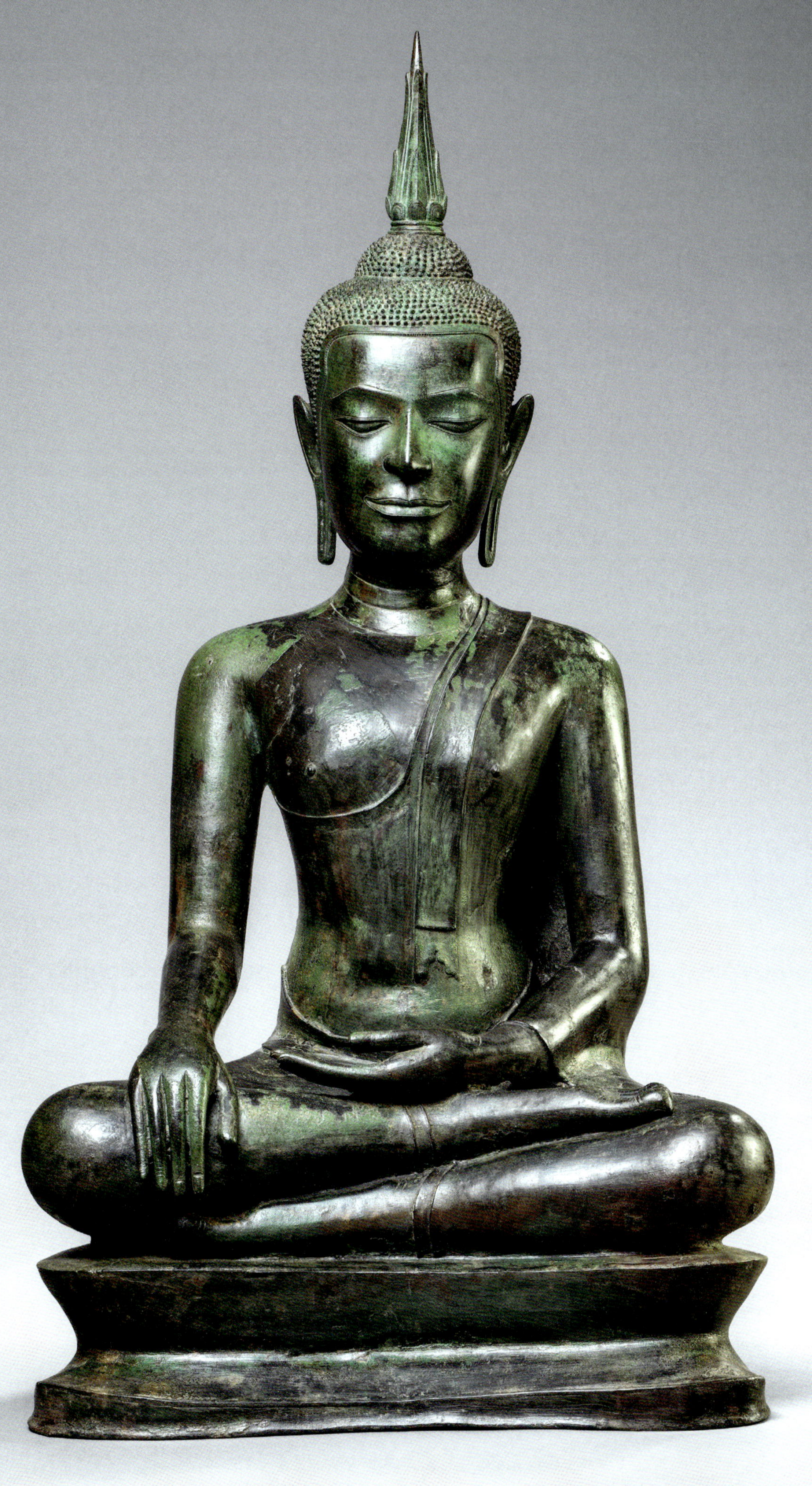

Padmapani, Lotus-Bearing Avalokiteshvara

Nepal, c. 10th century

Gilt copper and pigment
10 ½ × 8 ⁹⁄₁₆ × 6 in. (26.7 × 21.8 × 15.3 cm)

Avalokiteshvara, perhaps the most popular god in the Nepali Buddhist pantheon, is more commonly depicted as a standing figure than in this regal seated posture. The bodhisattva supports the pose with his left hand on the pedestal behind him while holding the stem of a lotus, the flower identifying this aspect of the deity as Padmapani, "lotus-bearer." His right hand makes the open-palmed, wish-fulfilling gesture (*varada* mudra). The supremely elegant sculpture captures the essence of the bodhisattva's perception of the human condition, with his hand reaching out to his devotees and a graceful inclination of the head embodying Avalokiteshvara's common epithet, "He who looks down with compassion." A halo of flames further symbolizes the bodhisat-tva's pristine awareness. The generous, well-proportioned pedestal represents the natural rounded form of a broad-petaled lotus flower with stamens surrounding the obconical receptacle. Buddha Amitabha, the bodhisattva's spiritual progenitor, appears as a standing effigy on a crown panel tied to the tall chignon (*jatamukuta*). Amitabha is more commonly depicted as a seated figure in the crowns of Nepali images of Avalokiteshvara, but here the effigy recalls rare, earlier examples with a standing figure in the crown, such as the renowned seventh- or eighth-century wood Phagpa Lokeshvara, now in the Potala, Lhasa.[1]

While this regal seated posture is rare in Nepali sculptures of Avalokiteshvara, it was evidently more common in eastern India, where a number of eighth- and ninth-century Pala-period (eighth–twelfth century CE) examples have been found in Bengal and Bihar.[2] The posture and sculptural detail of these earlier Indian statues may have informed the composition of this circa tenth-century Nepali example. The low central crown panel that allows an uninterrupted view of the effigy of Amitabha Buddha attached to the chignon is the common crown format of the eastern Indian bronzes but highly unusual in Nepal, where a seated effigy normally adorns a large central crown panel directly above the forehead.[3] The lotus pedestal with broad petals in a staggered sequence on the upper and lower levels is also comparable to the bases of the Indian examples.

The statue is modeled in the characteristically sensuous manner of Kathmandu Valley sculpture, cast in pure copper and fire gilded. In common with the majority of Licchavi and Transitional period (c. 400–1200 CE) bronzes, the jewelry is not embellished with inset gems, a decorative feature that became prevalent in later periods. Traces of azurite blue in the hair and gold paint on the face and neck, still remaining thickly applied at the back, indicate that the statue has been used in Tibetan worship in which the bodies of deities are often painted during ritual devotion. It was not uncommon for such fine Nepalese works of art to make their way to foreign lands. Early Nepali bronzes are found in ancient Tibetan monastery shrines and in the Chinese imperial collections, where they were revered for their true association with the motherlands of Buddhism and for the genius of the Newar artists who produced them. **DW**

Notes
1. Ian Alsop, "Phagpa Lokeśvara of the Potala," *Orientations* 21, no. 4 (April 1990): 51–61, and Ulrich von Schroeder, *Buddhist Sculptures in Tibet*, vol. 2 (Visual Dharma, 2001), 823, pl. 195D.
2. Nihar Ranjan Ray, Karl Khandalavala, and Sadashiv Gorakshkar, *Eastern Indian Bronzes* (Lalit Kalā Akademi, 1986), figs. 41, 123, 124.
3. See for comparison a tenth-century Nepali gilt-copper Padmapani seated in a more traditional "royal ease" (*rajalilasana*), with a seated effigy of Amitabha in the central crown panel, in Von Schroeder, *Buddhist Sculptures in Tibet*, vol. 1, 493, pl. 157D.

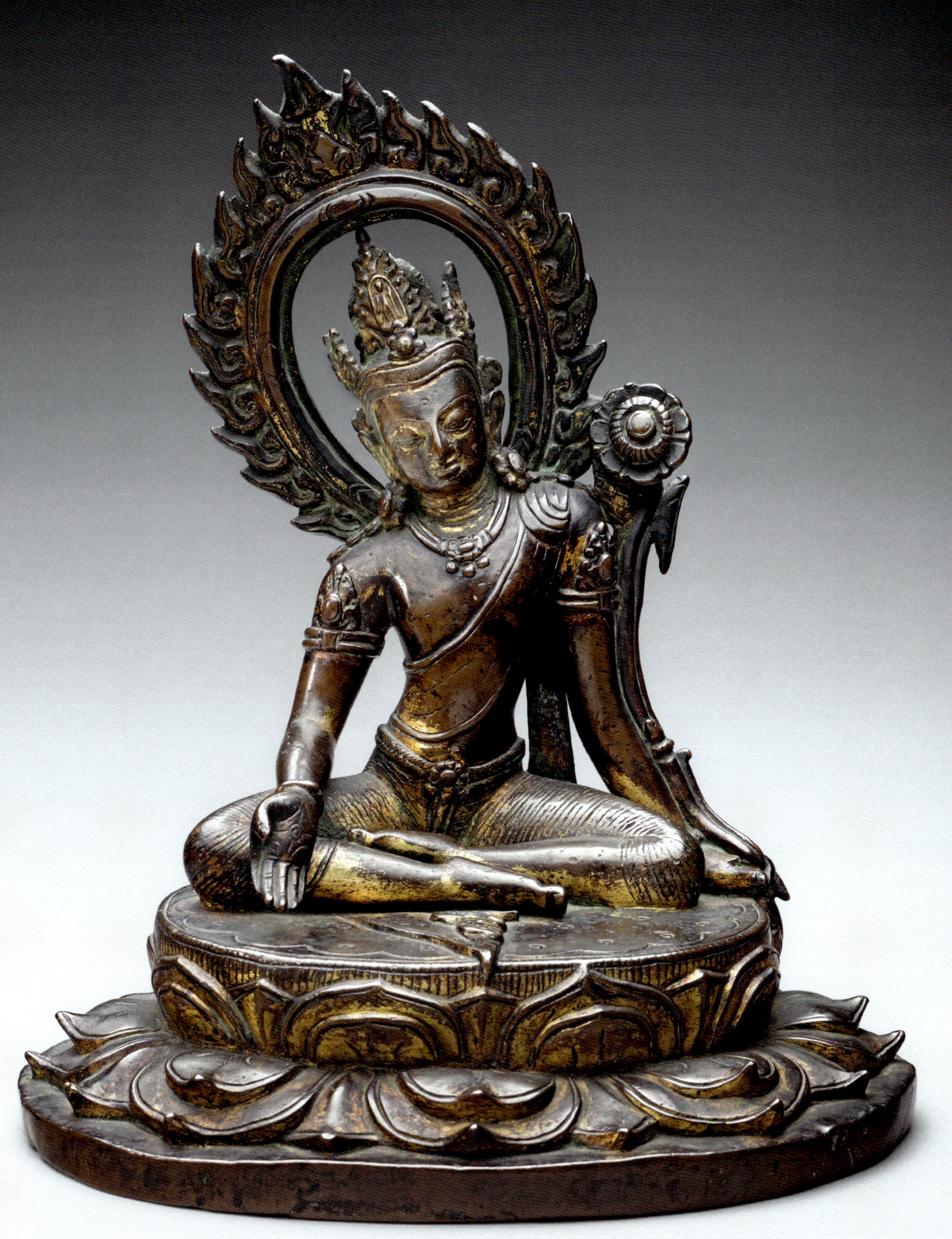

Bodhisattva Manjushri Kumara

Nepal, 10th–11th century

Parcel-gilt silver
2 ⅝ × 2 × 1 ½ in. (6.6 × 5.1 × 3.8 cm)

The bodhisattva Manjushri is depicted as a youthful prince (*kumara*) with rounded countenance and preadult physique. The god of Buddhist wisdom and knowledge sits with the right leg folded in the meditation posture and the left slightly raised (*ardhaparyankasana*). His right hand makes the open-palmed wish-fulfilling gesture (*varada* mudra), and the left holds the stem of a blue lily flowering at the shoulder, as prescribed in the sacred texts.[1] The necklace of tiger-claw pendants is a specific attribute of Manjushri, and the young prince's hair is gathered into five separate bunches, one on top and four at the back of the head. A single crown panel is tied around the lock at the top of the boy's head. The five locks of hair allude to the five syllables of the Sanskrit invocation *a-ra-pa-ca-na* used in devotions to the deity; the recitation of each syllable is said to have specific benefits, from eliminating dangers to ultimate awakening.[2] Dr. Pratapaditya Pal notes that the description of Manjushri as a young boy is continuously emphasized in the Indian religious texts, and in South Asia it is the Newar sculptors of the Kathmandu Valley who adhered most faithfully to this prescribed iconography.[3]

The intricate and finely incised geometric and floral patterns of the lower garment and scarf around the thighs are typical of later Nepali Transitional–period (c. 879–1200) sculpture from the Kathmandu Valley. The casting medium of silver, however, is a rare departure from the gilded copper for which Newar artists were renowned and indicates a special commission. The iconographic color of this aspect of Manjushri is white, making silver a natural choice for its gleaming white sheen. The small size and the precious metal suggest a treasured, personal devotional aid. The deity is visualized with golden adornments, hence the selective parcel gilding of the crown panel, earrings, tiger-claw necklace, dhoti, and flower in elegant contrast to the silver body.

Manjushri is particularly popular in Nepal, where the god is associated with the mythical origin of the Kathmandu Valley. A legend related in the Svayambhu Purana recounts how Manjushri came to Nepal from China and with one blow of his sword opened a deep gorge at Chobhar to drain the valley.[4] A beautifully sculpted stone image of Manjushri as a youthful standing prince is worshipped at Manjushri-tol, Kathmandu; the statue is dated by inscription to 920 CE and appears to be the earliest representation of Manjushri in the valley.[5] A Nepali copper image of the deity in the Metropolitan Museum of Art, with a rounded face and a youthful physique similar to the Xuzhou example, has been dated to the tenth or eleventh century.[6] The same dating has been ascribed to a Nepali wrathful form of Manjushri, also now in the Metropolitan Museum of Art, with geometric- and floral-patterned garments very much like this silver figure.[7] A date of tenth or eleventh century is thus likely for this rare, gem-like parcel-gilt silver statue of the boy prince Manjushri. **DW**

Notes
1. Marie-Thérèse De Mallmann, *Introduction à l'iconographie du Tântrisme Bouddhique* (Librairie d'Amérique et d'Orient, 1986), 252.
2. Denise Patry Leidy and Donna Strahan, *Wisdom Embodied: Chinese Buddhist and Daoist Sculpture in the Metropolitan Museum of Art* (Metropolitan Museum of Art and Yale University Press, 2010), 120.
3. Pratapaditya Pal, *The Arts of Nepal: Part I, Sculpture* (E. J. Brill, 1974), 123.
4. Ibid., 122.
5. Mary Slusser, *Nepal Mandala: A Cultural Study of the Kathmandu Valley*, vol. 2 (Princeton University Press, 1982), fig. 474.
6. Ulrich von Schroeder, *Indo-Tibetan Bronzes* (Visual Dharma Publications, 1981), fig. 85D.
7. Pratapaditya Pal, *Nepal: Where the Gods Are Young* (Asia House Gallery, 1975), fig. 35.

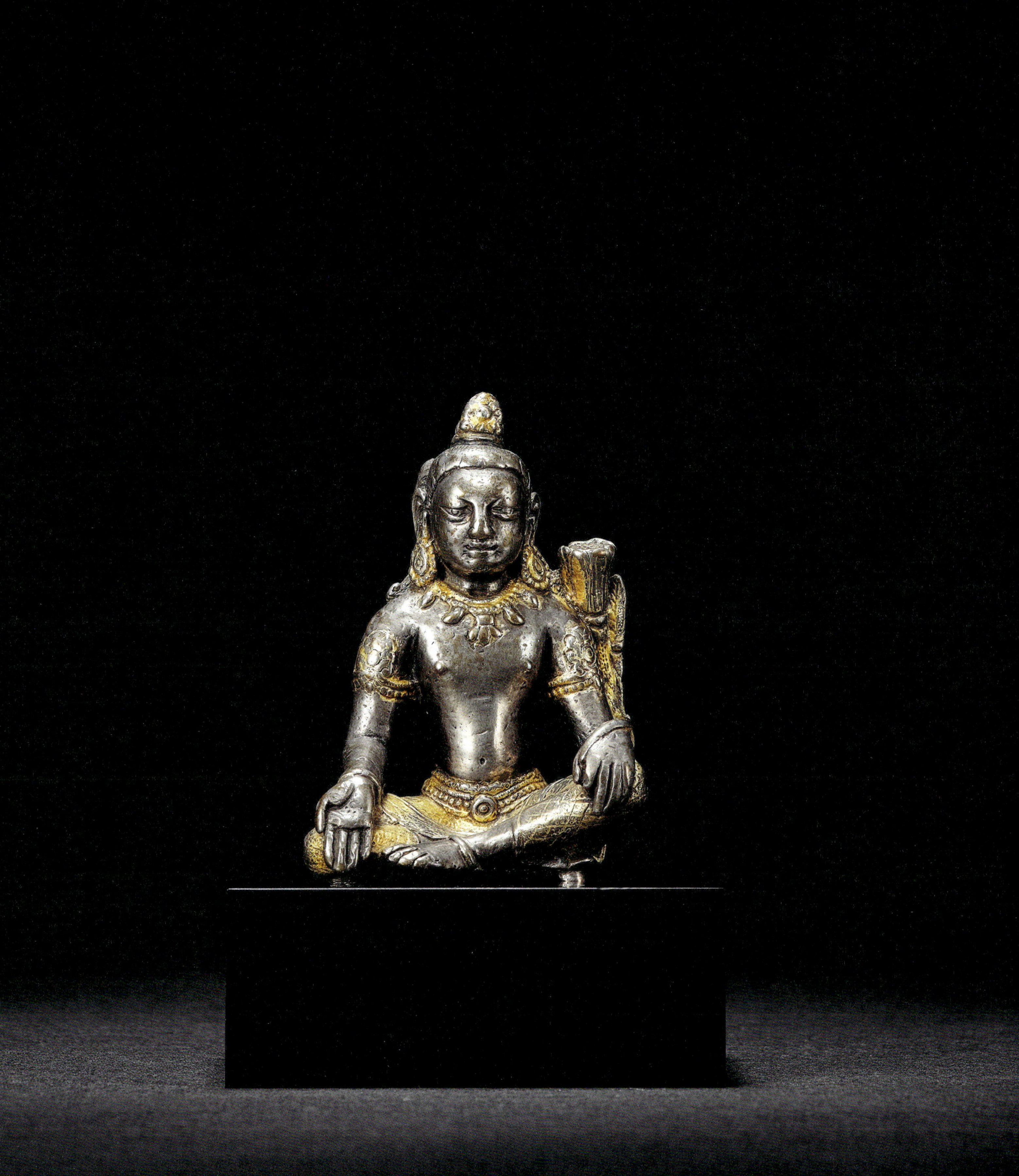

One of the Five Wisdom Buddhas, Possibly Akshobhya

Tibet, c. 12th century

Gilt copper
48 ⁷⁄₁₆ × 18 × 11 in. (123 × 45.7 × 27.9 cm)

The deity, adorned with jewelry, stands in an upright posture (*sama-pada*), and a sacred thread (*yajnopavita*) is draped over his left shoulder and around the torso. The identity of the figure is unclear from visual evidence. Hand gestures (mudra) often provide clues, but in this case both hands have been broken off and replaced, and the modern reconstructions have arbitrary gestures that cannot be used for iconographic identification. The nose, lips, and left leg and foot are also modern restorations, and the damage was likely sustained during the cultural upheavals in Tibet in the latter half of the twentieth century. The jewelry and the sacred thread are intact, and these attributes suggest the sculpture could represent a bodhisattva or a Wisdom Buddha.[1] Four similar sculptures are known from the same set of desecrated standing bronzes.[2] An example in the Rubin Museum of Art and one in the George Ortiz Collection are both severely damaged but have not been restored.[3] Together, these unrestored statues, both previously described as bodhisattvas, might provide evidence for the identification of the Xuzhou example and the group as a whole. The Rubin and Ortiz figures have their left hands in the attitude of meditation, a mudra usually associated with seated figures. The lowered right hand of the Ortiz example makes the wish-fulfilling gesture (*varada* mudra). The combination of meditative gesture and varada mudra is the iconographic indication of the Wisdom Buddha Ratnasambhava. If the Ortiz figure depicts a standing Ratnasambhava, the group might then be identified as standing manifestations of the Five Wisdom Buddhas: Amitabha, Akshobhya, Amoghasiddhi, Vairochana, and Ratnasambhava. The right forearm of the Xuzhou figure is lowered like that of the Ortiz Ratnasambhava. Among the Five Wisdom Buddhas, only Ratnasambhava and Akshobhya are depicted with lowered right arms, and the Xuzhou figure might thus depict Akshobhya. In which case, the modern right hand would have originally made the earth-touching gesture (*bhumisparsha* mudra), and the left would have been in the same meditative position as the Ortiz and Rubin examples.[4] Another from the series has both forearms raised, with hands together in a complex gesture, and may represent Vairochana.[5] Another has both hands in the meditation posture (*dhyana*) and may thus represent Amitabha.[6] By process of elimination, the Rubin example would represent Amoghasiddhi, with the missing right hand originally raised in *abhaya* mudra.

The upright, frontal stance may support the identification of a Buddha over a bodhisattva,[7] whose traditional posture is fluid, as in the subtle poise of a series of standing bodhisattvas at the Tibetan monastery of Sera.[8] The sculptural style of the Xuzhou figure is comparable to the Sera bodhisattvas, which date to a similar period around the twelfth century. Statues from both groups include a sash (*udarabhanda*) around the waist, a common feature of early Nepali sculpture but rarely seen in Tibetan works. In Nepal, where artists are familiar with both Hindu and Buddhist iconography, the sash is seen predominantly but not exclusively on Hindu sculpture, suggesting a well-informed Newar hand in the modeling of both sets of important Tibetan temple statues. **DW**

Notes

1. Wisdom Buddhas represent the various enlightened qualities of the Buddha.
2. Allowing for lost limbs, the bronzes in the group are the same size, have closely comparable necklace and crown designs, and all stand in samapada, with the uncommon feature of a sash around the waist, demonstrating the homogeneity of the group.
3. J. Van Alphen, Beth Citron, Karl Debreczeny, David P. Jackson, Christian Luczanits, Elena Pakhoutova, and Kathryn Selig Brown, *Collection Highlights: The Rubin Museum of Art* (Rubin Museum of Art, 2014), 130; Pratapaditya Pal, *Himalayas: An Aesthetic Adventure* (Art Institute of Chicago, 2003), 183, cat. no. 119.
4. A large Nepali gilt-copper crowned standing sculpture with precisely this combination of mudras is seen in a shrine in Dolpo. See Ulrich von Schroeder, *Indo-Tibetan Bronzes* (Visual Dharma Publications, 1981), 339, where the figure is identified as Vajrapani.
5. Pal, *Himalaya*s, cat. 118. The arms are in their original raised position, but the hands appear to have restoration: Originally, the fingers are likely to have made the gesture of enlightenment (*bodhyagri*); see for comparison a standing Vairochana in the imperial collections, Beijing, with hands in bodhyagri mudra, the Palace Museum, ed., *Cultural Relics of Tibetan Buddhism Collected in the Qing Palace* (Forbidden City Press/Woods Publishing Company, 1992), pl. 44.
6. Unpublished, personal communication, email from Jane Casey to David Weldon, December 19, 2018 (photograph taken July 28, 2003).
7. In a discussion on the iconography of two examples from this group, Dr. Pal notes that samapada is an unusual stance for a bodhisattva. Pal, *Himalayas*, 182.
8. Ulrich von Schroeder, *Buddhist Sculptures in Tibet*, vol. 2 (Visual Dharma Publications, 2001), 948–49, figs. XV-9, XV-10.

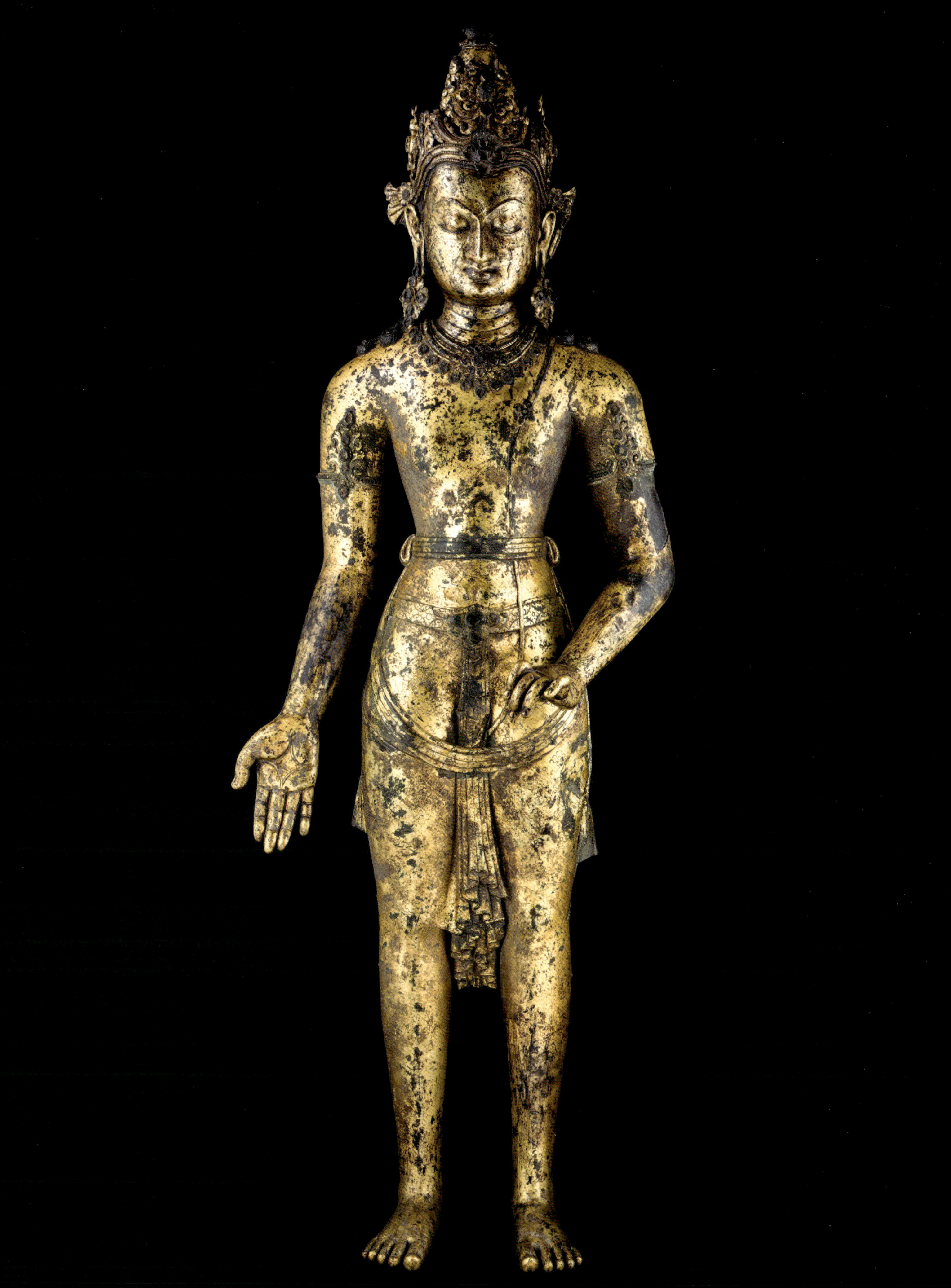

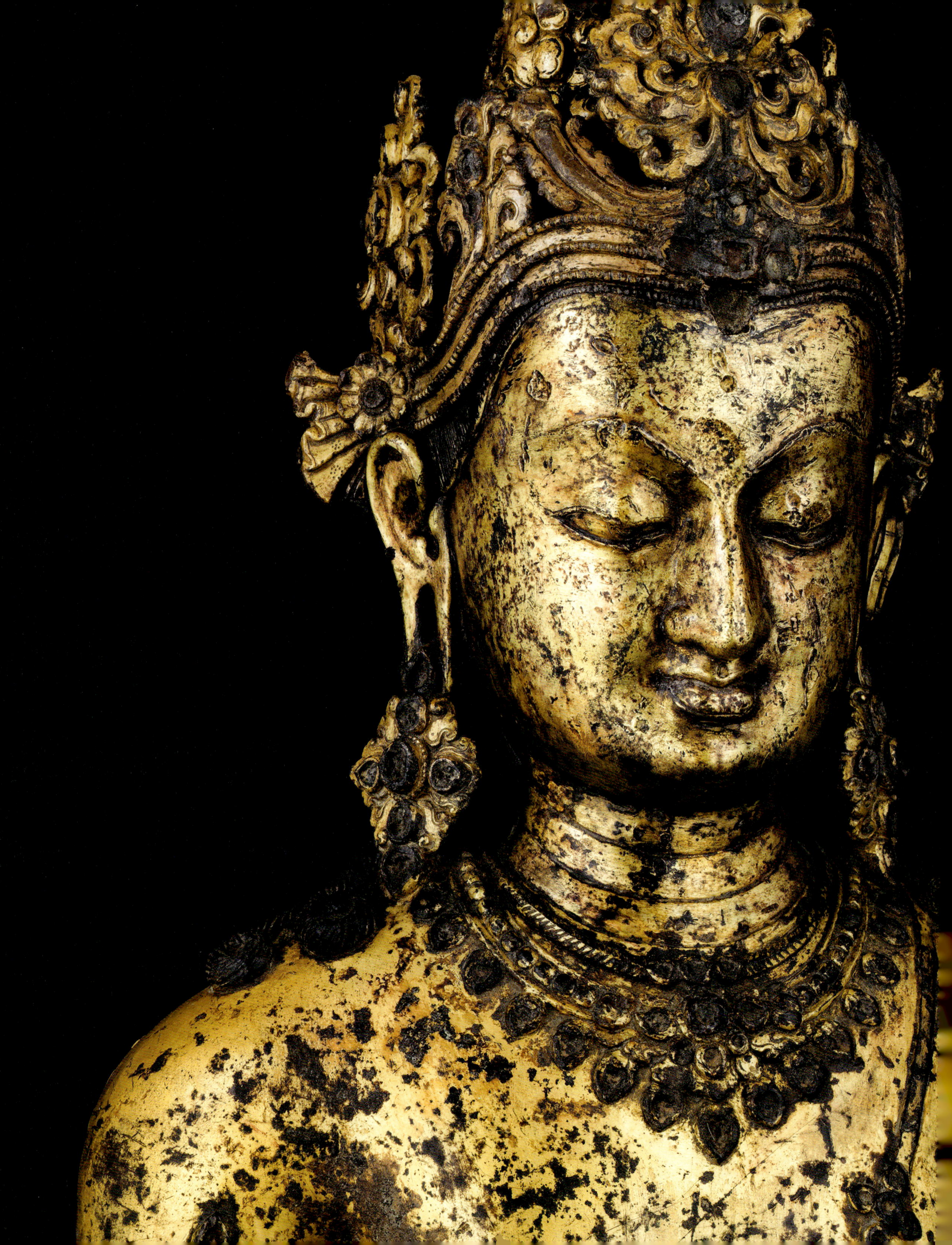

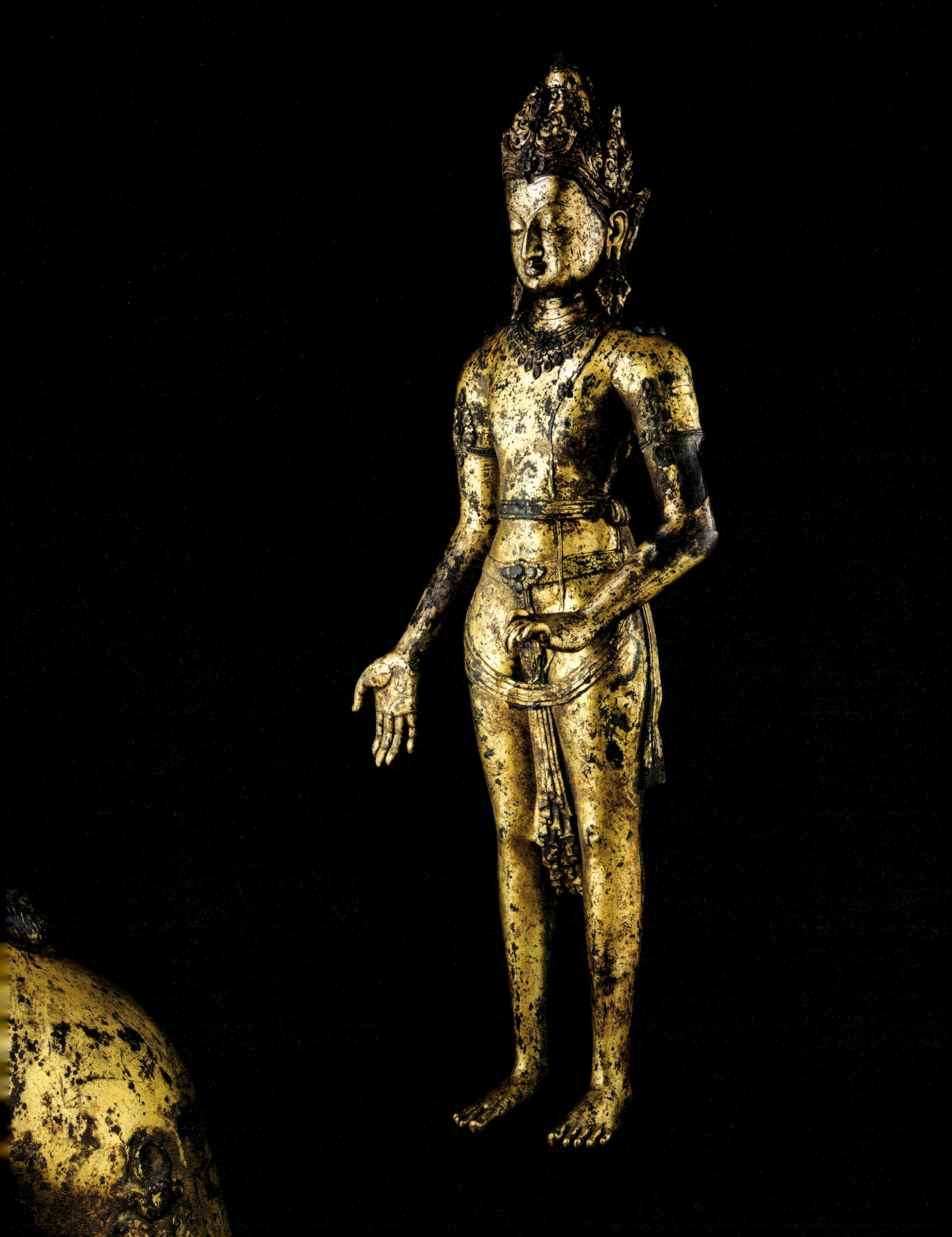

Buddha Maravijaya, Calling the Earth to Witness

Tibet, c. 13th century

Copper alloy, copper and silver inlay, and pigment
3 ⅞ × 3 × 2 ½ in. (9.9 × 7.6 × 6.4 cm)

This small but beautifully rendered image recalls the moment just before the Buddha's enlightenment, when he vanquished the distractions and doubts (*maravijaya*) that posed the final obstacles to spiritual liberation. This iconography became popular in eastern India during the medieval period (c. seventh–twelfth centuries), when Buddhist pilgrims journeyed across Asia to receive blessings and teachings in the Buddhist homeland. Tibetans were among the most ardent of international pilgrims. At great personal cost, they ventured over the Himalayas through treacherous mountain passes, eventually arriving on the Indian plains with its vastly different climate and its sophisticated material culture. Eastern India's monastic universities were renowned as architectural wonders. Beacons of higher learning, they were inhabited by some of India's finest Buddhist scholars and by thousands of students from India and across Asia.

The seventh-century Chinese pilgrim Xuanzang described Nalanda, where he studied for five years, as an exceptional center for Buddhist studies.[1] He noted it also trained students in fine arts, medicine, mathematics, astronomy, and politics. The nine-story library at Nalanda known as Dharmagunj (Mountain of Truth) was the largest and most renowned repository of Buddhist literature in its time. Tibetans sometimes resided for years as students at monastic universities such as Nalanda and Vikramashila. The thirteenth-century Tibetan pilgrim Dharmasvamin (1197–1264) wrote of the Buddhist homeland, "This country stretches from Vajrasana [Bodh Gaya] towards the four quarters . . . and is the very centre of the World."[2] Of the main image inside the Mahabodhi Temple at Bodh Gaya, he noted, "Even people with little faith when standing in front of the image felt it impossible not to shed tears."[3]

This image was made in Tibet but closely follows models from eastern India.[4] Eastern Indian medieval copper-alloy sculpture sometimes used gold, silver, and copper inlay to superb effect.[5] In this sculpture, the eyes are inlaid with silver and the lips with copper; the nails of the hands and feet are also inlaid with copper, as is the wide hem of the robe. Wear to the face (particularly the nose and eyebrows) of this small sculpture reflects handling by previous owners, who may have carried the object in a personal shrine or placed it on a personal altar. The presence of gold paint on the face and blue pigment on the hair reflects Tibetan ritual practices. The ritual application of paint to the face and hair would have been completed by the painting of the eyes and lips. The facial pigment was intended to make the image as lifelike as possible, and it was sometimes applied during a ritual in which the presence of the deity is invoked and invited to dwell within the sculpture. A larger and perhaps slightly later Tibetan sculpture resembles this one closely. The Maravijaya Buddha in the Nyingjei Lam Collection is similar in the rendering of the torso and in the design of the robe, although the Nyingjei Lam sculpture also has silver beading running down one side of the copper-inlaid hem of the robe.[6] Originally, the Xuzhou sculpture would have been placed on a throne or lotus base. **JC**

Notes

1. See Hiuen Tsiang [Xuanzang], *Si-Yu-Ki: Buddhist Records of the Western World*, 2 vols., trans. Samuel Beal (Chinese Materials Center, 1976).
2. See Dharmaswamin, *Biography of Dharmaswamin*, trans. George Roerich (K.P. Jayaswal Research Institute, 1959), 63.
3. Ibid., 65–66.
4. See for example seated Buddha sculptures of about the tenth century from eastern India, published in Ulrich von Schroeder, *Indo-Tibetan Bronzes* (Visual Dharma Publications, 1981), nos. 58A–G. See also some eleventh- and twelfth-century sculptures in Ulrich von Schroeder, *Buddhist Sculptures in Tibet*, vol. 1 (Visual Dharma Publications, 2001), nos. 85A–F.
5. See published examples in Von Schroeder, *Buddhist Sculptures in Tibet*, vol. 1, nos. 78–81, 85, 97; Jane Casey, Naman Ahuja, and David Weldon, *Divine Presence: Arts of India and the Himalayas* (5 Continents Editions, 2003), 96–97.
6. David Weldon and Jane Casey Singer, *The Sculptural Heritage of Tibet: Buddhist Art in the Nyingjei Lam Collection* (Laurence King Publishing, 1999), 104–5.

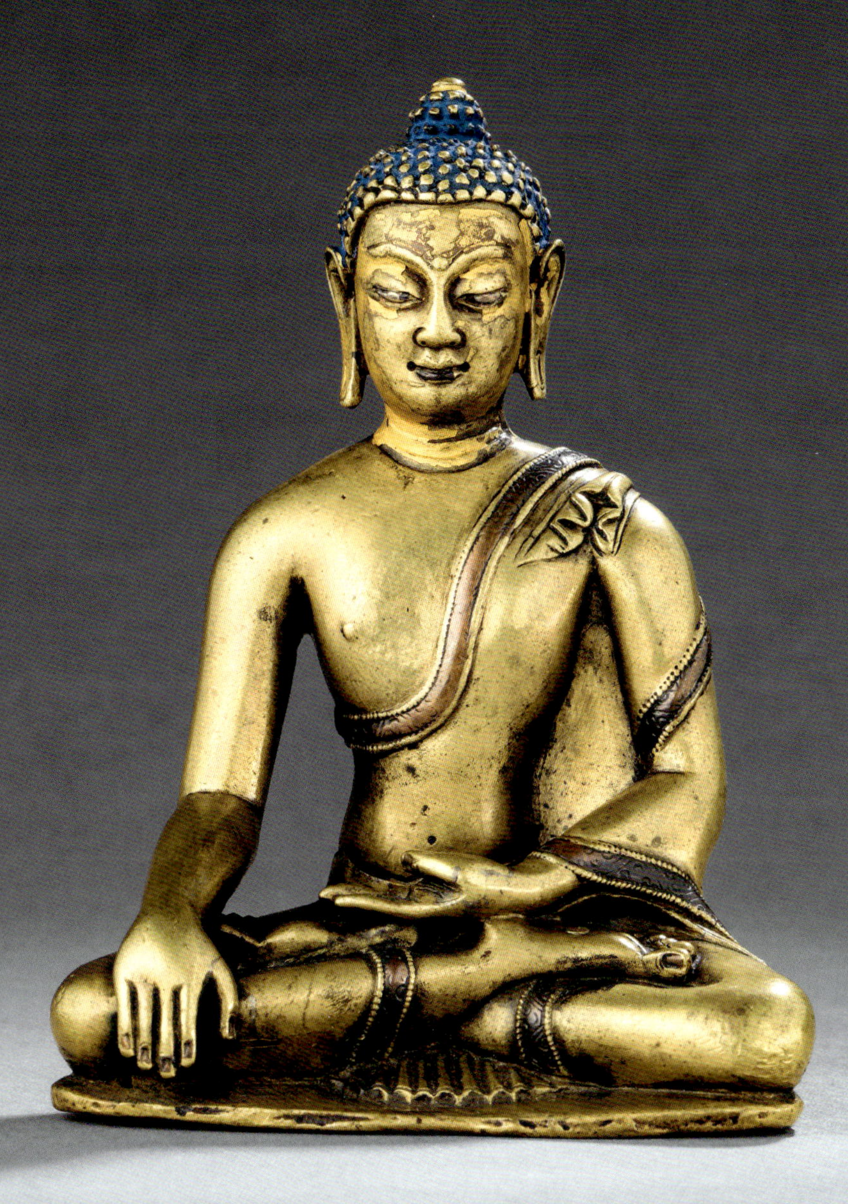

Buddha Shakyamuni

Tibet, c. 13th century

Gilt copper with silver inlay, pigment
16 ⁷⁄₁₆ × 11 × 7 ½ in. (41.7 × 27.9 × 19.1 cm)

The Buddha sits with legs crossed in the yogic posture (*vajrapary-ankasana*). The right hand is raised in the open-palmed gesture of reassurance and protection (*abhaya* mudra), with the left hand reaching forward to the ground before him. The image displays auspicious marks (*lakshana*) of an enlightened being, including the cranial protuberance (*ushnisha*), a symbol of supreme wisdom; the mark on the forehead (*urna*), here in the form of a gem setting; long earlobes; and webbed fingers. Remains of matte gold on the neck and azurite blue in the hair are indicative of Tibetan worship, in which the bodies of deities are often ritually painted.

The Buddha wears a patchwork mendicant's garment with the stitches delineated by silver beading inlaid between each panel and along the hems.[1] The silver inlay indicates the Tibetan origin of the statue, while the sculptural style is wholly Nepalese. Silver is rarely used to embellish bronzes in Nepal, but Newar artists adapted their indigenous traditions to suit Tibetan patronage. Nepalese artists had a continuous presence in Tibet, from the sculptors commissioned by King Songtsen Gampo (reigned 617–650 CE) to carve the beams and lintels of the Jokhang in Lhasa to those who constructed the towering gilt-bronze stupas at Densatil Monastery, now destroyed, to the painters of the finest fourteenth- and fifteenth-century Tibetan thangkas for Ngor Monastery patrons. Nepalese stylistic features of this Buddha include the broad forehead with tapering oval face and a protruding lower lip, typical of classical Newar sculpture throughout the Licchavi and Transitional periods (fifth–twelfth century CE).[2] Later Nepalese sculptural styles differ dramatically in musculature and the shape of the face, and the depiction of webbed fingers diminishes over time. The classical features and the elegant and powerful sculptural presence with broad shoulders and slim waist suggest a date of about the thirteenth century. The use of metal inlay to delineate stitchwork is a common Tibetan feature of the period, seen for example on the patchwork robes of the circa thirteenth-century silver *Crowned Buddha* formerly in the Pan-Asian Collection and the circa thirteenth-century portrait bronze of Phagmo Drupa in the Cleveland Museum of Art.[3]

The combination of abhaya mudra and the gesture of the left hand that mirrors the earth-touching mudra (*bhumisparsha*) of Maravijaya Buddha is uncommon in Himalayan sculpture. A statue in Musée Guimet with the same mudras has been described as Amoghasiddhi,[4] whose right hand commonly makes the abhaya mudra, but whose left typically rests in the lap rather than reaching forward. The abhaya mudra is a traditional gesture of the Buddha in Indian art from the Kushan (first–fourth century CE) to the Pala period (eighth–twelfth century CE),[5] and it may suggest an alternative identity for this iconography. The patchwork mendicant's garment is perhaps the most compelling attribute with which to identify this rare figure as an aspect of Buddha Shakyamuni. The simplest of robes stitched together from cast-off fragments of cloth serves as a potent symbol of the historical Buddha's renunciation of mundane existence. **DW**

Notes

1. The gray hue dispersed over the gilded surface in the vicinity of the beading is tarnish that has migrated from the silver.
2. These features are epitomized by the seventh-century standing Buddha in the Kimbell Art Museum. See Ulrich von Schroeder, *Indo-Tibetan Bronzes* (Visual Dharma Publications, 1981), 307, fig. 75F.
3. Jane Casey, Naman Ahuja, and David Weldon, *Divine Presence: Arts of India and the Himalayas* (Casa Asia and 5 Continents Editions, 2003), 141, cat. no. 44; David Weldon and Jane Casey Singer, *The Sculptural Heritage of Tibet: Buddhist Art in the Nyingjei Lam Collection* (Laurence King Publishing, 2000), 135.
4. Von Schroeder, *Indo-Tibetan Bronzes*, fig. 112C. See for comparison the similar iconography of a gilt bronze at Christie's, New York, March 27, 2003, lot 90.
5. For Kushan seated Buddhas with the right hand in abhaya and the extended left hand resting on the folded lower leg, see Stanislaw J. Czuma, *Kushan Sculpture: Images from Early India* (Cleveland Museum of Art, 1985), cat. nos. 12, 13, 15. And for Pala Buddhas with abhaya mudra, see Von Schroeder, *Indo-Tibetan Bronzes*, fig. 60A, 264–79 passim.

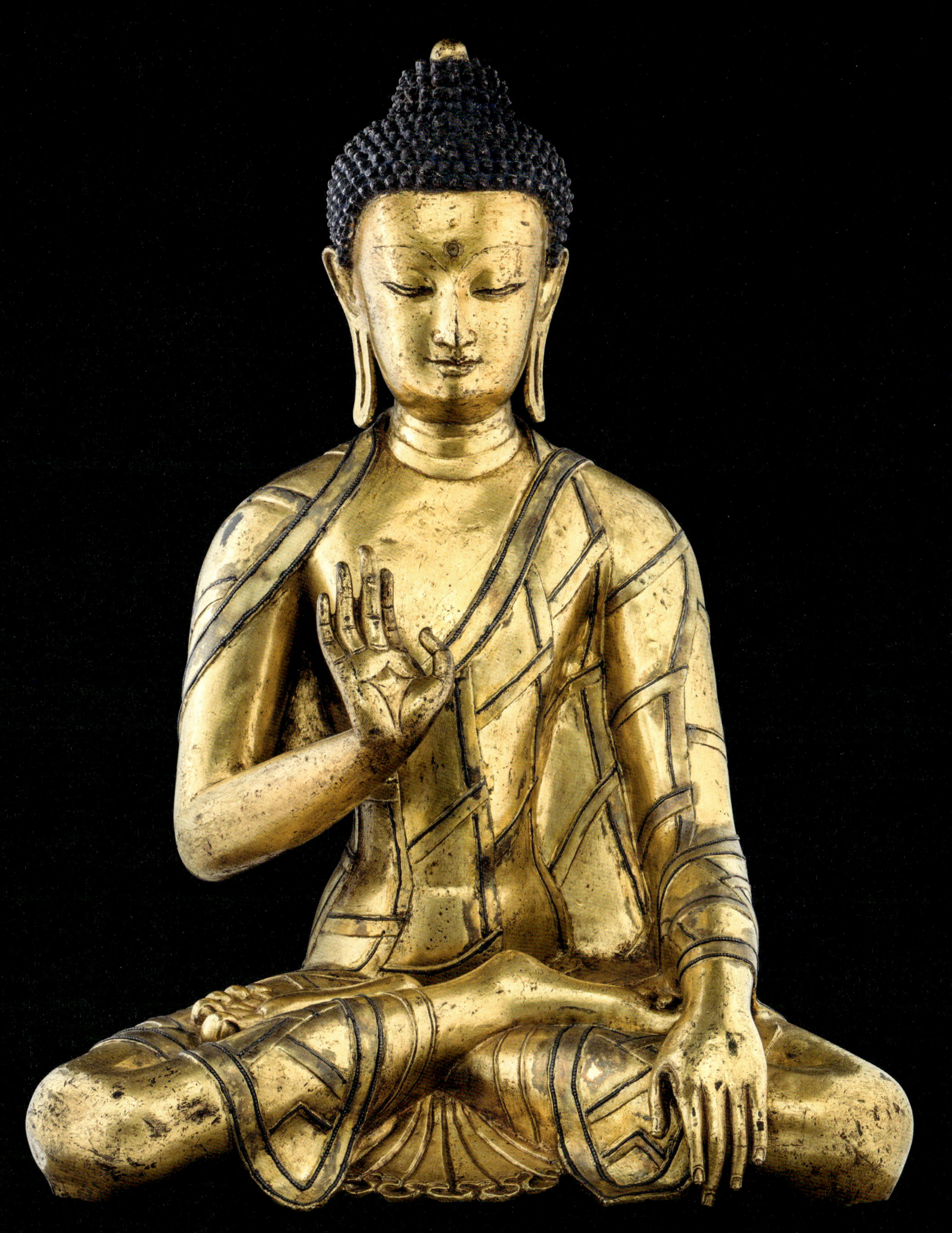

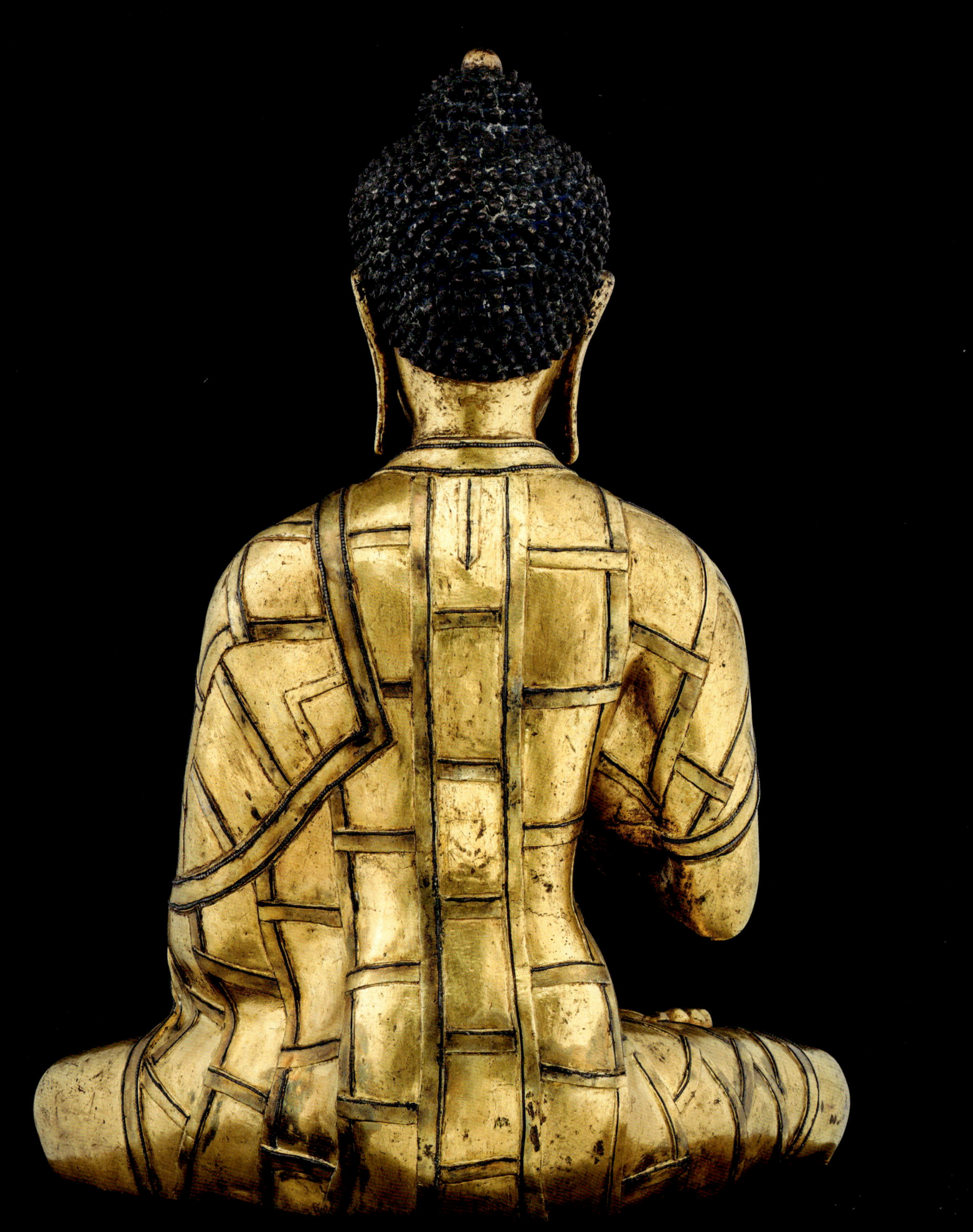

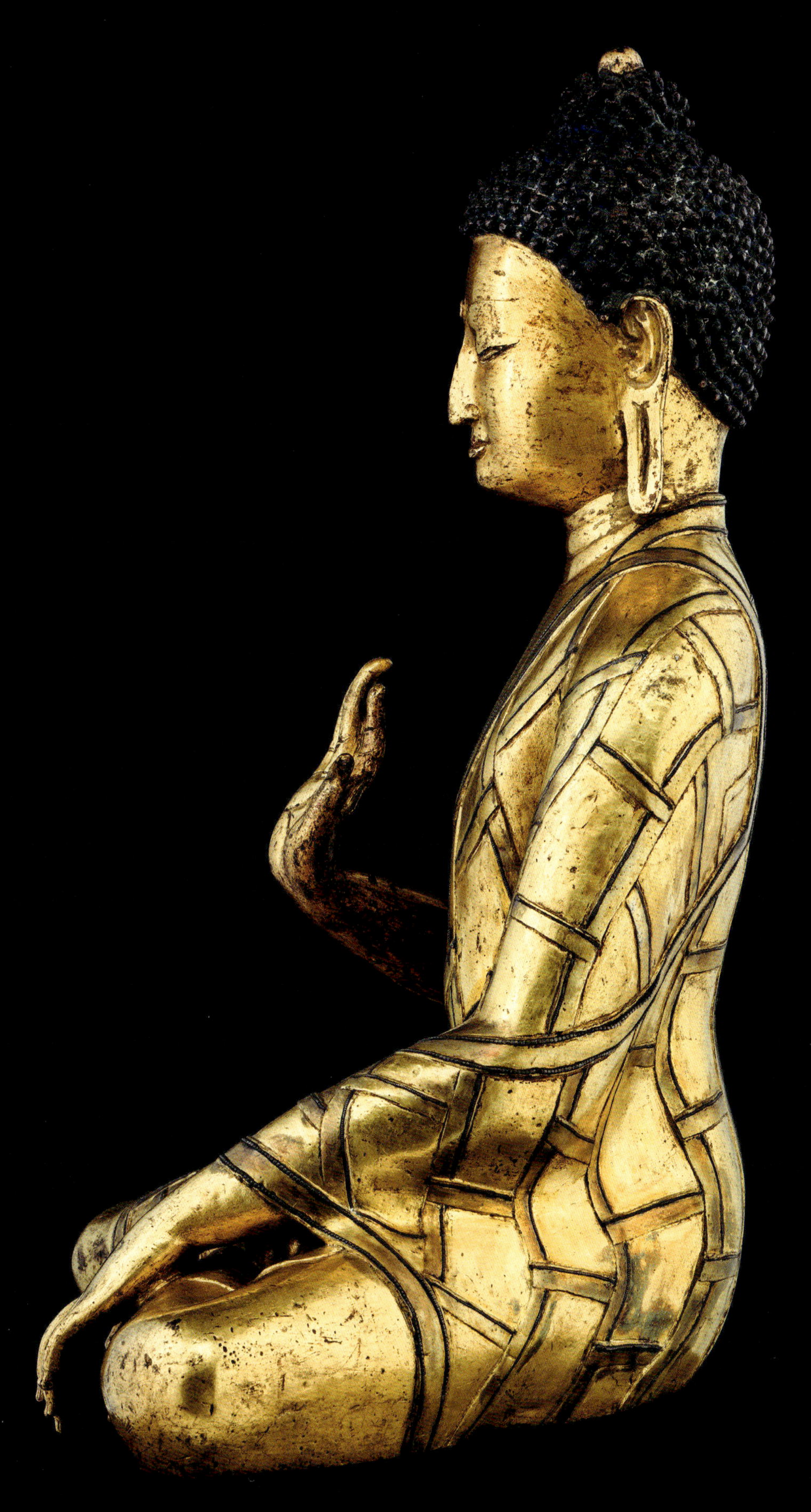

Anucara Varahi, a Boar-Head Goddess

Tibet, 15th–16th century

Copper alloy with silver inlay, pigment
2 ⅞ × 3 ¼ × 2 in. (7.4 × 8.3 × 5.1 cm)

The Buddhist goddess Varahi is seated on a lotus pedestal with her knees raised, toes curled, and the soles of her feet pressed together, wearing beaded necklaces over her naked torso and a loincloth around her waist. The porcine features of the head resemble that of an Indian or Central Asian wild boar with a ridged mane reaching down to the shoulders and white ivory tusks depicted in silver.

Varahi serves as an attendant (*anucara*) to Green Tara, the great Buddhist Savioress, in a pentad of female deities that includes Marici, goddess of the dawn, who is often depicted with a secondary head of a sow; Pratisara, a protector goddess and embodiment of early Buddhist texts; and Ekajata, a fierce one-eyed form of Tara and wrathful protectress of Tibetan Buddhism.[1] Varahi has counterparts in Indian Hindu culture, where the sow-headed deity is one of the Matrika, the seven mother goddesses, and shakti of Varaha, the boar-headed avatar of Vishnu. Female animal-headed *dakini*s in Indian mythology predate both Hinduism and Buddhism, and individual manifestations are linked to the twenty-four power places of the Indian Himalayas: The sow-headed dakini is associated with the principal Himalayan site of Mount Kailash.[2] Tantric Buddhist practitioners regard therianthropic deities with the head of an animal or bird as symbols of the primordial mind, a resource to be accessed in the attainment of spiritual knowledge and enlightenment.[3] The vajra-handled knife (*kartri*) held in Varahi's right hand is modeled on the Indian butcher's flaying knife and symbolizes the means to cut through veils of ignorance and obstructions on the path to the enlightened state. The blood-filled cup (*kapala*) held in her left hand is cut from a human cranium and serves as a symbol of impermanence and the ephemeral nature of mundane existence.

The surface of the bronze is abraded through centuries of handling. Details are smoothed and softened. The beaded jewelry is mostly worn away, with the original design only clearly visible around the neck in areas less accessible to touch. The fingers of the left hand have lost significant definition, becoming almost one with the skull cup. The beaded upper rim of the lotus pedestal is now almost completely smooth, save for the area protected by the protruding feet. The accumulated wear is due to handling and suggests that the figure was a personal devotional image, perhaps a talisman, that may have been passed down through generations rather than preserved untouched in a monastery shrine room. The lotus petals at the front of the base have lost almost all definition, with those at the sides retaining more of their original shape and helping to indicate a date for the statue. The broad petal with a simple flourish at the tip, together with the plain, undecorated back of the pedestal, would suggest a date of about the fifteenth or sixteenth century, a period when non-gilt Tibetan bronzes were often enhanced with silver inlay, seen here in the gleaming white silver tusks of this rare and unusual figure.[4] **DW**

Notes
1. The group of five goddesses appears in the Narthang Pantheon. See Lokesh Chandra, *Buddhist Iconography* (International Academy of Indian Culture, 1991), 253–54, figs. 654–58.
2. Glenn H. Mullin, with Jeff J. Watt, *Female Buddhas: Women of Enlightenment in Tibetan Mystical Art* (Clear Light Publishers, 2003), 149.
3. Ibid., 150.
4. Compare the pedestal of a circa fifteenth-century Mahakala with silver inlay, in Gilles Béguin, *Art sacré du Tibet: Collection Alain Bordier* (Éditions Findakly, 2013), 175–76, cat. no. 89.

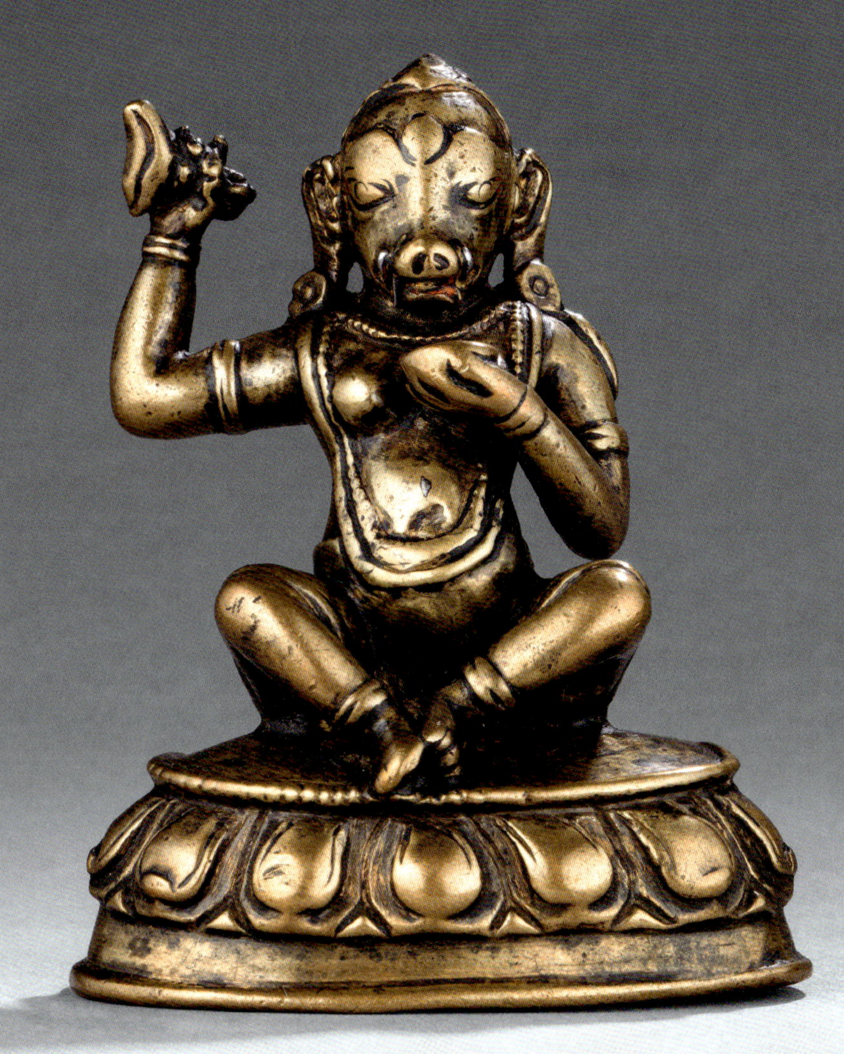

Padmapani, Lotus-Bearing Avalokiteshvara

China, Northern Wei dynasty, dated 470 CE

Gilt bronze
10 ⅞ × 5 ¼ × 4 ¼ in. (27.4 × 13.3 × 10.8 cm)

Padmapani (lotus bearer) is one of the thirty-three manifestations of Avalokiteshvara (Chinese: Guanyin) described in the twenty-fifth chapter of the Lotus Sutra (Saddharma Pundarika Sutra). Told in parables in a manner similar to Confucian moral writings, the Lotus Sutra was easily grasped by a Chinese audience; its early translations had an enormous impact on Buddhist practices and art forms.[1] Details such as the abundant jewelry, the garments and scarf, and the distinctive hairstyle presented on this piece were inspired by Gandharan and Central Asian sources. Direct contact with these sources increased dramatically during the fifth century, resulting in a flourishing of Buddhist art.[2] The figure holds in his left hand a lotus, the symbol of Padmapani, and grips in his right hand a long, flowing ribbon. The halo and elaborate flaming mandorla are integral to the cast form. The top section of the mandorla is missing.

The superior quality of the casting, the scale, and the stylistic factors suggest that this piece was created for a high-ranking member of the Northern Wei society. The inscription incised on the reverse of the plinth reads: "Fourth Year of the Huangxing period [equivalent to 470 CE], Wang Zhongtian patronized a figure of Padmapani for his parents, with the hope that the parents can be in the presence of Padmapani."[3] The surname indicates that the patron was Chinese; the date marks this as one of the earliest dated freestanding Chinese representations of Avalokiteshvara. The dedication of an image of Padmapani to his parents by the patron demonstrates how the Chinese of the Northern Wei translated and combined Buddhism with existing religious practices, in this case ancestor worship. Ancestor worship focused on the afterlife of the deceased, which was provided by their descendants with sumptuous burials and proper performance of rituals and offerings.[4] Buddhism introduced different concepts about death, rebirth, and karma. Rather than a direct transition of the soul to an afterlife, Buddhism taught about the cycle of rebirth (samsara) and the possibility of liberation from this cycle. Avalokiteshvara exemplifies the essence of the bodhisattva ideal — an enlightened being who chooses to remain in our world to help all sentient beings achieve enlightenment. Guanyin, the deity's name in Chinese, literally means "One Who Hears the Cries of the World," reflecting its role as the Bodhisattva of Compassion. This is particularly significant in Chinese Buddhism, where Guanyin became the most beloved bodhisattva, the one to whom devotees turn in moments of crisis and suffering. **MK**

Notes
1. An influential translation of the Lotus Sutra was completed between 401 and 413 by a team assembled in Chang'an by Kumarajiva, about sixty years prior to the creation of this sculpture.
2. A major statement is to be seen at the massive Yungang cave complex. Patronized by the imperial family of the Northern Wei, this complex was located near their capital of Pingcheng.
3. Translation in Sotheby's, Hong Kong, *Chinese Art Through the Eye of Sakamoto Gorō: Early Buddhist Bronzes*, October 5, 2016, lot 320.
4. See essay on pages 32–37 for a more complete discussion of this and the other notes for this entry.

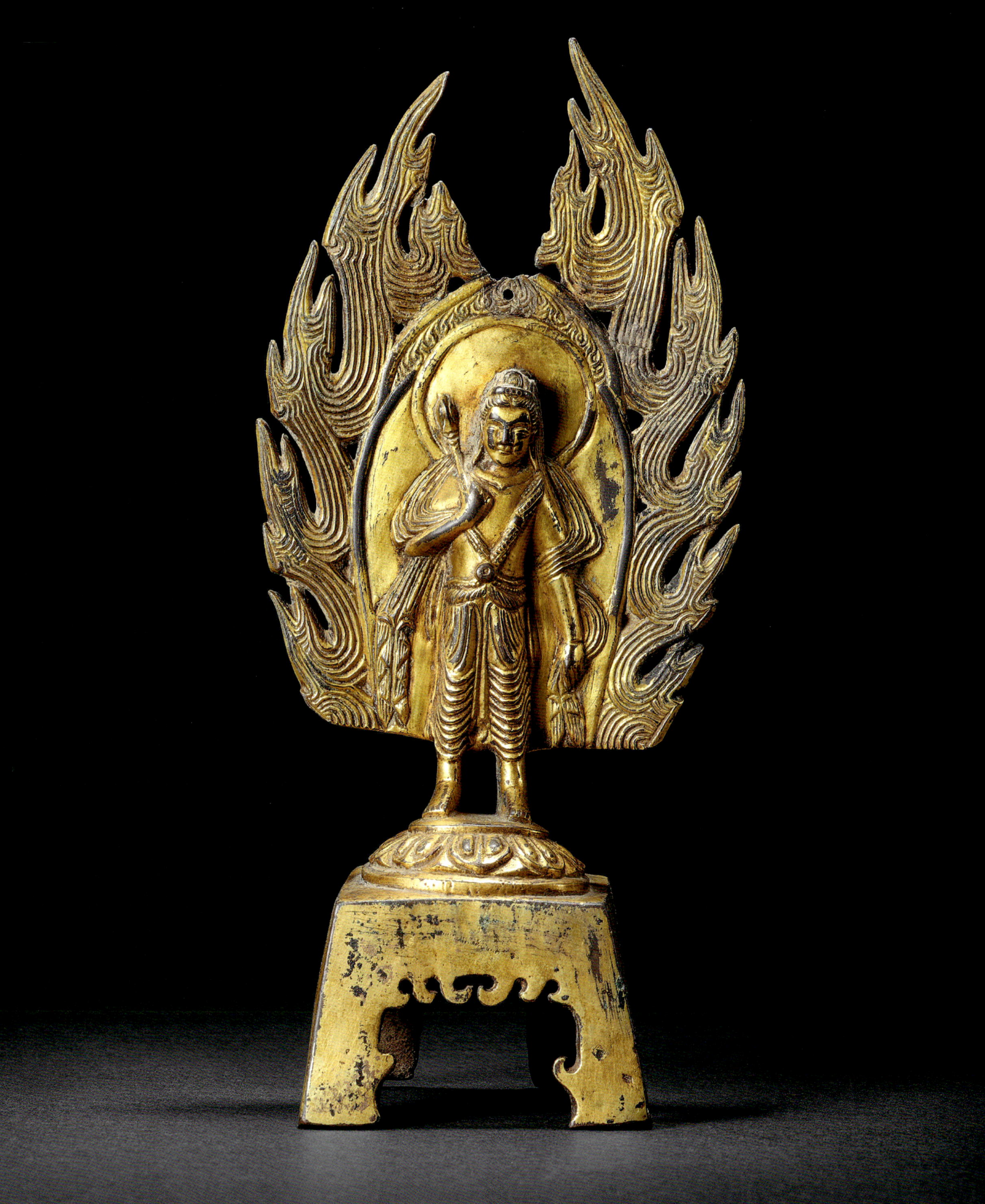

Standing Buddha

China, Northern Wei dynasty, dated 471 CE

Gilt bronze
10 ¼ × 5 ¼ × 4 ¼ in. (26 × 13.3 × 10.8 cm)

Presented in gilt bronze, this slender central figure wears simple robes draped across the shoulders and gathered at the knees. The figure is in high relief on a leaf-shaped mandorla; directly behind the head is a halo made up of radiating lotus petals. Five seated Buddhas, each with its own mandorla, occupy the area outside the halo. Incised onto the back of the mandorla is a figure seated under a broad-leafed tree with his right leg pendant. The sculpture is supported by a domed base with four legs. The front of the dome is decorated with interwoven designs; the inscription incised on the side and back reads: "Huangxing fifth year, third month, twenty-seventh day [corresponding to 471]; Xincheng County [near modern Zhengzhou in Henan Province] resident Qiu Jinu had one image made for [his] father and mother. May father and mother be reborn up to heaven and directly meet all Buddhas. Should they be reborn into this world, may they be dukes, kings, and elders."[1] As with the inscription on the sculpture in the Xuzhou Collection dated 470 (cat. 18), the content here is a combination of Chinese ancestor worship and Buddhist concepts.

Stylistically, this sculpture relates to contemporary pieces in stone from Yungang, the immense series of Buddhist caves, commissioned by the Northern Wei imperial family near their capital at Pingcheng (modern Datong, Shanxi Province). Interpreting its iconography presents some challenges. One possible interpretation of this ensemble is based on the Buddhist concept of time, where the past, present, and future are interconnected and coexist. In this scheme, the five seated figures on the mandorla represent the Buddhas of the Past; the main standing image is Shakyamuni, the Buddha of the Present; and the pensive bodhisattva on the back represents Maitreya, awaiting rebirth as the Buddha of the Future. **MK**

Note

1. Translated by Hao Sheng. The same patron commissioned a sculpture of Avalokiteshvara now in the British Museum, providing a rare instance of two surviving pieces from this period commissioned by the same donor.

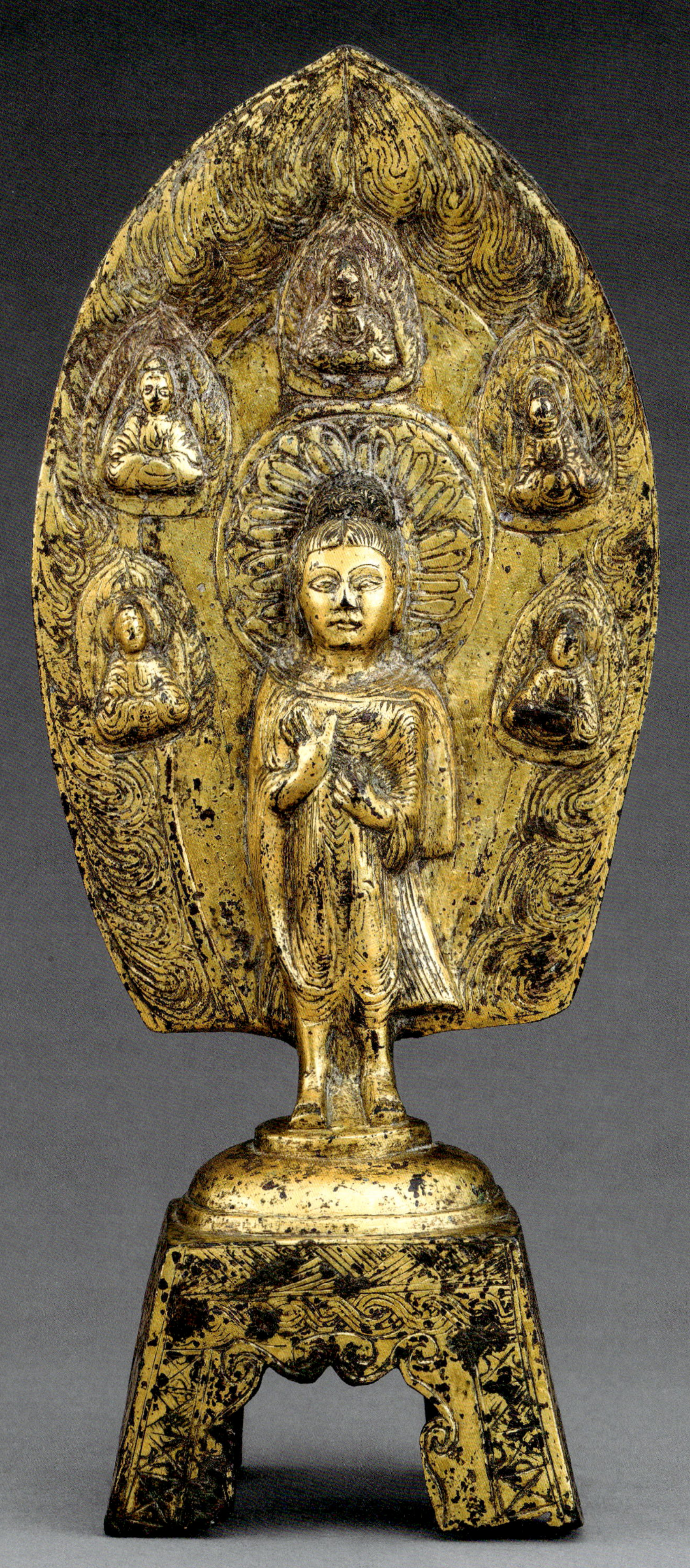

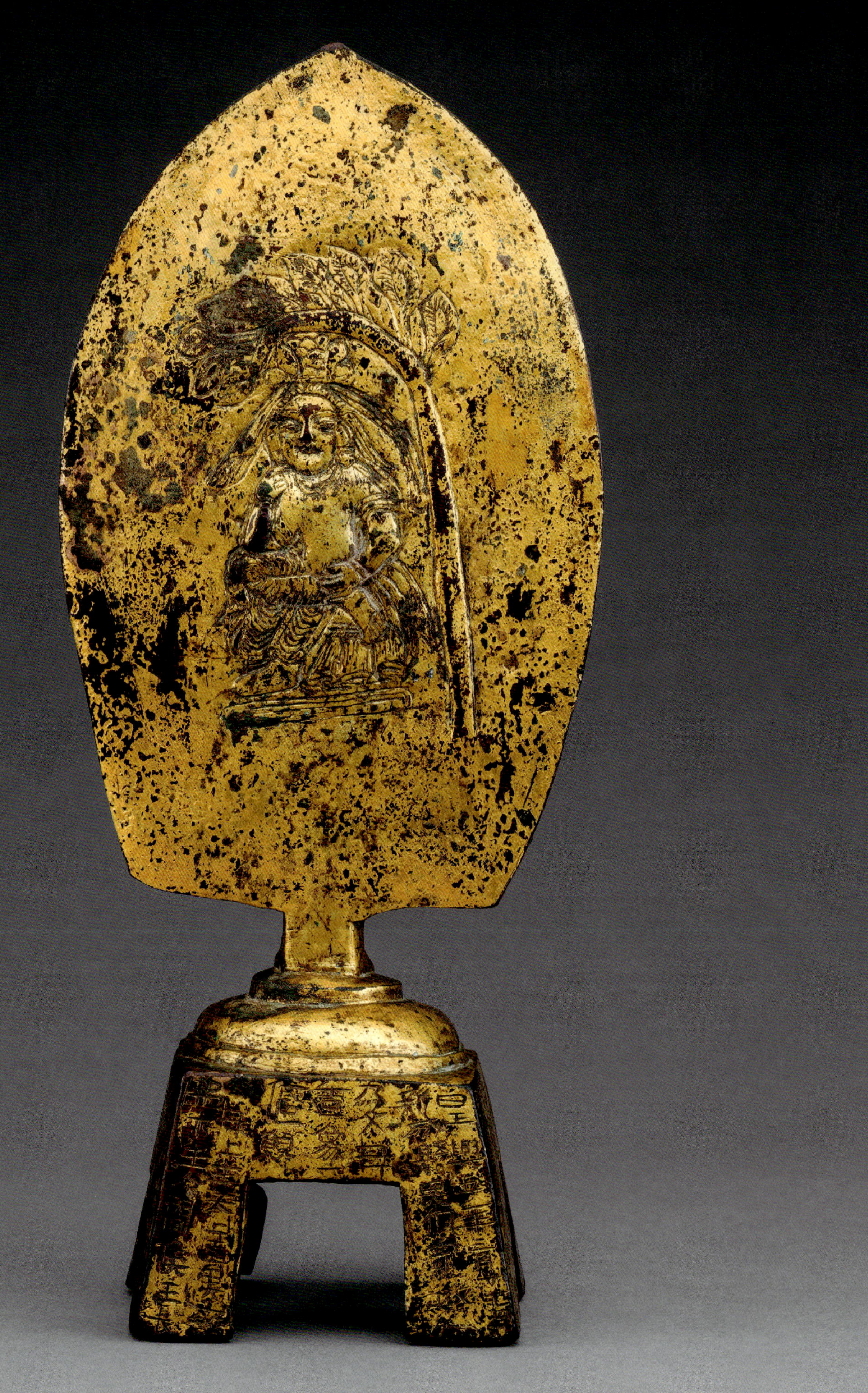

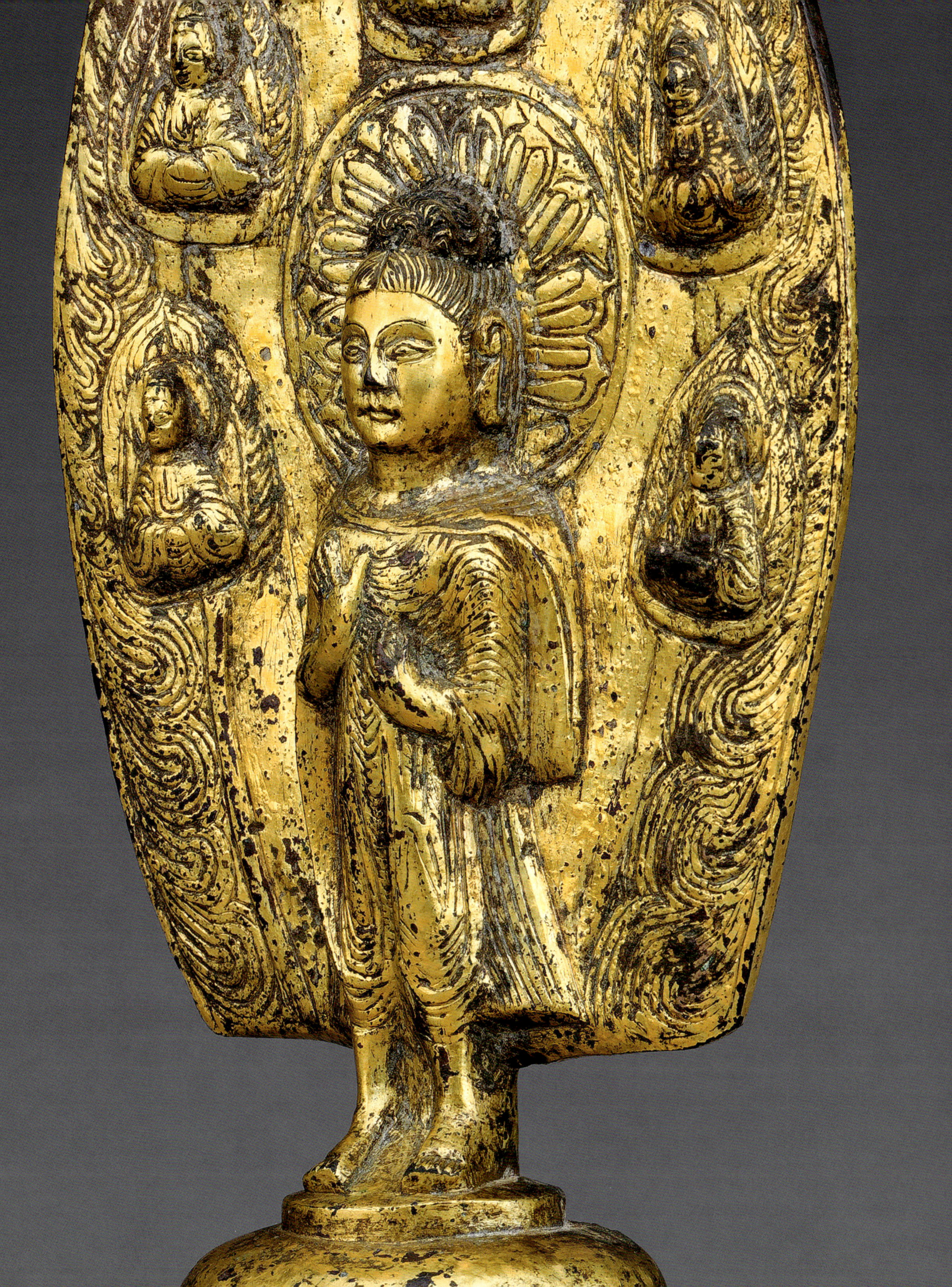

Buddhist Triad

China, Northern Wei dynasty, dated 526 CE

Limestone
23 ⅞ × 13 ¼ × 8 in. (60.5 × 33.7 × 20.3 cm)

This sculpture of a seated Buddha with two attendants embodies the "lean-boned and lofty countenance" aesthetic found in Northern Wei sculpture created after the move of the capital to Luoyang in 492. The Buddha is seated at the center of a boat-shaped mandorla incised with flames and foliage, his right hand raised in *abhaya* mudra and his left in *varada* mudra. He is dressed in heavy robes with stylized folds, has a smile distinctive to the period and a lotus-shaped nimbus, and is flanked by a pair of standing bodhisattvas with their hands held in *anjali* mudra, each standing on a lotus blossom behind a lion. The four-legged base with its barbed edge references contemporaneous sculptures in bronze. It is inscribed: "The Great Wei Dynasty, second year of the Xiaochang Reign (526 CE), ninth month, twenty-third day. Monk Faxing made with reverence two jade images of Shakyamuni, respectfully for the emperor, teachers and disciples, parents and relations, and all sentient beings. May all benefit from the merits of this image and reach enlightenment. This is my dedication."[1]

Freestanding sculptures were created for environments very different than those found in cave temples. Cave temples were built into cliffs, often some distance from urban centers.[2] Most freestanding sculptures were used in family shrines and temples within urban centers.[3] Following the move of the Northern Wei capital to Luoyang in 494, stone began to compete for these urban markets that had previously been dominated by bronze. This context presented issues for artisans working in stone. A comparison between the sculpture in stone illustrated here and a bronze altarpiece dated 524 in the Metropolitan Museum of Art is instructive.[4] Although the Buddha in stone is seated and the figure in bronze is standing, in broad stylistic terms the two pieces are similar, with the same body type, facial features, and heavy robes. However, the figures on the stone piece are integrated into the surface of the mandorla, whereas the bronze has a great deal of openwork and movement in three dimensions. This difference is in part a response to the artisans' familiarity with the medium. Those working in stone did not have the confidence to create fine openwork at this early period. This confidence increased dramatically in the years that followed.

The tradition of commemorative stele (*bei*) served as a source of inspiration for stone stele of this period and offers an additional explanation for the closed form of this sculpture. Bei, which began to appear in the third century BCE, could be quite large and were often flat stone slabs, though some were round or drum shaped. They were used to mark tombs and other important sites; the commemorative text chiseled into the surface might be surrounded by decorative motifs. Early examples of bei did not feature three-dimensional representations of the human figure, but their basic form and decorative schemes served as a foundation for Buddhist stele, which were freestanding and found in cave complexes, urban temples, and other environments.[5] **MK**

Notes

1. Translated by Hao Sheng.
2. The pilgrimages taken to visit these cave temples by upper levels of society were quite involved, and the major caves were designed to awe these visitors. The sculptors working at Longmen employed ingenious techniques to solve issues found in rock-cut temples. Most sculptures within caves were by necessity attached, limiting the possibility of explorations in full three dimensions or for extensive penetrations of space into the stone. Since most of the individual caves had only a single entrance and therefore a single source of light, works that were to the sides of the entrance were carved at a taper, with the wider side toward the light source. This gave them a greater sense of three-dimensionality than what is apparent when they are viewed outside their original context. For examples, see the donor panels from the Central Binyang cave at Longmen now in the collections of the Metropolitan Museum of Art and the Nelson-Atkins Museum of Art in Kansas City. A different approach was dictated for those works that were directly in line with the source of light.
3. Yang Xuanzhi provides details about urban temples in Luoyang; many were converted from residences donated by members of the local gentry. See W. F. J. Jenner, *Memories of Old Loyang: Yang Hsüan-chih and the Lost Capital (493–534)* (Oxford University Press, 1981). As with other art of the time, the translation of residential architecture into forms appropriate for Buddhist practice resulted in a merging of elements from both. See Nancy S. Steinhardt, *Chinese Traditional Architecture* (China Institute, 1984) and *Chinese Architecture in an Age of Turmoil, 200–600* (University of Hawaii Press, 2014).
4. *Buddha Maitreya (Mile) Altarpiece*, Northern Wei dynasty (386–534), dated 524 (fifth year of Zhengguang reign), gilt bronze, the Metropolitan Museum of Art, Rogers Fund, 1938, 38.158.1a–n; https://www.metmuseum.org/art/collection/search/42162.
5. See Dorothy Wong, *Chinese Steles: Pre-Buddhist and Buddhist Use of a Symbolic Form* (University of Hawaii Press, 2004).

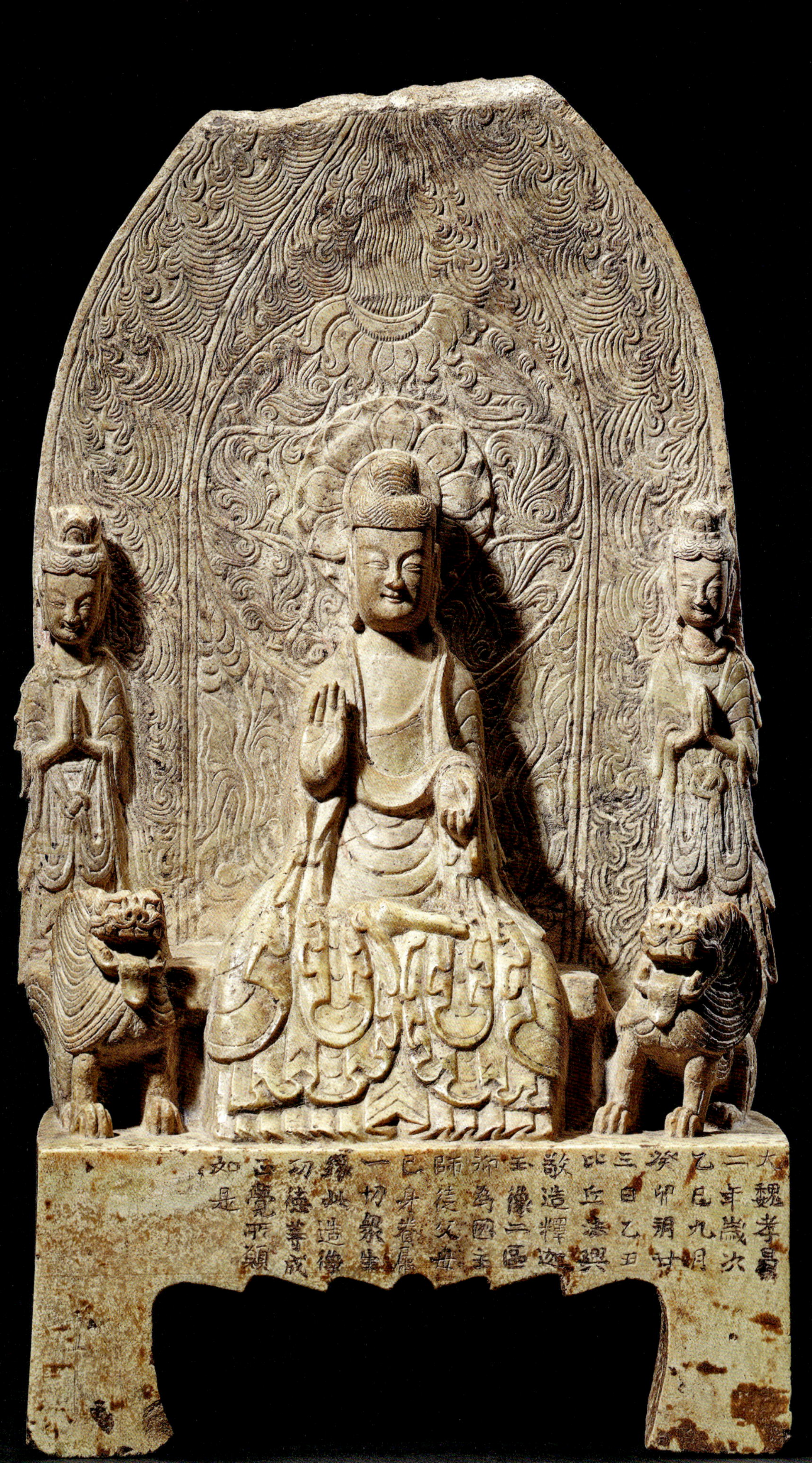

大魏孝昌
二年歲次
乙巳九月
癸卯朔廿
三日乙丑
比丘僧興
敬造輝像
一區上爲
國王帝主
師僧父母
及眷眷屬
一切衆生
緣此福德
咸同正覺
如是像成

Buddha Head

China, Tang dynasty, 8th century

Hollow-core dry lacquer
18 ¹⁄₁₆ × 11 ¼ × 12 in. (45.8 × 28.6 × 30.5 cm)

In 589 the Sui dynasty (581–618) unified China, bringing an end to centuries of division between north and south. The Tang dynasty seized control of this unified state in 618 and continued China's military and cultural expansion, defeating the kingdoms along the Silk Road and bringing them into the status of vassal states. Trade and cultural contact also expanded along sea routes as China became a major maritime power. After a brief disruption starting in 690, the Tang dynasty resumed in 705 and entered a period of wealth and stability that lasted until 744. This head of a Buddha, a prime example of High Tang Buddhist sculpture, demonstrates the synthesis that was a feature of the arts created during this period, incorporating elements from Central Asia, India, and native Chinese traditions.

The Buddhist temples in China were politically powerful and extremely wealthy during this period; as a result, their festivals increased in frequency, size, and splendor. While most of these festivals involved opening temples and monasteries to the public, some included processions in which important works of art were presented.[1] Weight and ease of use were clearly important considerations in creating art for use in such processions, and were one reason for going through the very challenging process of creating a sculpture such as this spectacular head in dry lacquer.[2] This head is thought to be the remnants of a full representation of a Buddha; extrapolating from it, the overall sculpture must have been considerably larger than life-size.[3] It has been suggested that this head and two others made using the same technique that are closely related were part of an ensemble.[4] Such a group would have been visually powerful yet light and easy to carry; presenting similar sculptures in bronze or stone in a procession would have been extremely difficult.[5]

Further evidence that this piece was created for use in processions can be found in the features of the face, which are somewhat simplified to make the most powerful impact from a distance. While much of the decoration on the large *ushnisha* has been lost, remnants of flowing hair can be seen near the ears and in small areas in the front. The ears are very large, with long, pierced earlobes (a sign of nobility in India frequently found in Buddhist art). The arched eyebrows join to the aquiline nose, making a single visually powerful unit. The inset circle between the eyebrows is the Buddha's third eye, representing enlightenment; most likely it was originally inlaid with glass.[6] The slightly downcast and partially closed eyes are inlaid with black glass surrounded by white pigment. The face has full cheeks, partially pursed lips, a double chin, and circular folds around the neck. There are traces of red on the lips, and the entire figure was once likely brightly colored, as befitting a work of art to be celebrated in a public procession. **MK**

Notes

1. See Robert E. Buswell, *Encyclopedia of Buddhism* (Macmillan, 2004), 249–50, and Kenneth Chen, *Buddhism in China: A Historical Survey* (Princeton University Press, 1964), 275–85. The diary of the Japanese monk Ennin's visit to China from 838–47 contains many descriptions of local festivals. He did not have an opportunity to view imperially sponsored processions since his visit corresponded to a persecution of Buddhism and other foreign religions. See Edwin O. Reischauer, *Ennin's Diary: The Record of a Pilgrimage to China in Search of the Law* (Ronald Press Company, 1955). Those in the capital and involving the imperial court were great spectacles; an example in which sculptures were carried in procession is the Festival of the Buddha's Birthday. It occurred on the eighth day of the fourth month and was marked by two events — the procession of Buddha images and the bathing of the Buddha. Yang Xuanzhi (Hsüan-chih) provides a description in his *Memories of Old Luoyang*: "On the previous day (the 7th) all images in the city, over a thousand in number, were first transported to the Ching-ming [Jingming] Temple, and on the following day they were then carried through the streets of the capital in the direction of the imperial palace where they were personally reviewed by the emperor. Golden flowers sparkled in the sunlight, ornamented parasols floated about like clouds, the banners and pennants formed a forest, fumes from the incense resembled the mist, music and chants resounded and shook heaven and earth." Buswell, *Encyclopedia of Buddhism*, 249–50.
2. For a complete technical analysis of this piece, please see Donna Strahan's essay in this catalogue.
3. Strahan estimates it would have been seven and a half feet tall as a seated figure.
4. Regina Krahl, "Divine Features in Lacquer," Sotheby's Hong Kong, sale HK049, lot 120.
5. For example, Yang Xuanzhi, in his description of the Jingxing convent, states, "It had a golden statue on a carriage that stood 30 feet high and was covered with a precious canopy from which hung pearls and golden bells on all four sides; flying devas, musicians, and dancers gazed down on the statue from beyond the clouds. The excellence of its craftsmanship beggared description. On the day the statues were brought out in procession, 100 Forest of Wings guardsmen were ordered to carry it, and musicians and performers were also sent by royal command." See Jenner, *Memories of Loyang*, 182.
6. Ibid.

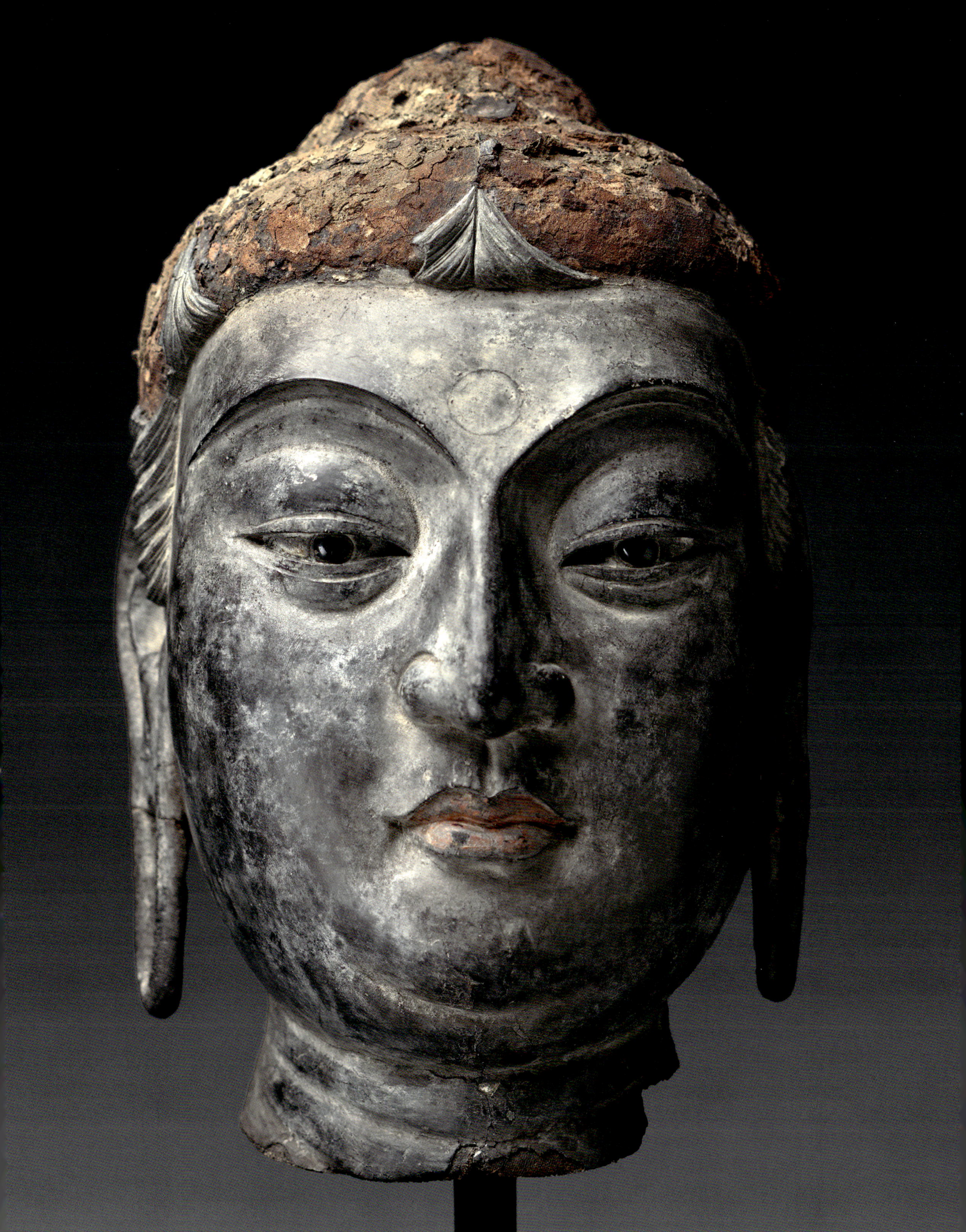

Avalokiteshvara as Acuoye Guanyin

China, Dali kingdom, probably 12th century

Gilt bronze
19 ½ × 4 ½ × 3 ½ in. (49.5 × 11.4 × 8.9 cm)

The Dali kingdom occupied an area centered in modern Yunnan Province. Located on one end of the major trade route between China and Southeast Asia popularly known as the Burma Road, it came into being in 937 after the collapse of Nanzhao kingdom. The rulers of the Dali kingdom came from the Duan family, who had been eminent during the Nanzhao. Not Chinese, the inhabitants of Dali were probably the ancestors of some of the many ethnic groups now living in southwestern China and Southeast Asia. They had their own spoken and written language. Much of the wealth in the region came from trade, the sale of horses, and military expeditions. During the Nanzhao period, military campaigns were carried out in Annam (modern Vietnam), Burma (Myanmar), Tibet, and Tang dynasty China. Historical records indicate that Buddhist monks and possibly artisans were among the captives brought back to the capital following successful campaigns. Others came through diplomatic and religious relationships. The Dali kingdom was conquered by Kublai Khan of the Yuan dynasty in 1253.

Although the region had its own religious traditions, Buddhism was present and in 831 was declared the state religion by the last Nanzhao king. It continued as the state religion during the Dali kingdom. A local form of Vajrayana Buddhism known as Azhali was practiced; according to historical texts, it was founded about 821–24 by a monk from India. It was related to Vajrayana Buddhism practiced in Tibet and Burma.

Buddhist art produced during the Dali kingdom combines elements from China, Tibet, Southeast Asia, the Pala kingdom, and indigenous styles to produce forms unique to the area. Of particular importance are a group of standing images of the bodhisattva Avalokiteshvara (Chinese: Guanyin); the sculpture illustrated here is an example.[1] Legend of this distinct iconography tells its miraculous origin from an Indian monk of the 600s, who introduced the worship of Avalokiteshvara to the region and was himself considered an incarnation of the bodhisattva.

Many of its features relate to those on an eleventh-century seated Avalokiteshvara from the Pala kingdom in the Xuzhou Collection (see page 10).[2] These features include hair drawn up under a crown into a tall topknot. In both cases, the lobes of the ears are very long and decorated with heavy rings; other jewelry includes elaborate necklaces and multiple armbands. Both figures are bare chested, tall, slender, and wear a thin dhoti secured at the waist by a jeweled belt and elaborate sashes. The Dali kingdom had access to Pala through trade relations and military exploits in Burma and through Tibet. The facial features of the Dali Avalokiteshvara are more closely related to those found in works from Southeast Asia. The left hand is in the gesture of religious discussion (*vitarka* mudra) and right in the gesture of gift-granting (*varada* mudra). **MK**

Notes
1. There is some debate about the origin of the term Acuoye. Some scholars have stated that it is a transliteration of the Sanskrit term *acharya*, which means "preceptor." Acharya played a critical role in the religious and political practice in the Dali kingdom. They were allowed to marry; their titles were hereditary, and they served as advisers to the government. Others have suggested that Acuoye is a transliteration of the Sanskrit term *ajaya*, which means "all victorious." See Christie's, New York, October 2002, lot 193, for a bibliography for this sculpture. Some information presented here comes from Patricia Berger's unpublished notes on a group of Dali sculptures in the collection of the Asian Art Museum of San Francisco.
2. See Susan L. Huntington, "Compassion in a Mountain Abode: A Pala Period Image of Avalokiteshvara," *Orientations* 48, no. 5 (September/October 2017): 78–87.

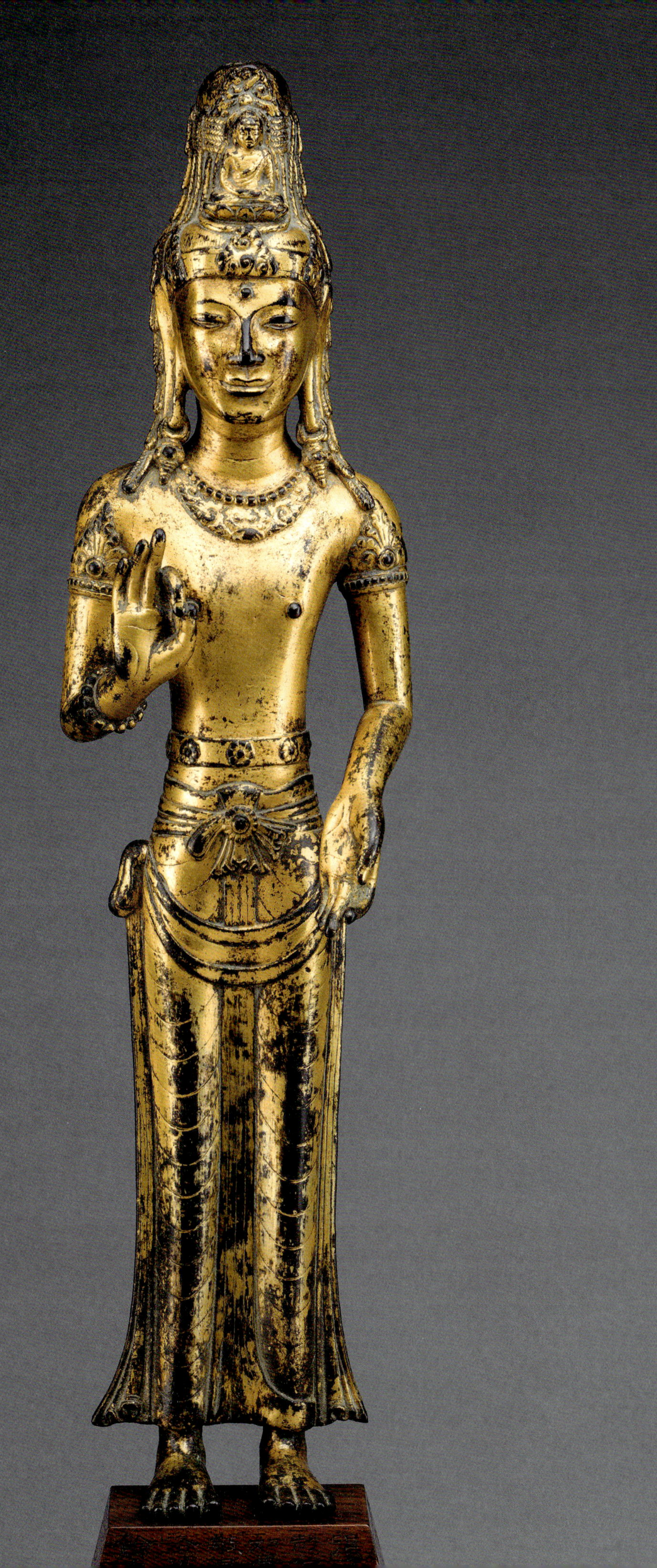

Buddha at Birth

Korea, Three Kingdoms period, 7th century

Gilt bronze
4 ¾ × 1 ¾ × 1 ½ in. (12.1 × 4.4 × 3.8 cm)

This image of the Buddha at Birth (Korean: Tansaeng Bul) was made about three centuries after Korea adopted Buddhism from India.[1] Two pairings of visual attributes constitute the Buddha-at-Birth iconography. The first involves one hand pointing up and the other pointing down. The second combines a youthful body with the head of an enlightened Buddha, signified by the protrusion on the head (*ushnisha*), the stretched earlobes, and also often the "third eye" between the eyebrows — here eroded.

According to legend, when Queen Maya picked a flower from a tree in Lumbini park in Kapilavastu, Nepal, the baby Buddha issued forth from her side and began walking seven steps in each of the four directions. He then declared, "I alone am honored in Heaven and Earth; I will alleviate all sufferings of the world." Upon hearing this prophesy of salvation, heavenly beings and dragons showered him with fragrant holy water.[2] Buddhist temples around the world reenact this auspicious shower by pouring pure or perfumed water onto a Buddha-at-Birth image placed at the center of a wide shallow basin.[3]

While the hand gestures recall the moment of the infant's speech, the pairing of a young body with the head of an enlightened Buddha conveys the narrative arc of prophesy to fulfillment. It glorifies the infant's first steps as a symbolic move toward freedom from rebirths — Nirvana.

Unlike most of the surviving Buddha-at-Birth images with adolescent bodies, this Korean work maximizes the childlike charm that early seventh- and eighth-century Koreans prized. This penchant is also seen in other Buddhist image types from this period, for example, a boyish seventh-century Amitabha Buddha at the National Museum of Art of Korea.[4]

Seventh- and eighth-century Korean works often used the S-shaped curve of the contrapposto posture to create a sense of latent energy. In this figure, subtle movement is further indicated by the left foot positioned a bit outward and forward. A view from behind confirms this suggestion of incipient movement, as the forward-leaning leg tilts the dhoti slightly to the right.

The attention given to all sides of the baby Buddha affirms scholars' assumption that today's practice of participants surrounding a wide round basin and taking turns sprinkling water onto the icon dates to the earlier centuries of the birthday ritual. Unlike most small gilt-bronze images made mainly for frontal viewing, this image clearly anticipates adoration from all angles.

Another detail that distinguishes this work from most other known East Asian Buddha-at-Birth images is the ease with which it indicates heaven and earth.[5] Rather than extend his entire arm, this infant points upward with only his forearm. While the baby's future dominion over heaven and earth is hinted at, the focus is the optimistic beginnings of a new life. This impression is consistent with another tradition associated with these images in Korea. Among the thousand Buddhas displayed at Jikjisa in Gimcheon, Gyeongsang Province, is a small Buddha of this type; a long-held belief asserts that if a woman beholds it before seeing any other Buddha images surrounding it, she will conceive a son.[6] **KH**

Notes

1. Korea's official acceptance of Buddhism occurred in 372 CE during Korea's Three Kingdoms period, when the ruler of Former Qin, Fu Jian (reigned 357–385) sent Shundao to the northern kingdom of Goguryeo bearing Buddhist scripture and icons. The term "Infant Buddha" is also used in English publications, but there is no East Asian language equivalent to that designation. In today's India, there is little trace of any ritual centered upon a Buddha-at-Birth image. In China, icons of the type remain only from the Song dynasty (960–1279) and after.
2. We do not know specifically when Buddha-at-Birth iconography began to circulate in Korea. However, based on Korea's gifting of such an image to Japan (see cat. 26), it is reasonable to conclude that the image type was set prior to early sixth century. See Hiromitsu Washizuka et al., *Transmitting the Forms of Divinity: Early Buddhist Art from Korea and Japan* (Japan Society and Harry N. Abrams, 2003), 210.
3. For more information on the ritual tradition and art history, see Tanaka Yoshiyasu, *Ancient Statues of the Infant Buddha*, trans. Juliet Carpenter, exh. cat. (Asuka Historical Museum, 1978), available online at https://www. nabunken.go.jp/english/e-catalogue/5.html (accessed March 15, 2025).
4. Kim Lena, ed., *History of Korean Buddhist Art* (Mijinsa, 2011), 32, cat. 1–31. The object is also featured in Washizuka et al., *Transmitting the Forms of Divinity*, 222–31, cat. 16.
5. For additional comparisons, see Washizuka et al., *Transmitting the Forms of Divinity*, 240–41, cat. 25; 208–9, cat. 9; 210–11, cat. 10; 292–93, cat. 53.
6. Kim Wi-seok, "Tansaengbul" in *Encyclopedia of Korean Culture*, http://www.encykorea.aks .ac.kr/Article/E0058783 (accessed March 17, 2025).

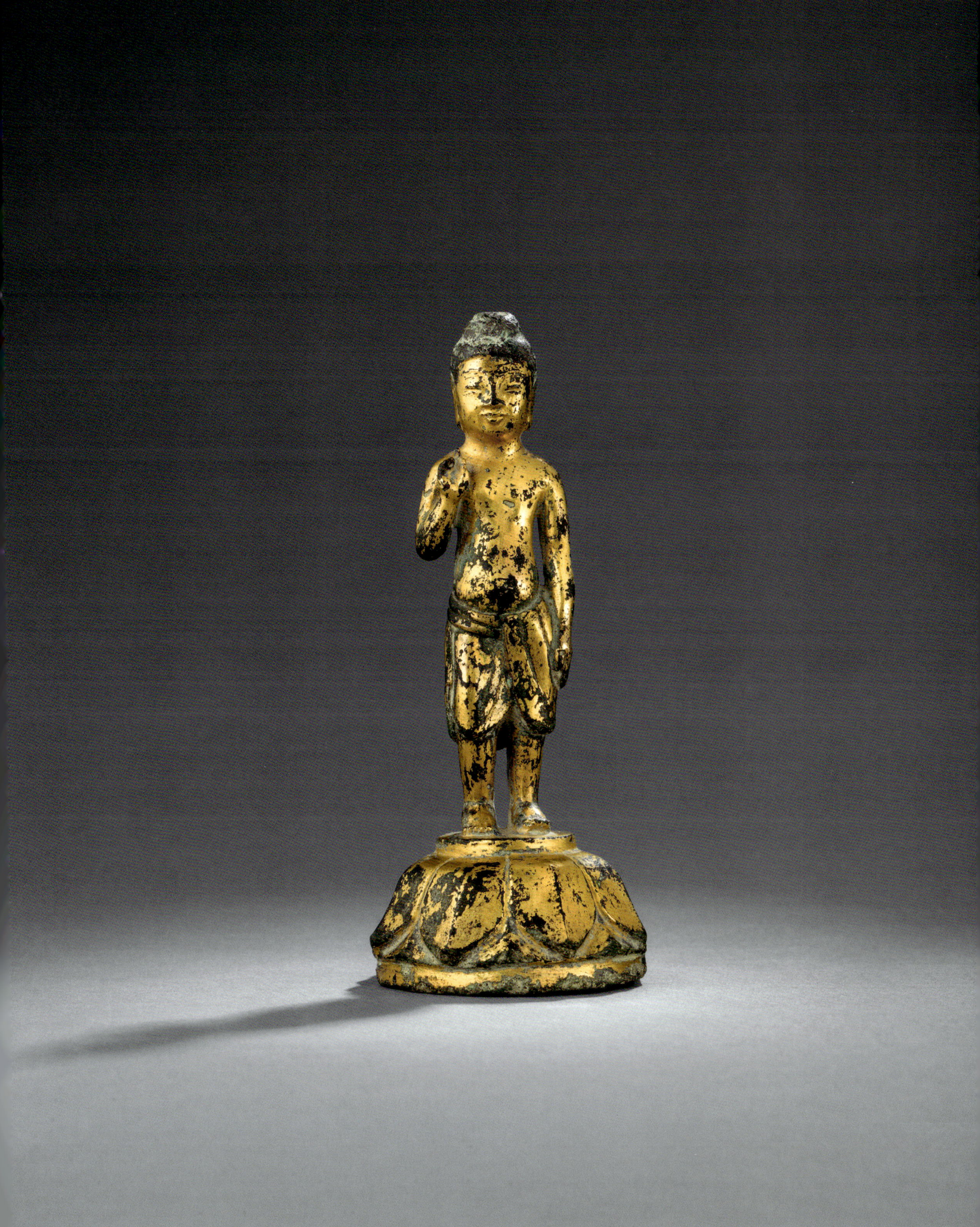

Standing Buddha

Korea, Unified Silla, 8th century

Gilt bronze
4 ¾ × 1 ¾ × 1 ½ in. (12.1 × 4.4 × 3.8 cm)

Exquisite small-scale images like this one were made as potent symbols of divine efficacy. Most Korean portable icons from the eighth century gesture the "fear not" and "wish granting" mudras, promising reward for those who sponsored divine likenesses and pray to them in domestic settings or on the person. But among them, those that also feature a particularly modeled body and garment constitute an especially valued typology of icons known as the "Udayana type."

According to legend, King Udayana of India (reigned sixth century BCE), suffering an intense longing for Buddha Shakyamuni during his brief absence, commissioned a sandalwood image of the beloved teacher. Upon his return, Shakyamuni blessed this first sculpture of himself and ordered it to stand in as his substitute after his Nirvana. Essentially, the Udayana story is about the merits of an elite patron and his image-making and worship.

Among the various ways in which artists visualized this legendary first image, the iconography that accrued the richest reception history in East Asia is that which this Xuzhou Buddha represents. The formula consists of the two mudras and a robe, with "wet drapery" folds that cling to the body, covering both shoulders and with a high U-shaped neckline.

This iconography and style follow a general artistic trend that Chinese sculptors of the Tang dynasty developed by appropriating, in turn, sculpting techniques developed in Gandhara and Mathura of India that focus on a curvaceous body thinly veiled under Greco-Indian–style garments. Such figures became so prevalent throughout late seventh- and eighth-century East Asia that scholars have coined the term the Tang International style.

While faithfully adopting these classicizing and exoticizing elements from the early Indian and Chinese models, Unified Silla–period sculptors also made significant adjustments according to their own local aesthetic. One prevailing tendency was to apportion the head and body of the divine subjects to be closer to that of a child.[1] However, the mandorla attached to the back, with its patterns in open metalwork (another popular technique during that time), counterbalances the impression of solid, material existence and adds a sense of transcendent beauty.

This particular Udayana iconography in the Tang International style became so popular that it was eventually applied also to representations of Buddhas other than Shakyamuni — including the Buddhas Amitabha and Bhaishajyaguru. This development and the fact that at least one other iconography had also been formulated to represent the first image have raised questions among scholars about the viability of the term "Udayana type."[2]

Nevertheless, around the time when this piece was made, sketches of Buddha images similar to it very likely circulated within East Asia, bearing written labels recalling the Udayana legend.[3] Centuries later, Japanese sandalwood Buddhas bearing the same iconography were labeled Udayana Buddha.[4] Such endurance of the visual trope cannot be ignored as we consider what powerful efficacy this small-scale icon must have signaled to its makers and worshippers. **KH**

Notes
1. See a similarly proportioned and modeled gilt-bronze Buddha in Kim Lena, *History of Korean Buddhist Art* (Mijinsa, 2011), 54–56, figs. 67, 72–74; also see Hapcheon Museum, *Small Statues of Buddha Embraced by Our Arms* (Hapcheon Museum and National Jinju Museum, 2021), 33, cat. 10 from Gyeongju Hwangryongsa temple site, collection of the National Research Institute of Cultural Property of Gyeongju.
2. See Hamada Tamami, "On the Udayana King Images in the Vicinity of Early Tang Luoyang," *Ars Buddhica* 287 (2006) about a seated, bare-torso-type Udayana image that had appeared in Luoyang, China, with some influence — but for a relatively short duration.
3. Sculptural or painted "Auspicious Images" of the Buddha actively circulated throughout East Asia during the Tang dynasty. These famous images associated with India and Central Asia, including those associated with the Udayana legend, were consistently shown gesturing fear-not and wish-fulfillment mudras and wearing Indian-style wet drapery of high or looser neckline.
4. There is also a celebrated thirteenth-century copy of the Seiryoji Buddha, which in turn was valued as an authentic copy of Udayana sandalwood image. See Ive Covaci, ed., *Kamakura: Realism and Spirituality in the Sculpture of Japan*, exh. cat. (Asia Society and Yale University Press, 2016), 38–41, fig. 1. The "Seiryoji Buddha" is attributed to Song dynasty artists Zhang Yanjiao and Zhang Yanxi and dated to 985. Also see *Buddhist Art Paradise: Jewels of the Buddhist Art Collection* (Nara National Museum, 2021), 352, no. 6. The Nara Museum Udayana image bears an inscription indicating that it was made by a sculptor named Genkai and was dedicated in 1273.

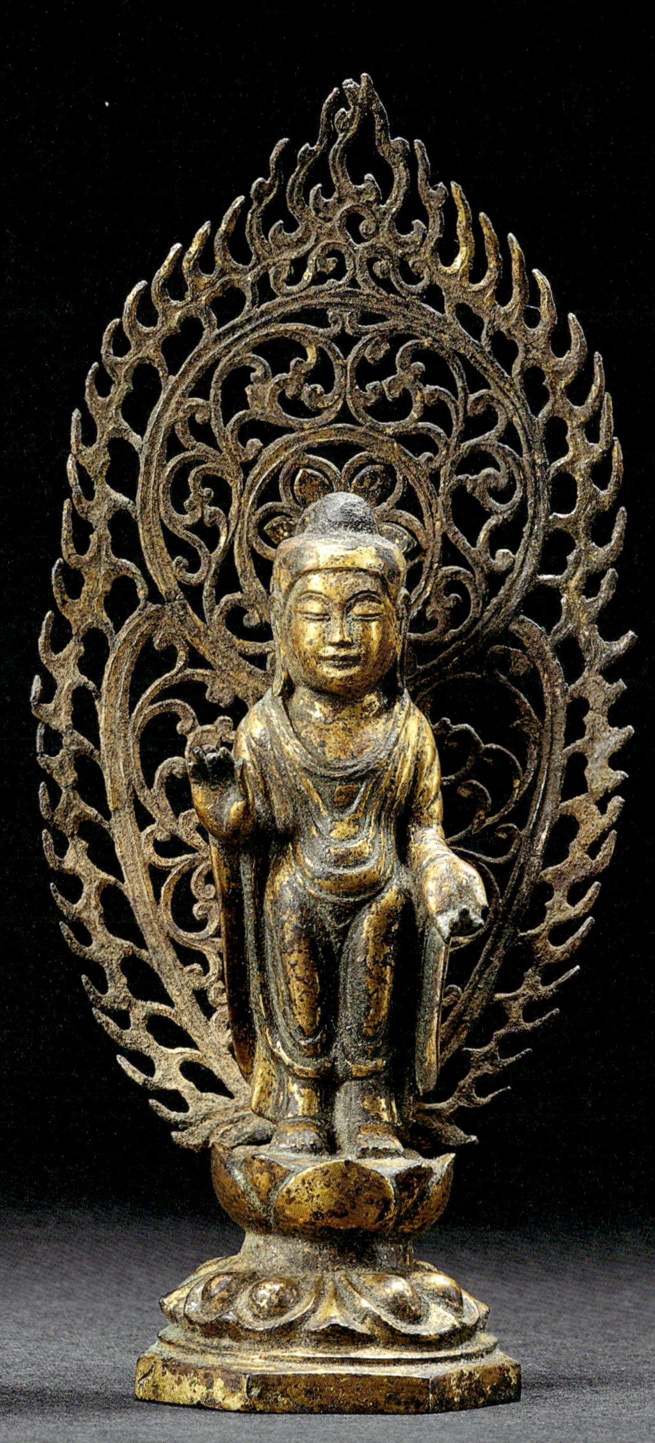

Standing Buddha

Korea, late Unified Silla–early Goryeo period, late 9th–early 10th century

Gilt bronze
4 ⅛ × 1 ⅝ × 1 ¼ in. (10.5 × 4.2 × 3.1 cm)

This work features characteristics of both early Korean Buddhist images from the sixth and seventh centuries as well as those from around the tenth century. One detail that associates it with the earlier period is the waterdrop-shaped aureole featuring seated Buddhas of the Past.[1] The halo calls to mind a cache of similarly shaped and decorated aureoles that survive from the Three Kingdoms period. Early Korean Buddhists adopted from the Northern Wei dynasty of China a taste for solid, pointed, oblong backdrops with floating seated Buddhas as a favorite motif.[2] Moreover, the inscription engraved on the back of this Buddha's halo is written in a script commonly found on those of Northern Wei and Three Kingdoms periods. Korea's National Treasure No. 119, dated to 539 CE, is one of the latter examples.[3]

Another feature that recalls early sculpture of the preunification centuries is the flat and angular treatment of the body that is antithetical to the pursuits of the Tang International aesthetic (see cat. 24). The present Buddha's deep-carved fabric folds and its plastic articulation of loose sleeves and hanging skirt are signature features of sixth- and seventh-century Korean sculpture that were inspired by fifth- and sixth-century Chinese models. These tendencies of the preunification era returned for revisionist classicism during the closing decades of the ninth century, when Silla, the unifier of the Three Kingdoms, waned and dissenting powers pledging fealty to the defeated kingdoms began to rise throughout the peninsula. Among them was Wang Geon, who would unify the peninsula once again and found the dynasty of Goryeo (918–1392). The present Buddha demonstrates this mixing of aesthetic achievements of the collapsing Unified Silla dynasty and those developed during the periods prior to unification.

This Buddha's round, wide face shows undeniable traces from the Unified Silla period. Its broad, arched eyebrows canopy hooded eyelids over downcast eyes. The small mouth has dimpling corners that lift up the fat cheeks. The upper torso, with its rounded rectangular shoulders, builds on the basic structure of preunification precedents, but the volume is more substantial than the exaggeratedly slender scales favored by the Goguryeo artists of the Three Kingdoms period, to which the inscription on the back of this work pays indirect allegiance.[4]

The inscription reads: "Wang Yu, a lay disciple of the temple Jeungshimsa of Goryeo humbly made [this image]." The dynastic name Goryeo was used for both Go[gu]ryeo of the preunification period and for Wang Geon's later kingdom, signaling their connection. But this work's stylistic melding of the two periods suggests that it is the later Goryeo that is being referenced here. Jeungshimsa likely refers to an important temple established in 860 CE near the city of Gwangju in Cholla Province.[5]

Overall, this exquisite object is a valuable palimpsest of art history from one of the most intriguing periods of transitions and creativity in Korean history. **KH**

Notes
1. The halo is attached by a pin though a protruding knob on the back of the Buddha's head inserted through an eyelet in the halo.
2. For other examples of the three seated Buddhas motif, see Hiromitsu Washizuka et al., *Transmitting the Forms of Divinity: Early Buddhist Art from Korea and Japan* (Japan Society and Harry N. Abrams, 2003), 238–39, cat. 24, and 204–5, cat. 7.
3. Inscribed "7th year of Yeonga (539 CE)."
4. National Treasure 119 exemplifies the typical slender silhouette of the early Goryeo (Goguryeo) period sculptures. The solid physique seen in this work is, in fact, closer in volume to some of the works made in preunification Silla and Baekje territories than to the works made in Goguryeo. *Standing Buddha* from the temple site of Suksusa, Yeongpung, North Gyeongsang Province, in the collection of Daegu National Museum is a good example from the early seventh-century Silla dynasty, reprinted in Washizuka, *Transmitting the Forms of Divinity*, 218–19, cat. 14.
5. This work is also discussed by Tanabe Saburosuke in *Buddha's Smile II — Transcending Time and Space*, Tajima Mitsuru, eds., exh. cat. (London Gallery Tokyo, 2010), 316, 352–53. The temple was established by a prominent master of Seon (Chinese: Chan; Japanese: Zen) Buddhism, a sect that emerged during the final decades of the Silla dynasty as it was championed by the rebelling clans to oppose the conservative Gyojong school supported by Silla's central government.

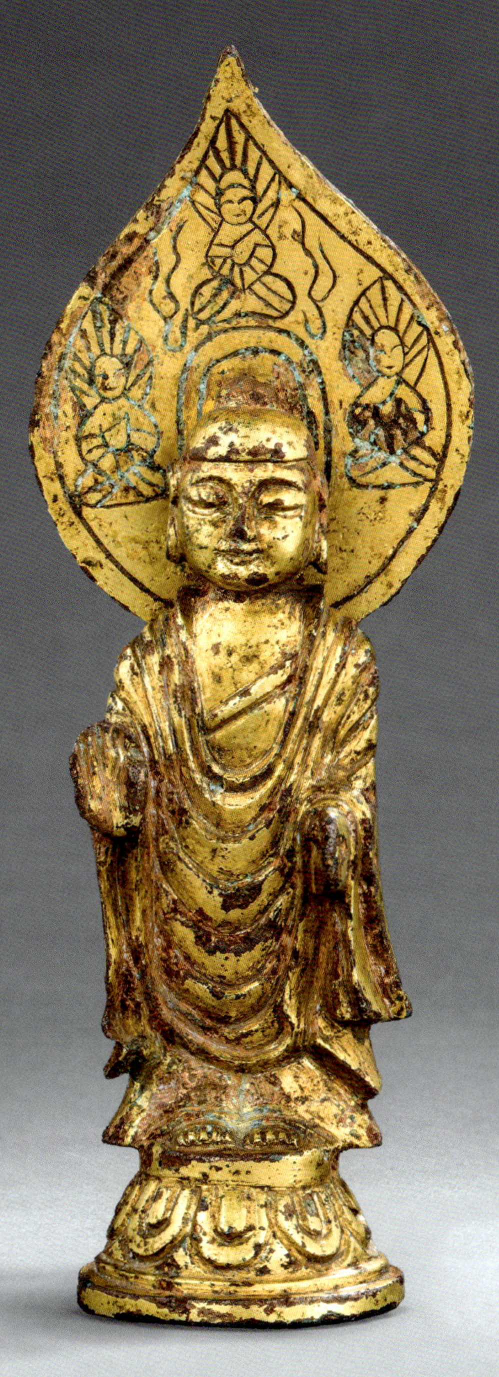

Buddha at Birth

Japan, Nara period, 7th century, basin added later

Gilt bronze
3 9⁄16 × 1 3⁄16 × 1 3⁄16 in. (9 × 3 × 3 cm)

Like cat. 23, this figure also represents the Buddha at Birth. According to *The Origins of the Gangōji Monastery*, King Seongmyeong of the Korean kingdom of Baekje introduced Buddhism to Japan in 538 CE along with a Buddha-at-Birth image.[1] The same text reports that, by the year 606 CE, a birthday ritual of bathing a baby Buddha sculpture was in practice in Japan. Replete with salvific promises, the iconography would have seemed an ideal set of visual signs with which to spread the new religion. Moreover, the portability of the object type would have been an added benefit.

Compared to the toddler-type *Buddha at Birth* (cat. 23), this adolescent figure's lean, elegant body is rigid, with his entire arm outstretching to declare his purpose. Whereas the former has a bright, innocent smile with full half-moon eyebrows and lips, this one has wide, arched brows and a mouth that give it a somber, pensive expression, as if focused on the magnitude of his future task.

This seventh-century Japanese work finds informative comparisons in two well-known works: Korea's National Treasure No. 808 in the collection of the Horim Museum and the Japanese Important Cultural Property from Shōgenji, Aichi Prefecture.[2] Stylistically dated to the late sixth century, the Horim Buddha at Birth is also an adolescent image with slender arms outstretched upward and down. But whereas it demonstrates the Korean penchant for earthly naturalism, this work here shows the artist's exacting precision, privileging the effect of transcendence over earthly presence. The Shōgenji Buddha at Birth (Japanese: Tanjōbutsu) also displays idealism in the modeling of the smooth torso and in the scalloped flare of the skirt, but these efforts fall short of matching the degree of perfectionism achieved in this work.[3]

This image showcases verticals and curves that reverberate with great precision. The vertical lines and shapes, including the chest cavity, the pendant ends of the belt, and the oblong space between the legs, create a sense of unity and perfection. The linearity is further reinforced by the alignment of seemingly incidental yet methodically spaced points in space that the eyes are guided to connect. The fingertip of the right-hand index finger is perfectly aligned with the central verticals that frontally bisect the body. It also caps other verticals of the image in the round, including those viewed from the back and multiple oblique angles of view.

Echoes of rounded and pointed arches also abound. To cite only a few, gliding along the bent arms, the viewer's eyes are led along the outline of an aureole encasing the entire figure. It is a slim, leaf-shaped mandorla with the Buddha's raised finger marking its pinnacle. Below the feet, finely cast petals adorning the bottom tier of the double-lotus pedestal complement the silhouette of the implied mandorla. These are exquisitely subtle but effective visual strategies that invite viewer participation to hallow the icon. **KH**

Notes
1. "Origins of the Gangōji Monastery and Its Assets," often abbreviated to *Gangōji Garan Engi*, compiled by an unnamed Buddhist monk in 747 CE. Tokutarō Sakurai, ed., *Nihon Shisō Taikei 20: Jisha Engi* (Iwanami Shoten, 1975), 7–22.
2. See Tanaka Yoshiyasu, *Ancient Statues of the Infant Buddha*, trans. Juliet Carpenter (Asuka Historical Museum, 1978), available online at https://www.nabunken.go.jp/english/e-catalogue/5.html (accessed March 15, 2025).
3. Another fine example in the Smithsonian Museum, National Museum of Asian Art, demonstrates the same point: *The Buddha at Birth*, Asuka period, seventh century, gilt bronze, F2005.9a–b.

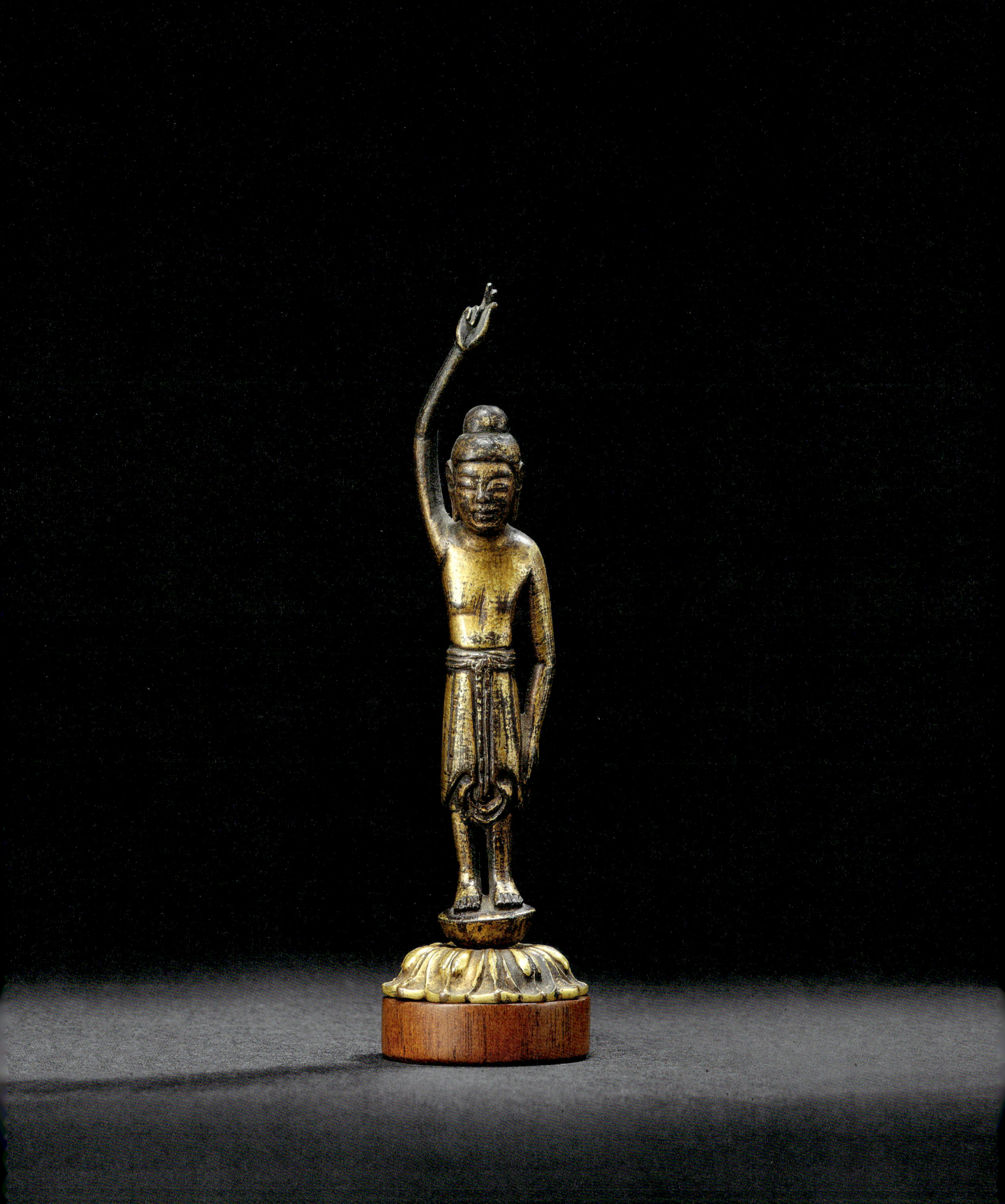

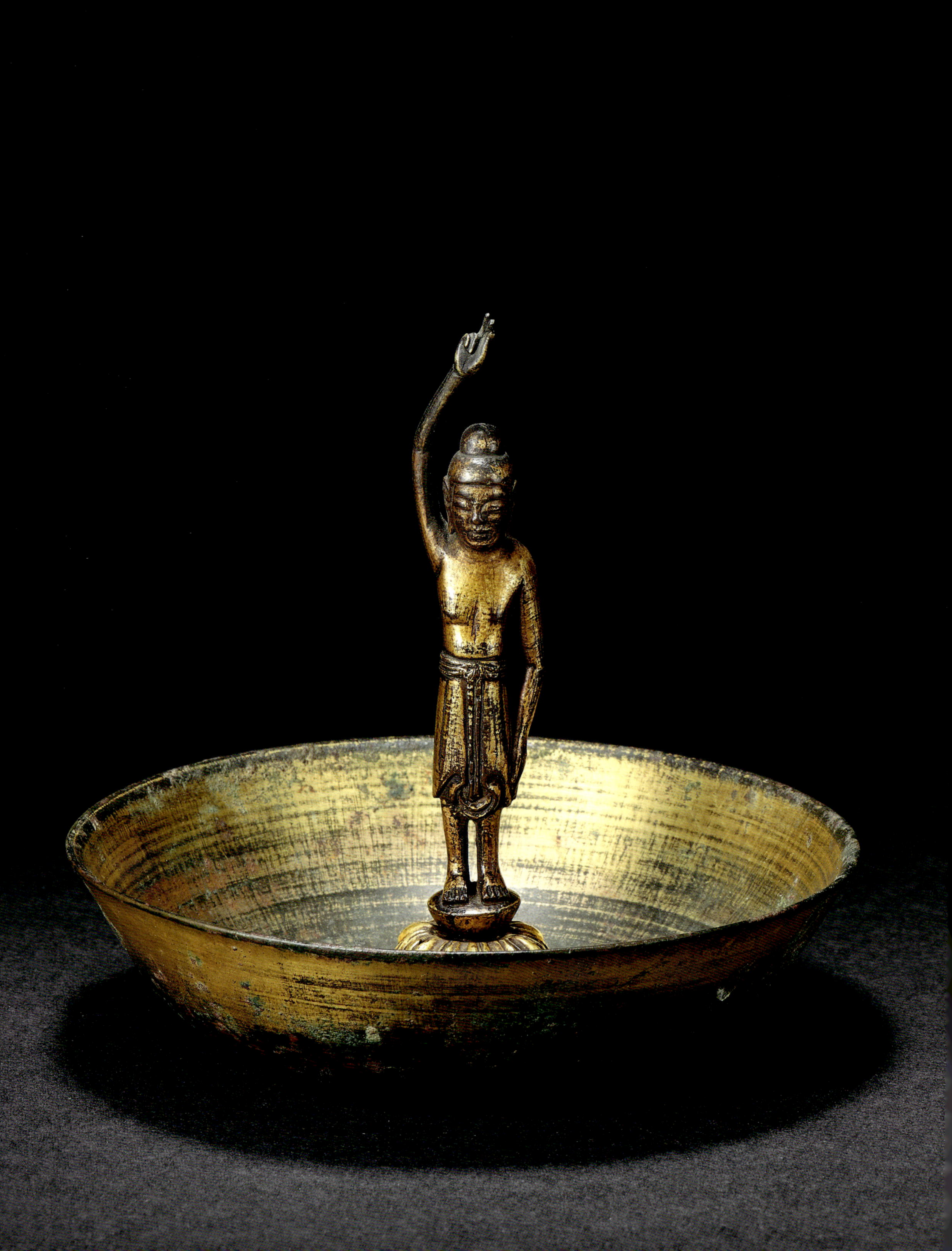

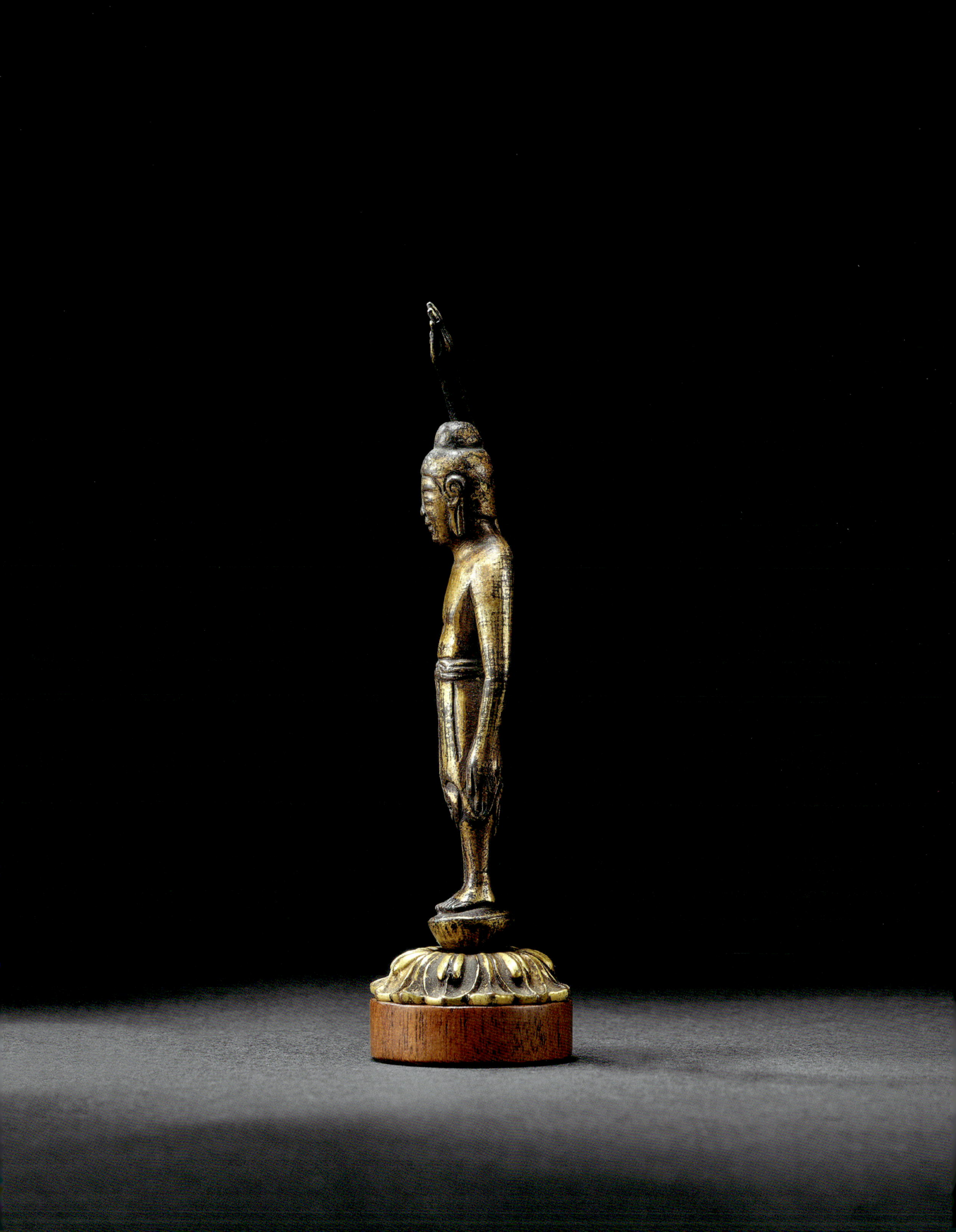

Avalokiteshvara as Nyoirin Kannon

Japan, Kamakura period, 1185–1333

Gilt bronze
3 ⅜ × 2 ¼ × 2 in. (8.6 × 5.7 × 5.1 cm)

Among the many bodhisattvas who help humankind reach Buddha-hood, the most beloved is Avalokiteshvara (Japanese: Kannon). Scriptures and folklore attest to the deity's fulfillment of his vow to manifest in myriad forms to save souls in need — White-Robed Kannon, Eleven-Headed Kannon, or Thousand-Armed Kannon, to name just a few.[1] Sculptors and painters followed suit to materialize these abstract concepts. Among the most technically challenging of the forms was the Nyoirin Kannon, named for the wish-granting jewel he proffers.

Like most Kannon images, Nyoirin Kannon are richly adorned with jewelry, signaling his choice to stay connected to the material world and to serve as interlocutor between humans and the Buddhas. They also tend to have multiple arms to emphasize their extraordinary endowments and matching generosity.[2] When six-armed, four of the hands hold a symbol of generous teaching: the jewel promising a reward for sincere supplication, the "wheel of law" symbolizing the Dharma, a rosary asserting the power of prayer, and a lotus flower demonstrating the possibility of staying pure in a murky environment.

The remaining right hand touches the cheek, while the left hand either clenches or rests on a gathered end of his scarf on his seat — a gesture often interpreted as the Kannon's will to subdue all earthly agitations, including material greed. The iconography thus projects onto a single figure ideal religious means and end: prayer, contempla-tion, meditation, learning the doctrine, and spiritual purity, all leading to enlightenment.

The Nyoirin iconography emerged in Japan during the Heian period (794–1185) but ascended to a new level of prominence during the Kamakura period (1185–1333), during which military warlords vied for dominance.[3] People on all levels of the society sought comfort in possessing small images of the Kannon for private devotion. However, the Nyoirin Kannon seems to have been particularly popular among the ruling elite, who possessed the material wealth to sponsor its complex and expensive form.[4]

Families of Kamakura sculptors accumulated remarkable skills over generations, reaching new heights in realism to satisfy an evolving aesthetic that prioritized sensorial stimulation as key to reaching spiritual salvation. Esoteric Buddhism, including Tantric and Shingon schools, developed elaborate public and secret rituals for "enlivening" lifelike icons through ceremonies such as eye-dotting, inscribing prayers, and inserting prayer scrolls or reliquaries into the inner cavities of a sculpture.[5] Icons of Nyoirin Kannon were thought to ensure not only peace and wealth but also fecundity. A religious document from the period promises that a Nyoirin image can help male or female worshippers conceive a son by adjusting their levels of lust.[6]

The complex design of this figure required great skill in metal-working at a minute scale. Though it remains striking in its current state, this object must be imagined in its likely original condition and context: placed in a private altar in a Kamakura elite's home, brightly gilded, seated on the lotus pedestal with tiny precious gems glistening at the petal tips. **KH**

Notes

1. Avalokiteshvara's gender has a complex history resulting from an enduring tension between the traditional belief in male superiority in general and that in greater female capacity for compassion. More often than not, however, the bias in favor of the male spirit won the contest, and the deity was conventionally defined as a male.
2. Nyoirin Kannon comes with arms in multiples of two (for instance, two, four, six, and so forth). Six-armed versions are the most common, however, partly because the numerology of six recalls the Six Realms of Existence imagined of the Buddhist Universe from which the Kannon vows to save beings.
3. Japan's oldest extant Nyoirin statue is dated to approximately 840 CE and installed at the temple Kanshinji in Osaka. Other celebrated early examples include the Nyoirin images at Murōji (Nara) and one at Kannōji (Hyōgo Prefecture).
4. Larger statues of Nyoirin Kannon from the Kamakura period include: *Nyoirin Kannon*, dated 1275, Nara National Museum (formerly in the temple Kanshinji, Osaka), see Katharine Epprecht, *Kannon—Divine Compassion: Early Buddhist Art from Japan* (Reitberg Museum, 2007), pl. 20; *Nyoirin Kannon*, 13th century, Gangoji, Nara; *Nyoirin Kannon*, c. 1230–50, Kimbell Art Museum, Fort Worth; *Nyoirin Kannon*, early 14th century, Asia Society Collection, New York; *Nyoirin Kannon*, 13th–14th century, Minneapolis Institute of Arts; a two-armed *Nyoirin Kannon*, 13th–14th century, Bonhams, September 2019 sale.
5. For more information about this source and its content, see Ive Covaci, ed., *Kamakura: Realism and Spirituality in the Sculpture of Japan* (Asia Society and Yale University Press, 2016).
6. Ibid.

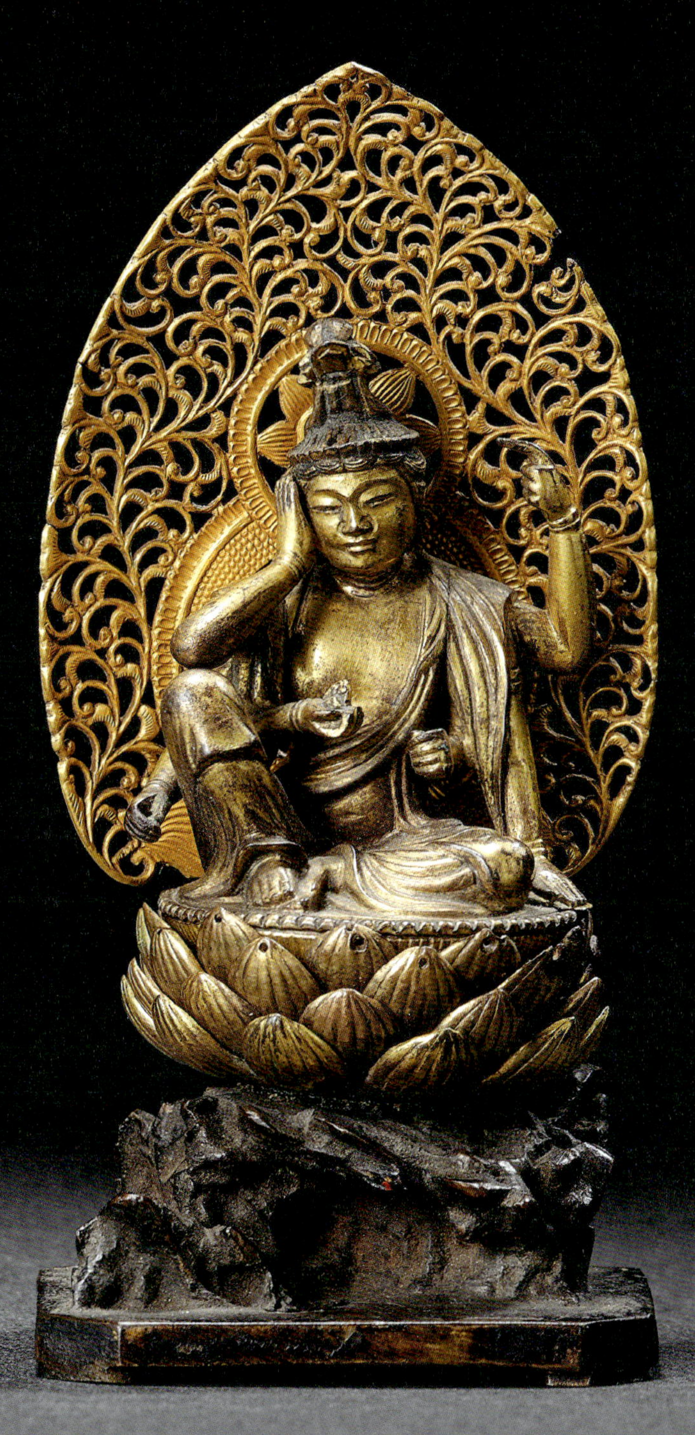

Jikokuten (Dhritarastra), Heavenly King of the East

Japan, Kamakura period, 13th–early 14th century

Gilt bronze with traces of gold
12 ³⁄₁₆ × 6 × 5 in. (31 × 15.2 × 12.7 cm)

From the pantheon of Hindu gods, Jikokuten (Sanskrit: Dhritarastra) is one of the Four Heavenly Kings (Japanese: Shitennō) who protect the Four Directions of the Buddhist universe. This one guards the East quadrant and often wears a military suit and armor painted with blue-toned pigments.[1] He usually holds a lance or a halberd in his raised left hand, while the right hand rests on the hip or holds a sword near the hip. The guardian of the South (Sanskrit: Virudhaka; Japanese: Zōchōten) also often has one hand raised and the other near the hip, so the two deities are sometimes confused. By the thirteenth and fourteenth centuries, however, the mirroring positions of the two deities' arms became more standardized.[2]

Two sets of Four Heavenly Kings images from Kōfukuji around the beginning of the Kamakura period may register the development. One set guards the four corners of the altar of the Central Golden Hall. Both Jikokuten and Zōchōten, in the left and right front corners from the main icon, respectively, stand with their left arm raised and right hand by hip. By contrast, among a slightly later set (now dispersed among different collections) only Jikokuten retains the above pose, while Zōchōten uses the opposite hands to mirror Jikokuten.[3] Similarly, in Daigoji, a prominent temple of Shingon Esoteric Buddhism, a horizontal assembly of six icons includes Jikokuten and Zōchōten protecting the central icons by bracketing them with their outermost arms raised.

For domestic altars of the military aristocrats, for whom small-scale images like this one were made, the Shitennō often needed to be abbreviated to a pair or a single representative.[4] For a pair, it was Bishamonten with either Zōchōten (God of Accretion and Growth) or Jikokuten (Keeper of the Realm).

Images of the Shitennō proliferated during the Kamakura period, when powerful warlords competed for dominance and became custodians of Japan's culture, religion, and arts. The military aristocrats partnered with Buddhist masters to fill public and domestic shrines with lavish sculptural objects. Compared to surviving large-scale Shitennō images made to guard Kamakura-period temple gates, extant smaller-scale sculptures are far fewer in number.[5] Metal sculptures like this example, formerly painted and gilded, are particularly rare.

Earlier Jikokuten images are typically figured as an older, enraged warrior with exaggerated facial wrinkles, heavy jowls, large glaring eyes, and a roaring mouth, suggesting a "barbaric" nature with which East Asians often associated foreign gods. The present work instead depicts a young, handsome East Asian face expressing controlled, stern disapproval.

The impulse to naturalize the foreign deity to fit Japan's own aristocratic sensibility is also evident in the treatment of the fabric, featuring textile patterns commonly found on Kamakura elites' expensive brocade silks. These accents are blended with suggestions of the deity's foreign origin, indicated by the lion mask at the waist and the animal-skin pattern throughout the armor. These juxtapositions of binary references enhance the work's overall aesthetic goal of synthesis and balance. **KH**

Notes

1. The Four Heavenly Kings melded conceptually with the preexisting Chinese symbols of the mythical spirits of the four directions — the Black Turtle of the North, the Vermilion Bird of the South, the Azure Dragon of the East, and the White Tiger of the West. Jikokuten naturally became an amalgam of the Azure Dragon, hence the association between him and the color blue.
2. Jikokuten iconography shifts again after the Kamakura period. Later images of Jikokuten often hold musical instruments.
3. The Nara Museum holds the Vaishravana (Bishamonten) and Virudhaka (Zōchōten), the Miho Museum holds the Dhritarastra (Jikokuten), and Kōfukuji holds the Virupaksha (Kōmokuten). For information about the set in the Central Golden Hall, see https://www.kohfukuji.com/property/b-0026/.
4. Bishamonten (Sanskrit: Vaishravana) of the North was the common choice.
5. Also see *Jikokuten*, 13th–14th century, from the Price Collection, https://www.christies.com/en/lot/lot-5658536.

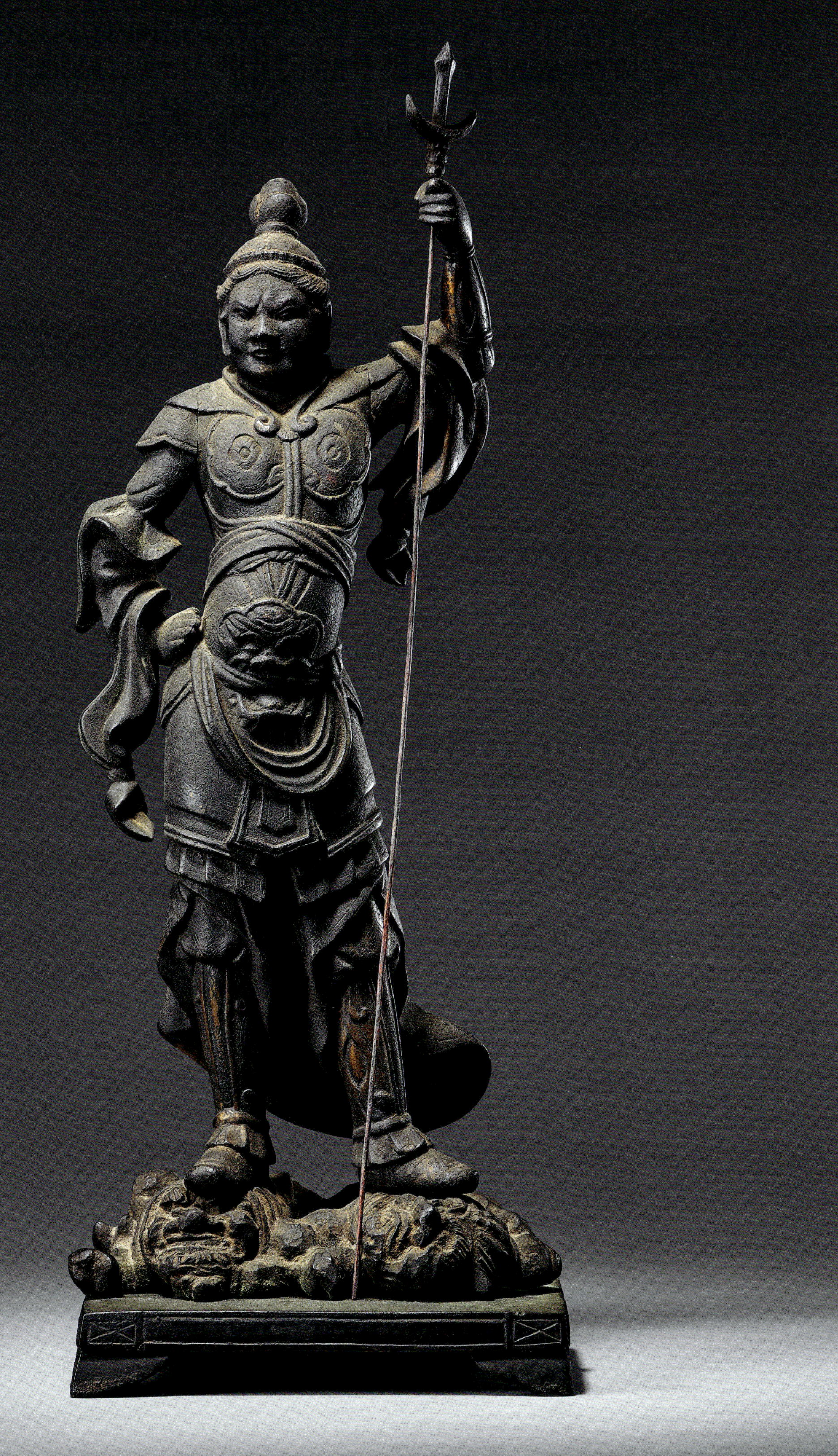

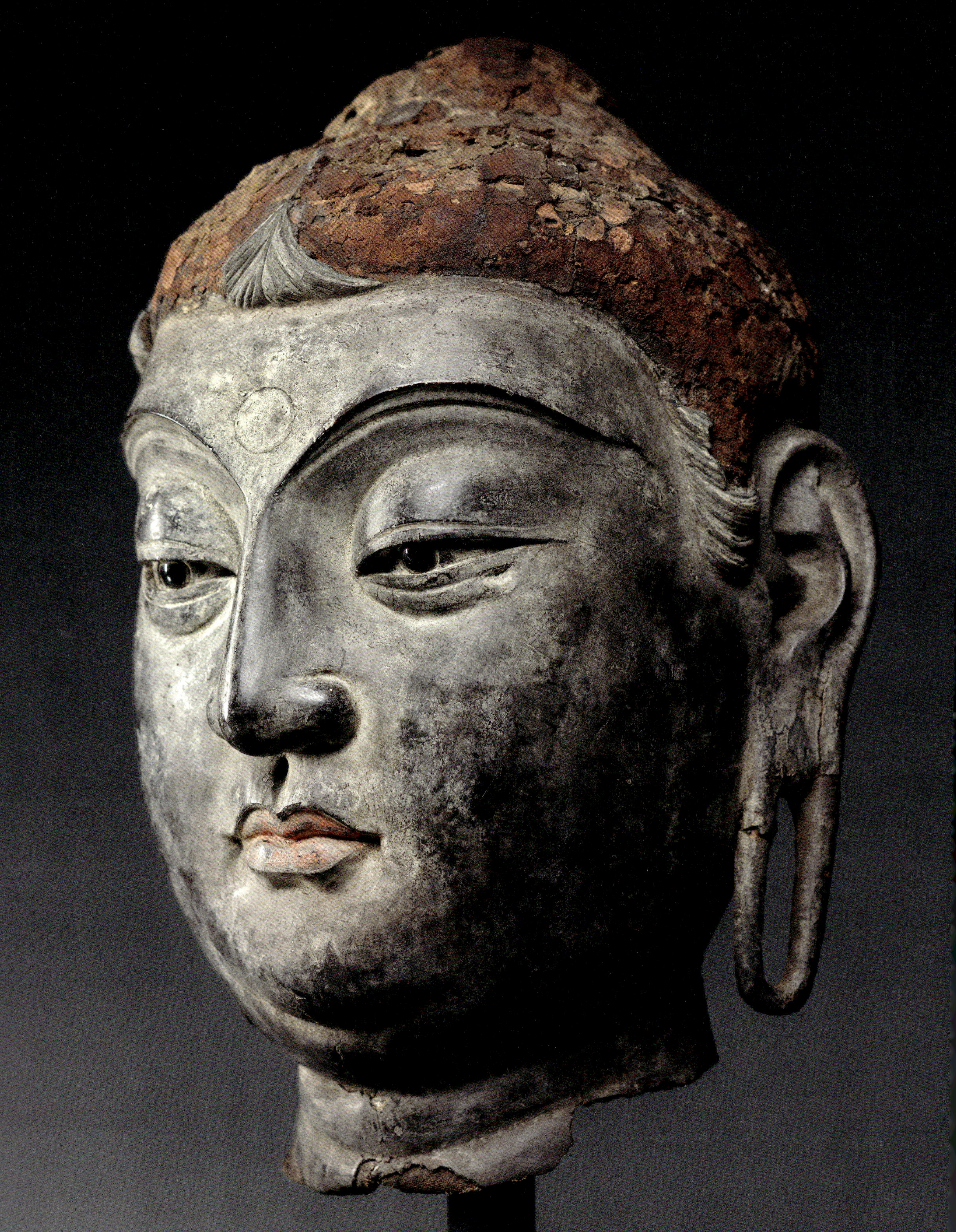

A Tang Dynasty Hollow-Core Lacquer Buddha Head

by Donna K. Strahan

This monumental *Buddha Head* was created during the eighth century by the hollow-core lacquer method in China (figs. 1 and 3). Not much is known about early Buddhist lacquer techniques because so few sculptures exist.[1] This head, along with three life-sized Buddha images, are among the earliest that survive today: one in the Walters Art Museum, another in the Metropolitan Museum of Art, and the third in the Smithsonian's National Museum of Asian Art (fig. 2).[2] This head was once part of a much larger sculpture. If it belonged to a seated Buddha, then that sculpture, unlike the other three, would have been larger than life, estimated at nearly seven and a half feet in height. The back of the head is missing, providing access to its interior (fig. 4).

Lacquer sculpture fabrication is a difficult, time-consuming, and expensive craft. Hollow-core lacquer sculptures were first formed over a modeled clay core. Then pieces of textile soaked in lacquer were added to the core. Last, layers of bulked lacquer were applied. Once the textile and lower lacquer layers were complete, the clay core was removed. Without the core, the hollow sculpture was very lightweight.

In order to study the appearance of the head's original clay core, prior to the addition of the lacquer and textile, a 3D scan of the interior was conducted. From this scan, a positive 3D print of the interior was produced, showing how surprisingly detailed the clay core had been (fig. 5).[3]

After the clay core was fabricated, strips of plain-weave textile with an S twist to the threads and eight to twelve threads per square centimeter (twenty to thirty threads per inch) were dipped in lacquer and placed piece by piece over the core. The textile aided in the durability of the brittle lacquer resin. The use of separate strips allowed for more control over the shrinkage or stretching of the textile and provided it more tensile strength to keep the lacquer from breaking into pieces. Additional textile strips were employed to enhance details over the core. The textile's fibers were examined by polarized light microscopy using polarization colors to confirm its identify as hemp.

Fig. 1

Buddha Head, China, Tang dynasty, 8th century, hollow-core dry lacquer (cat. 21).

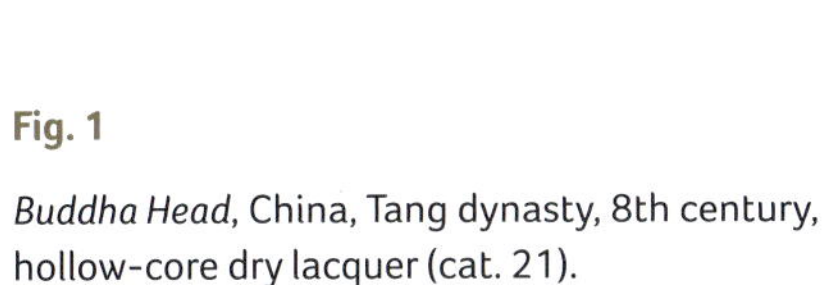

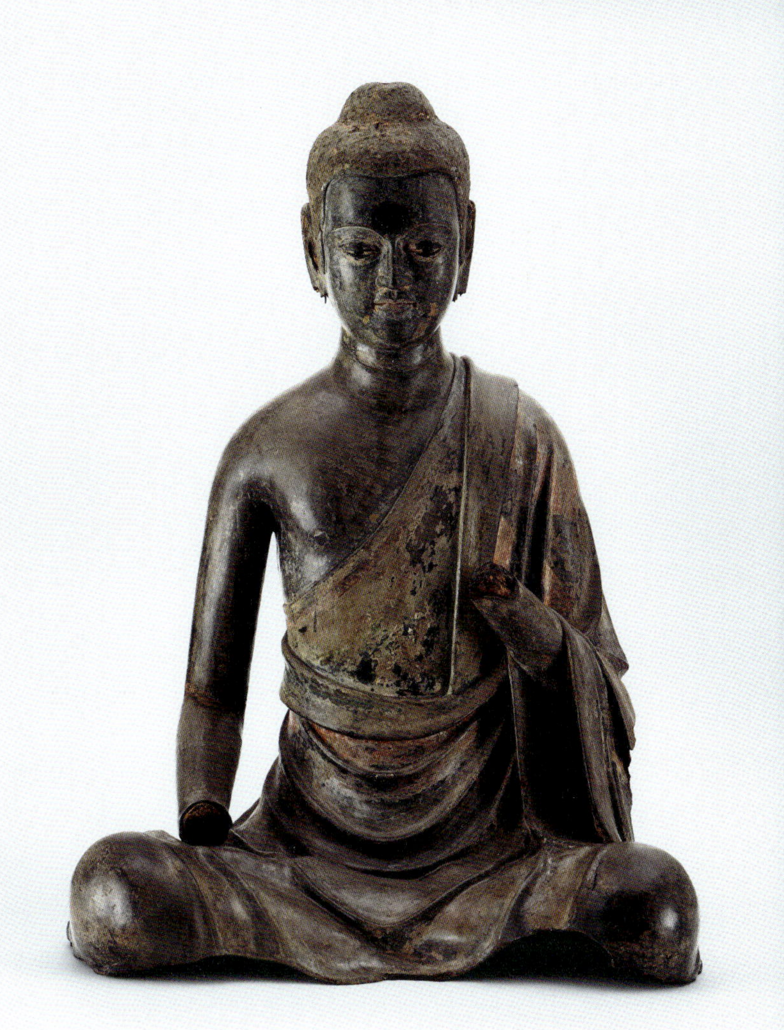

Fig. 2

Buddha, China, Tang dynasty (618–907), early 7th century, hollow-core lacquer with pigment and gilding, Freer Gallery of Art, purchase — Charles Lang Freer Endowment, F1944.46.

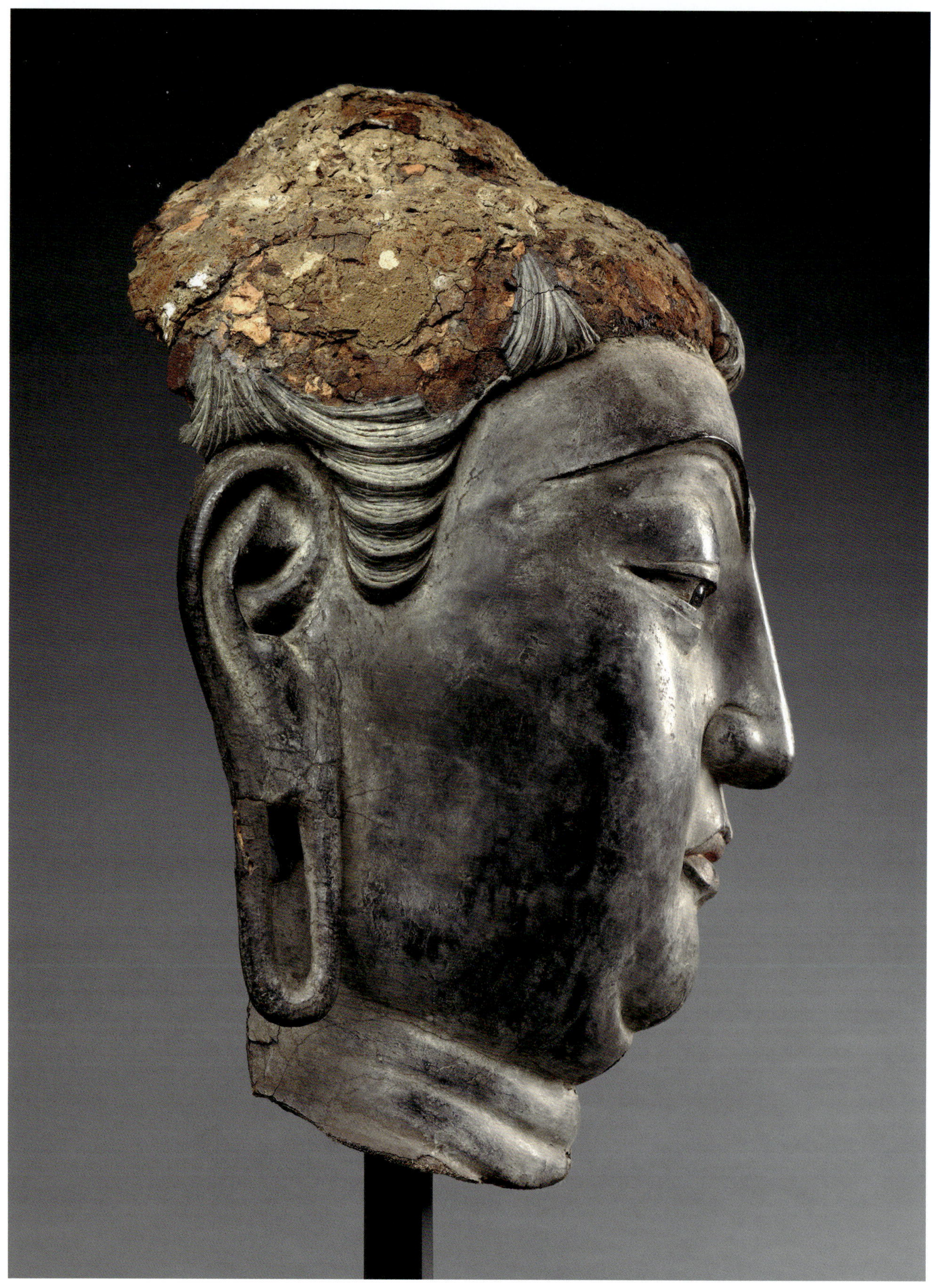

Fig. 3

Side view of *Buddha Head.*

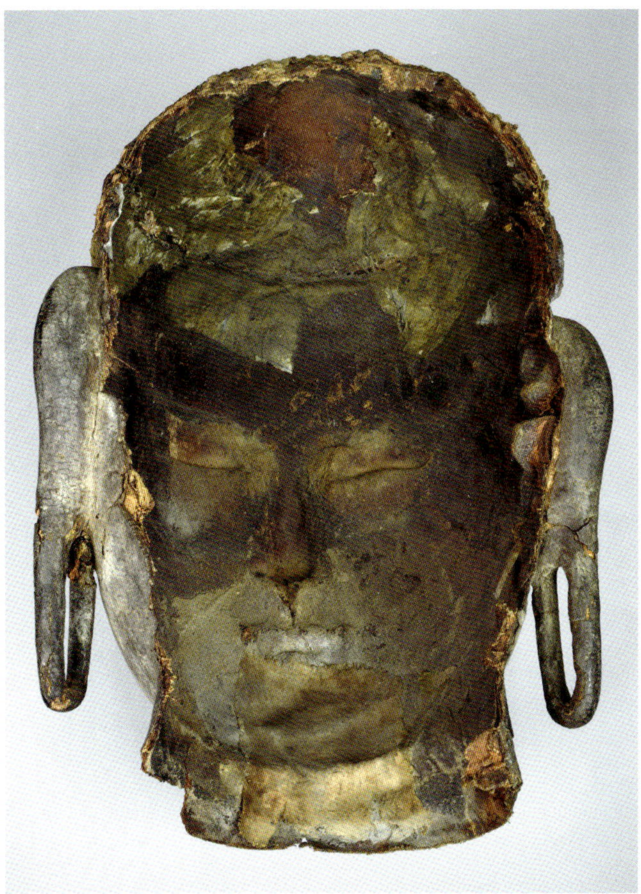

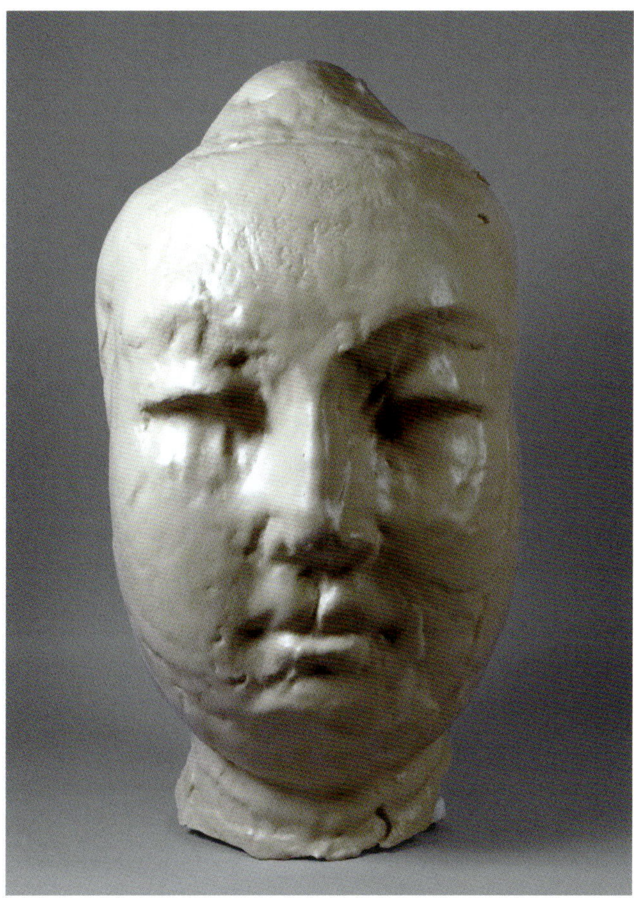

Fig. 4
Interior view of the head.

Fig. 5
Positive 3D print of the head's interior,
revealing the original shape of the clay core.

As the textile was applied, the top of the head was left open. Once the clay core was removed, access to the interior of the face was available to add the eyes, including a third eye in the forehead, now missing. The two existing glass eyes were held in place by lacquer putty that formed the lids, and a small separate piece of lacquer-wetted textile was added on the inside to hold them in place. One of the glass eyes has a stem extending toward the interior. The top section of the head was then attached after work on the interior was complete. Its attachment location can be seen on the interior of the head and in the X-ray radiograph, though it is not visible on the exterior (fig. 6).

Next, lacquer layers were applied on top of the textile strips. Asian lacquer is a resin, essentially a water-in-oil emulsion that cures to a tough, durable layer. It is produced from the sap of several trees belonging to the anacardiaceous family. Regardless of the type of sap used, the refining and fabrication techniques are similar. Caution is needed, as raw lacquer tree resin is toxic and causes a poison ivy–like contact dermatitis that may be severe. The most common tree species grown in China, Japan, and Korea is *Toxicodendron verniciflua*.

Once purified and applied to a surface, lacquer requires a temperature between 20 and 28 degrees Celsius (68 and 82.4 degrees Fahrenheit) and high relative humidity of at least 60 percent to harden into an impervious film. Each layer must cure before the next layer can be applied. Lacquer objects are usually made of multiple layers of lacquer, and many weeks of work, even up to a year, may be required to complete a single object.

When lacquer is used in the undercoating or ground of a sculpture, it is often bulked with fillers to seal and fill flaws in the support. These fillers may vary, depending on the quality of the lacquer. They may include raw or fired powdered clays, sawdust, rice paste, seashells, bone ash, wood ash, or a combination of these materials.

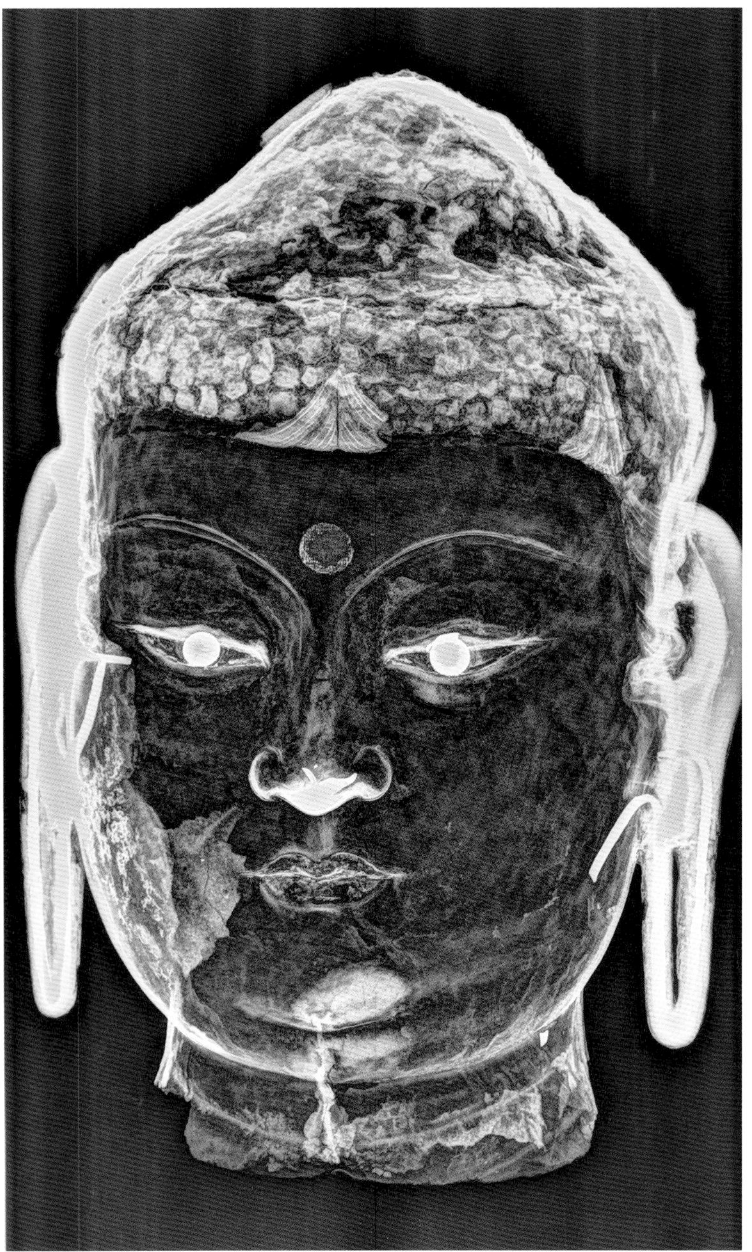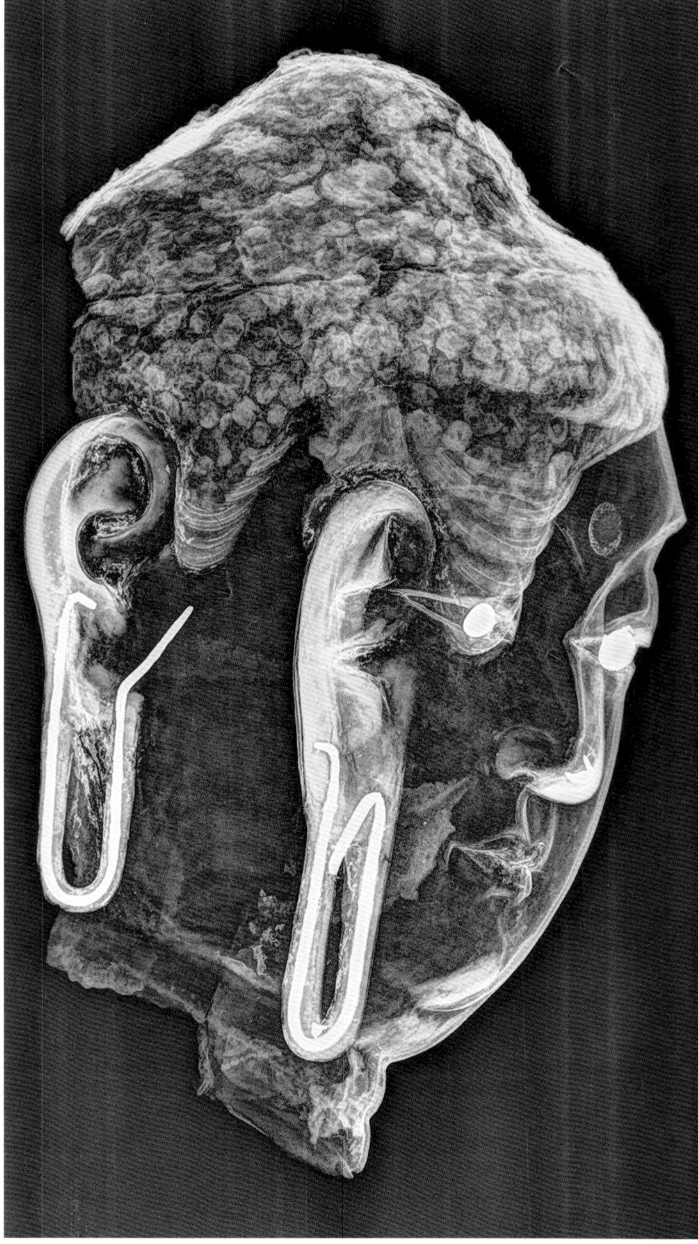

Fig. 6

X-ray radiographs of the head. The whiter
areas of the ears are remaining clay. The third
eye in the forehead is covered over and only
visible in X-ray radiograph. A denser ring
around the top of the head shows where it was
added after the interior work was completed.

The lacquer used for this head was applied in several layers above the fabric and core. It was analyzed and found to be *Toxicodendron verniciflua* lacquer.[4] In exploring the other components of the lacquer, the most prevalent material present was discovered to be ground, partially burnt bone. Bone particles were used to add bulk to the layers, along with with very small amounts of quartz and other silicates.[5] Those bone particles were clearly used as a filler to bulk up the lacquer to form a paste and to fill holes and mask flaws in the textile.

The lowest lacquer layer next to the textile is porous, with many large, twenty-micrometer-diameter bone particles, often partially burnt. The upper lacquer layers are denser and contain finer particles. Proteomics, an analytical method that identifies the proteins of different animals, determined the bone mixed in the lacquer is either horse or donkey (fig. 7).[6]

The only remains of the Buddha's sculpted hair are found on the forehead and sideburns. The hair was formed from a bulked lacquer putty. Both eyes are white with black, shiny pupils. Analysis confirmed that the pupils are leaded glass with some copper and iron present.[7] The earlobes are formed of U-shaped iron wires with a square cross section. Clay was applied over the wires, and multiple lacquer layers cover the clay. The remains of clay can still be found in the structure of the ears, as detected in X-ray radiographs (see fig. 6).

After the multiple layers of lacquer were applied and cured, the sculpture was painted. Such sculptures were often restored or repainted many times during their service. Though the head has several layers of paint from restorations, little of the color remains. The ground was identified as lead white, the pink flesh color as a mixture of red lead and vermilion, and the red in the lips as vermilion. Azurite blue was found on the hair and identified by polarized light microscopy and X-ray fluorescence. Traces of gilding on the flesh areas around the ears indicate that the face was originally gilded over the pigment layer.

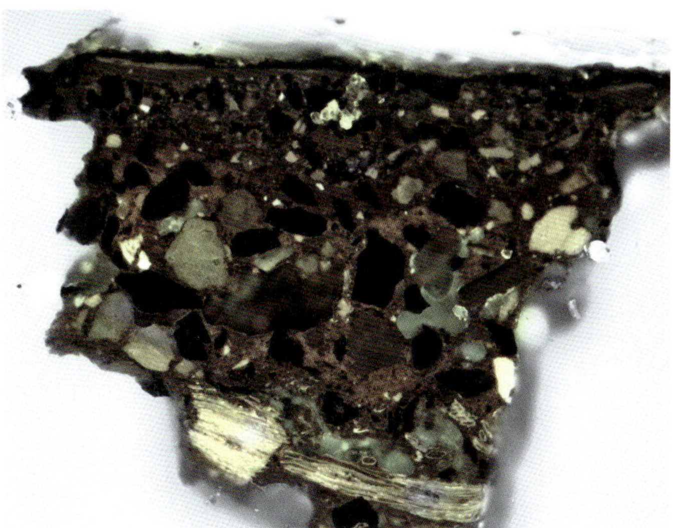

Fig. 7

Cross section of lacquer and textile.

The fabrication methods for this Buddha head are very similar to those of the three aforementioned life-sized Buddhas. They were made either by the wood- or hollow-core lacquer technique, with multiple layers of textile and bulked lacquer making up their general forms. Iron armatures were used to create their ears. The only difference among these sculptures is the type of bone mixed into the lacquer. The three complete seated figures were made with ground cow bone, whereas the bone particles in this head are horse or donkey.

This exquisite thirteen-hundred-year-old head was once part of a monumental sculpture made of expensive materials that was difficult and time-consuming to create. Analyzing its materials has shed new light on the fabrication methods of early Chinese hollow-core lacquer sculptures. The fragile nature of these materials makes its survival even more remarkable.

Notes

1. See Denise Patry Leidy, "Lacquer and Buddhist Sculpture in East Asia, Sixth-Eighth Centuries," in *Research on Early Chinese Lacquer Buddhas: Proceedings of the Sixth Forbes Symposium at the Freer Gallery of Art*, ed. Donna Strahan and Blythe McCarthy (Archetype Publications, 2023), 1–9.
2. See Strahan and McCarthy, eds., *Research on Early Chinese Lacquer Buddhas*. Available online at https://doi.org/10.5479/10088/116413.
3. Carolyn Thome, an exhibit specialist at Smithsonian Exhibits, scanned the head and 3D printed a positive from the interior geometry.
4. Pyrolysis-gas chromatography-mass spectrometry allowed the identification of many of the components added to the lacquer. However, others could not be identified, as they are present in too small an amount or the marker compounds that indicate they are there have not been determined.
5. The bone particles were visible using microscopy, and their identification was confirmed by energy-dispersive X-ray analysis in a scanning electron microscope at the Freer Gallery of Art.
6. Proteomics was carried out by scientists at the Smithsonian's Museum Conservation Institute.
7. Matthew Clarke, research scientist, Freer Gallery of Art, used X-ray fluorescence to analyze the left eye on January 9, 2017.

From the Twelfth Century to the Present, a Gilded Wisdom Buddha

by John Twilley

Scientific study has revealed unique aspects of the fabrication and subsequent history of this large, standing figure identified as one of the Five Wisdom Buddhas, possibly Akshobhya (see cat. 14). While technical investigations have brought much of its history to light, damage that it sustained in modern times also contributed to what we know by revealing parts of the construction that are normally hidden. Attempts to mitigate this damage with restorations led to modern additions that introduced confusion about what the original artist sought to depict. A linear trajectory for this account requires that we set aside discussion of the damage, and the laboratory tests done to understand its materials, to first concentrate on the fabrication of the sculpture, even though some of what we know about its construction came to light only due to the damage.

Himalayan sculptures depicting Buddhist deities have been fabricated both by casting molten metal and by cold-working (hammering) sheets of metal. Most often, this involves copper, or the copper alloy "bronze." Both cast and hammered types have often been gilded, so that they have remained brilliant over centuries. This example was cast from unalloyed copper, using the lost-wax method.

As with most large, hollow-cast sculptures, the fabrication process began with an armature fashioned from wrought iron by an ironsmith (fig. 1). Two rods with square cross sections were bent so that their ends reached from a common point in the hips to the planned positions of the heels. Another rod for the "spine" descended from the head to the hips and was welded to these two by the smith to form a sort of "wishbone" in the hips. This vertical bar supported a crossbar, or bars, at the shoulders (now also missing) that passed downward through each arm to the hands.

The sculptor modeled the general form of the figure around the armatures with wet, sandy clay reinforced with straw and allowed to dry. Combustion of the straw would provide porosity for the escape of hot gasses during the

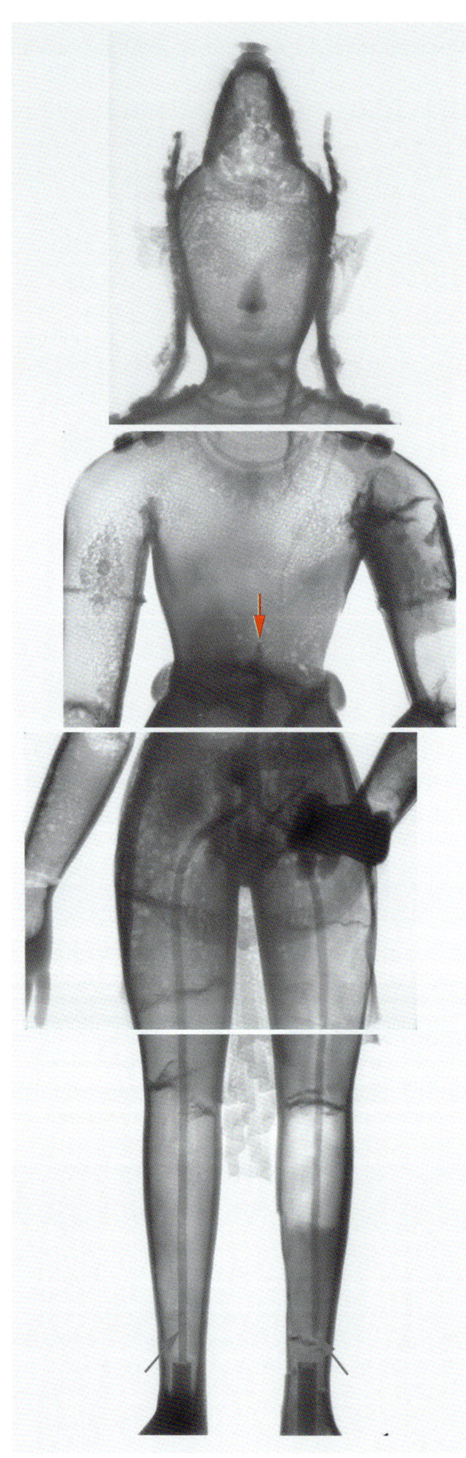

Fig. 1

Radiographs showing the full height of the Buddha. Red arrows mark the surviving part of the iron armature in the legs and hips.

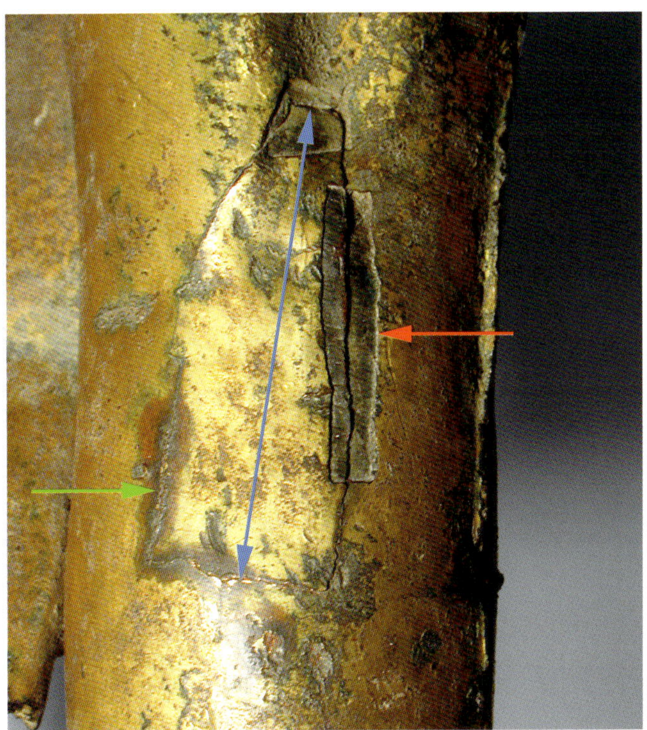

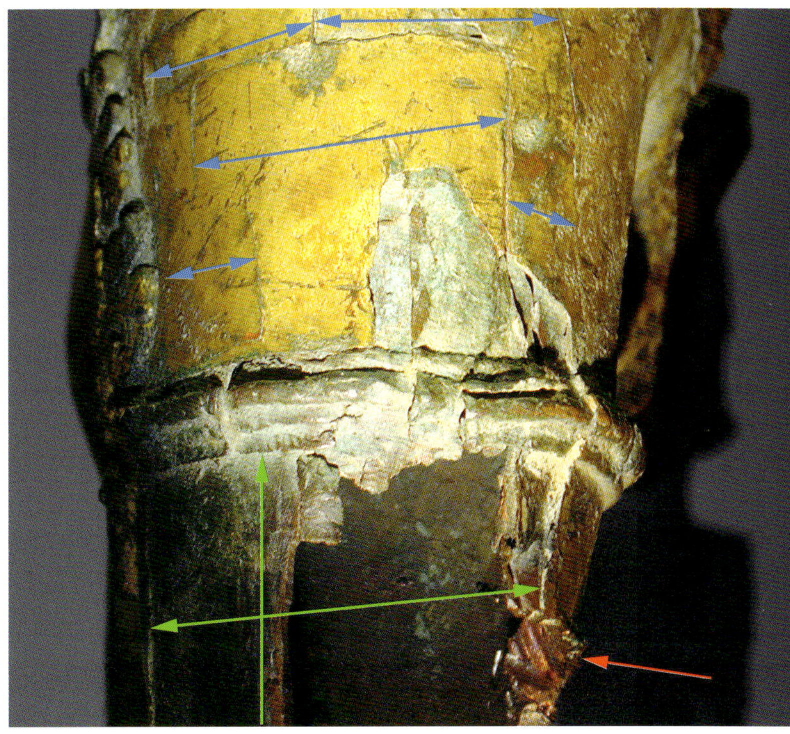

Fig. 2

Foundry patches at the rear of the right knee were damaged by flexing of the leg. Dark copper oxides (green arrow) disclose the boundary of the intact side of the large patch (blue arrows) beneath the gilding. A bridging patch, distinctive for this Buddha, has been lost from its socket on the right (red arrow).

Fig. 3

Blue arrows mark the edges of individual patches in an extremely complex set of interconnected foundry patches at the rear of the upper left arm. A large missing patch over the space designated with green arrows was lost during defacement of the sculpture — defacement that was so forceful that it bent back the wall of the casting (red arrow).

casting that was to come. Wax was applied over the dry clay in sheets and carefully modeled to the final contours of the body and jewelry. The crown and fabric ends were modeled entirely of wax. Wax rods that would become channels and sprues for the entry of molten metal were added. The entire figure with its sprues was encased in exterior clay "investment." Metal spacers, to maintain the separation between the casting core and the investment established by the wax layer, were inserted during this process, anticipating the burn out of the wax prior to casting. In this "lost wax" process, the wax and straw were burned out while copper was melted and subsequently poured into the resulting void left by the wax.

Upon cooling, much remained to be done after removal of the investment. The casting surface had to be burnished, spacers were finished off flush with the surface, and flaws were repaired by cold-working. Finer structures that could not be precisely cast, including lines of the face,

garment patterns, and jewelry details, were created or sharpened by the use of chisels and punches. Flawed areas of the casting had to be cut out and replaced. When this work was done, the surface was smeared with a pasty mixture of mercury and gold known as amalgam, followed by roasting of the entire sculpture to drive off the mercury as vapor, leaving a matte layer of gold bound to the surface (fire gilding). The gilded surface seen today is the result of burnishing that gold to a high polish.

The foundry finishing work was extremely thorough and involved copper patches unique for this Buddha. Many of the patches introduced to correct casting flaws are large ones that were provided with unusual bridging patches in a procedure intended to strengthen the work. These have become visible as a result of the development of copper-oxide trails along their outlines atop the gilding (fig. 2). Subsequent damage resulted in the displacement of the patches, revealing their details (figs. 2 and 3).

Most of these patches were introduced by using a sharp chisel to cut a shallow, rectangular recess around the surface area flawed by gas pores. (One in the left buttock is kidney-shaped in outline.) Copper was removed to a consistent depth across this rectangle, and a patch of the same dimensions was cut from a sheet of similar metal. The tightly fitted metal was then hammered to spread its edges against the walls of the recess, locking it in place (fig. 4). This form of cold-worked patching was nearly universal in preindustrial metal sculpture, ranging from Rome to China and points in between. The uncommon feature of the patches in this sculpture is the introduction of secondary patches, fabricated by the same methods, that bridge the edges of the larger primary patches (figs. 2 and 5). This step seems to have been taken to provide a more intricate system of interlocks between the patches and their recesses, thereby ensuring their permanence and immobility.

One of the traits of unalloyed copper is that it retains a high amount of oxygen while molten and releases this gas upon solidification, resulting in large numbers of gas pores that weaken the casting when they are concentrated in large numbers. The head is particularly affected by these, with a spongy appearance in the radiographs. Nonetheless, the skill of the artisans resulted in a nearly flawless surface appearance, unblemished by the porosity immediately underneath. The larger patches on the limbs were necessitated to strengthen these areas while eliminating visible pits.

The migration of copper to the surface of the gilding and its oxidation once there have made the outlines of copper patches visible in a way that they were not at the time that the sculpture was completed. Years of wear and the inevitable accumulation of soot from lamp flames in a temple have transformed the surface and muted what would have been a brilliantly reflective surface when new. No specific residues that would be a result of worship or

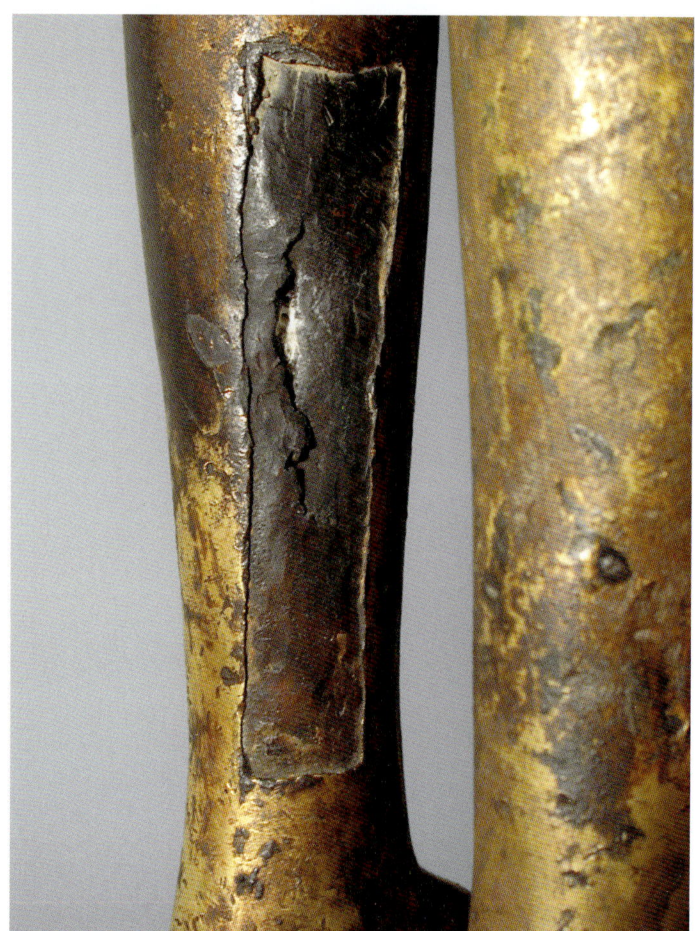

Fig. 4

The loss of a long patch on the inner side of the lower left leg shows how a socket was prepared by chiseling out a shallow rectangle of metal around the casting flaw during foundry finishing.

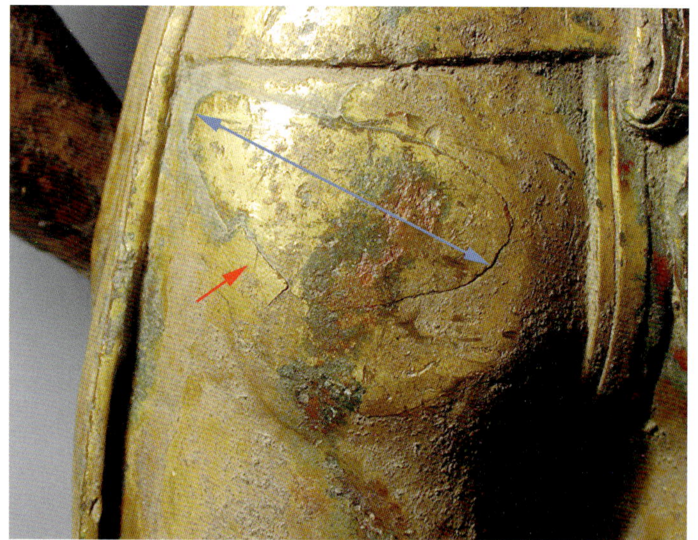

Fig. 5

An oval patch in the left buttock (blue arrows) was given a rectangular bridging patch (red arrow) of the type so distinctive for this sculpture.

ritual use were found. However, the sculpture has certainly been cleaned in the course of restorations that it received in modern times. So residues of devotion may have been lost. Many ancient sculptures have survived in burial, only to be rediscovered in modern times. The absence of attached mineral matter and absence of a burial patina (incrusting corrosion products) demonstrate that this Buddha belongs to another class entirely, one that still exists in the Himalayas today. It remained in active worship until the acts of desecration committed against it.

Parts of the interior construction are visible due to iconoclastic damage that it experienced, probably during China's Cultural Revolution of the 1960s, which entailed the destruction of many Buddhist sites in Tibet. The rear of the torso and head are open, and the edges of the opening were deformed. A connection from the "spine" to a rod projecting out the back of the figure that secured it in its place of worship is likely, because the violence with which it was taken down resulted in breakage and loss of the back of the figure. Distortions and some bending of the arms and legs during the forceful dismounting of the sculpture are apparent where original foundry patches have become dislodged, revealing some of the details of their construction that would normally be hidden.

Faces and gesturing hands are typically a target of the most vehement attacks, especially when those attacks are inspired by hatred or the desire to erase the ideals that they express; it seems doubtful that the face could have survived the forceful dismounting of the figure intact. The hands were lost, along with the left foot and forepart of the right foot, including the toes. Today, however, the hands and toes all appear intact. This is a result of restorations carried out after the sculpture left Tibet. In the aftermath of the attack on the sculpture, it would undoubtedly have been recovered by devotees and secreted away until a means could be found to remove the deity from further threats of desecration.

Some saw marks are visible on the edges of the missing rear where deformed metal was cut away in an effort to reduce the visibility of its brutalization. However, the rear was left open, providing a rare opportunity to see normally hidden aspects of its fabrication. Restorations were carried out that added new hands, a new left foot, and the missing forepart of the right foot. This entailed the making of newly cast components, brazing them in place and gilding their surfaces to match the adjacent original gilding. Where the original gilding was discolored by copper corrosion, matching discoloration was supplied to the new parts. Gilding was almost certainly reapplied to the face after filling any indentations caused by blows.

The hands convey essential concepts for an understanding of the deity and his role in Buddhist thought. Lacking full information about their original form, the restorer copied hands from other works without recognizing their misappropriation for this deity. As technical study of the sculpture began in the absence of any record of this work, essential questions concerned where restorations began and ended and the degree to which the sculpture had been changed in appearance and meaning by those changes.

Some of the information regarding the damage was apparent by direct observation. However, the carefully integrated restorations required more sophisticated methods, including radiography using gamma rays. The radiographs and metallurgical analysis of the alloy revealed a level of skill higher than that required for a typical bronze casting. These same analytical methods explained the high incidence of casting flaws and the origin of weaknesses that came to light with its desecration. The sculpture was cast from unalloyed copper containing 99.4 percent copper and 0.6 percent iron. The use of unalloyed copper required exceptional handling skill for a large quantity of molten metal at a temperature around 1,100 degrees Celsius (2,000 degrees Fahrenheit), significantly above those required for a bronze alloy.

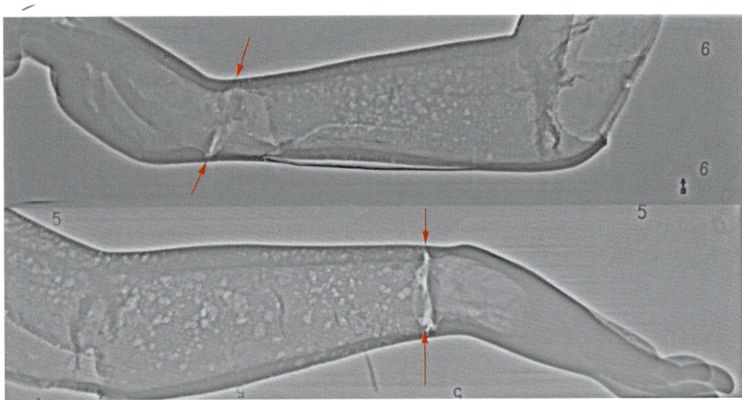

Fig. 6

Radiograph details of the arms with red arrows marking the end of the porosity associated with the original casting at the joints where modern hands cast from brass were added.

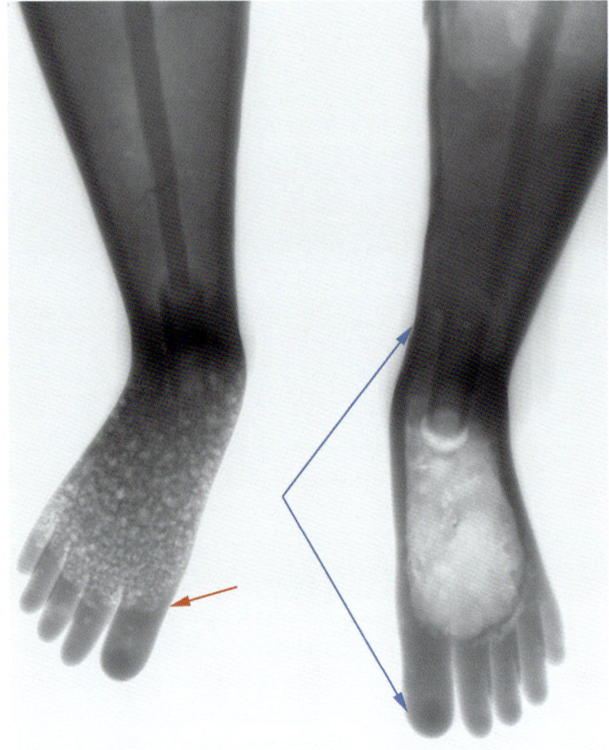

Fig. 7

Radiograph detail of the feet, showing gas porosity in the original solid right foot, and the use of a hollow brass casting without gas porosity for the replacement left foot (blue arrows). The right toes are also brass replacements (red arrow). (Modern hollow tubes have been inserted in both heels to allow mounting of the sculpture.)

The propensity for unalloyed copper to retain high amounts of oxygen while molten, and to release this gas upon solidification, resulted in abundant gas pores. The radiographs show that the head is particularly affected by these. Regions of the limbs that have become distorted are typically ones with prevalent porosity and patching that were less resistant to the damage wrought on the figure.

The gas porosity of the unalloyed copper used in the original casting allowed areas lacking this porosity in the radiographs to be identified as modern restorations. Along with the missing part of the rear, the damage that the sculpture received included the loss of both hands, the left foot, and the toes of the right foot, all of which are differentiated by their lack of gas pores in the aftermath of replacement (figs. 6 and 7). The metal used for these replacements is a modern brass alloy containing 91 percent copper and 9 percent zinc. After joining to the broken edges of the original sculpture, the restorations were fire gilded and the gilding blended with the original work. No evidence was found for regilding of the statue as a whole. In fact, the slowly evolved oxides outlining the patches atop the gilding, and occasional copper corrosion products on its surface, would not be present if it had been regilded in modern times.

Much attention has been paid to the face and the extent of restoration that it might have experienced. However, it is one of the stronger, thickest parts of the casting, and careful radiographic inspection shows that the porosity typical of the original work extends throughout the face (fig. 8). A patch in the cheek has the attributes of original foundry repairs seen elsewhere. It seems likely that the face has received some surface repairs for impact damage and regilding to blend these with their surroundings. But none of the pore-free alloyed metal additions

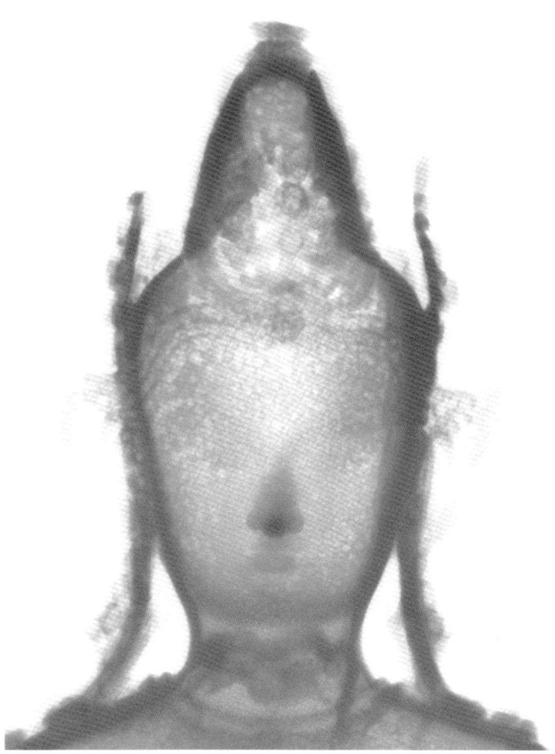

A radiograph of the face shows an abundance of uniformly
distributed gas voids in the copper casting, demonstrating
that there are no modern brass replacement components in
the face like those used for the hands and feet.

used for the restorations of the extremities were visible in
radiographs of the face. Additional evidence supporting
the lack of major restorations to the face comes from
inspection of the head interior through the damage at the
rear. Reshaping of the face from behind, from the rear
opening, is not evident.

Close study of the sculptor's casting and foundry
finishing techniques, and radiographic inspection coupled
with the tools of scientific investigation for alloy and gilding
analyses, have clarified the original making of the Buddha
image. Knowledge obtained by prior scientific studies of the
effects of burial on copper sculptures allows us to confirm
that this figure survived as an object of continuing devotion,
rather than in burial. Prior technical studies of the practices
of Newari sculptors, known for their role in the production
of devotional figures in Tibet, allow us to recognize unusual
and important innovations in this example. From that

knowledge, we can extrapolate details that have been lost
in its desecration. Scientific study, sometimes cast as a polar
opposite to faith, has, in this case, illuminated aspects of
the devotion that led to the making of the image and the
continuation of that devotion down through the years. The
survival of this statue over about nine centuries speaks to
the actions of generations of people with differing motiva-
tions, but also to the perseverance of the Buddhist faith.

Bibliography

Alphen, J. Van, Beth Citron, Karl Debreczeny, David P. Jackson, Christian Luczanits, Elena Pakhoutova, and Kathryn Selig Brown. *Collection Highlights: The Rubin Museum of Art*. Rubin Museum of Art, 2014.

Alsop, Ian. "Phagpa Lokeśvara of the Potala." *Orientations* 21, no. 4 (April 1990).

Beal, Samuel, trans. *Buddhist Records of the Western World*. Reprint edition. San Francisco, 1976.

Béguin, Gilles. *Art sacré du Tibet: Collection Alain Bordier*. Éditions Findakly, 2013.

Boucher, Daniel. "The Pratityasamutpadagatha and Its Role in the Medieval Cult of the Relics." *Journal of the International Association of Buddhist Studies* 14 (1991): 1–27.

Bunker, Emma C., and Douglas Latchford. *Khmer Bronzes: New Interpretations of the Past*. Art Media Resources, 2011.

Buswell, Robert E. *Encyclopedia of Buddhism*. Macmillan, 2004.

Buswell, Robert E., Jr., and Donald S. Lopez, Jr. *The Princeton Dictionary of Buddhism*. Princeton University Press, 2014.

Casey, Jane, Naman Ahuja, and David Weldon. *Divine Presence: Arts of India and the Himalayas*. Casa Asia and 5 Continents Editions, 2003.

Casey Singer, Jane. "Tibetan Homage to Bodh Gaya." *Orientations* 32, no. 10 (2001): 44–51.

Chandra, Lokesh. *Buddhist Iconography*. International Academy of Indian Culture, 1991.

Chandra, Pramod. *The Sculpture of India: 3000 BC–1300 AD*. National Gallery of Art, 1985.

Chang, K. C. Chang. *Art, Myth, and Ritual: The Path to Political Authority in Ancient China*. Harvard University Press, 1983.

Chen, Kenneth. *Buddhism in China: A Historical Survey*. Princeton University Press, 1964.

Choi, Sun-ah. "Zhenrong to Ruixiang: The Medieval Chinese Reception of the Mahabodhi Buddha Statue." *Art Bulletin* 97, no. 4 (December 2015): 364–87.

Covaci, Ive, ed. *Kamakura: Realism and Spirituality in the Sculpture of Japan*. Asia Society and Yale University Press, 2016.

Czuma, Stanislaw J. *Kushan Sculpture: Images from Early India*. Cleveland Museum of Art in cooperation with Indiana University Press, 1985.

Dalrymple, William. *The Golden Road: How Ancient India Transformed the World*. Bloomsbury Publishing, 2024.

d'Argencé, René-Yvon Lefebvre, and Diana Turner, eds. *5000 Years of Korean Art*. Asian Art Museum of San Francisco, 1979.

Deeg, Max. "The Historical Turn: How Chinese Buddhist Travelogues Changed Western Perception of Buddhism." *Hualin International Journal of Buddhist Studies* 1, no. 1 (2018): 43–75.

De Mallmann, Marie-Thérèse. *Introduction á l'iconographie du Tãntrisme Bouddhique*. Librairie d'Amérique et d'Orient, 1986.

Dharmaswamin. *Biography of Dharmaswamin*. Translated by George Roerich. K.P. Jayaswal Research Institute, 1959.

Douglas, Nick. *The Enlightened Ones in Sacred Buddhist Art*. Kreitman Gallery, 1980.

Eck, Diana. *Darsan: Seeing the Divine Image in India*. Columbia University Press, 1998.

Epprecht, Katharine. *Kannon—Divine Compassion: Early Buddhist Art from Japan*. Reitberg Museum, 2007.

Fontein, Jan. *The Sculpture of Indonesia*. Harry N. Abrams, 1990.

Guillon, Emmanuel. *Hindu-Buddhist Art of Vietnam: Treasures from Champa*. River Books, 2006.

Guy, John. "The Mahabodhi Temple: Pilgrim Souvenirs of Buddhist India." *Burlington Magazine* 133, no. 1059 (June 1991): 356–67.

Hamada, Tamami. "On the Udayana King Images in the Vicinity of Early Tang Luoyang." *Ars Buddhica* 287 (2006).

Hapcheon Museum. *Small Statues of Buddha Embraced by Our Arms*. Hapcheon Museum and National Jinju Museum, 2021.

Howard, Angela Falco, Li Kunsheng, and Qiu Xuanchong. "Nanzhao and Dali Buddhist Sculpture in Yunnan." *Orientations* (February 1992).

Huntington, John C. "Sowing the Seeds of the Lotus: A Journey to the Great Pilgrimage Sites of Buddhism, Part I." *Orientations* (November 1985): 46–61.

Huntington, Susan L. "Compassion in a Mountain Abode: A Pala Period Image of Avalokiteshvara." *Orientations* 48, no. 5 (September/October 2017).

Huntington, Susan L. *The "Pala-Sena" Schools of Sculpture*. E. J. Brill, 1984.

Jansen, Michael, and Christian Luczanits. *Gandhara, The Buddhist Heritage of Pakistan: Legends, Monasteries, and Paradise*. English ed. Verlag Philipp Von Zabern, 2008.

Jarrige, J. F., et al. *L'Age d'or de l'Inde classique: L'Empire des Gupta*. Éditions de la Reunion des musées nationaux, 2007.

Jenner, W. F. J. *Memories of Loyang: Yang Hsüan-chih and the Lost Capital (493–534)*. Oxford University Press, 1981.

Juliano, Annette L., and Judith A. Learner, eds. *Monks and Merchants: Silk Road Treasures from Northwest China, Gansu and Ningxia, 4th to 7th Century*. Harry N. Abrams, Asia Society, 2001.

Kandajjaya, Hudaya. "The Scheme of Borobudur." In *The Creative South: Buddhist and Hindu Art in Medieval Maritime Asia*. Vol. 2. Edited by Andrea Acri and Peter Sharrock. ISEAS, 2022.

Khandalavala, Karl, ed. *The Golden Age: Gupta Art—Empire, Province and Influence*. South Asia Books, 1991.

Kang, U-bang. *Korean Buddhist Sculpture: Art and Truth*. Translated by Cho Yoonjung. Art Media Resources, Youlhwadang Publisher, 2005.

Kim, Lena. *History of Korean Buddhist Art*. Mijinsa, 2011.

Kim, Wi-seok, "Tansaengbul (Buddha at Birth)." In *Encyclopedia of Korean Culture*. http://www.encykorea.aks.ac.kr/Article/E0058783.

Klimburg-Salter, Deborah E. *The Silk Road and the Diamond Path: Esoteric Buddhist Art on the Trans-Himalayan Trade Routes*. UCLA Art Council, 1982.

Knight, Michael. "The 338 Buddha Revisited." *Lotus Leaves* 15, no. 2 (Spring 2013).

Krahl, Regina. "Divine Features in Lacquer." Sotheby's Hong Kong, sale HK049, lot 120.

Kramrisch, Stella. "A Note" [Appended to K.P. Jayaswal's "Metal Images of Kurkihar Monastery"]. *Journal of the Indian Society of Oriental Art* 2, no. 2 (December 1934).

Lefèvre, Vincent, and Marie-Francoise Boussac, eds. *Art of the Ganges Delta: Masterpieces from Bangladeshi Museums*. Translated by John Adamson. Éditions de la Reunion des musées nationaux, 2008.

Leidy, Denise Patry. *The Art of Buddhism: An Introduction to Its History and Meaning*. Shambhala, 2008.

Leidy, Denise Patry, and Donna Strahan. *Wisdom Embodied: Chinese Buddhist and Daoist Sculpture in the Metropolitan Museum of Art*. Metropolitan Museum of Art and Yale University Press, 2010.

Leoshko, Janice. "The Significance of Bodh Gaya," 10–13. In *Pilgrimage and Buddhist Art*. Edited by Adriana Proser. Asia Society Museum, Yale University Press, 2010.

Leoshko, Janice. "Time and Time Again: Finding Perspective for Bodhgaya Buddha Imagery." *Ars Orientalis* 50 (Miraculous Images in Asian Traditions) (2020): 6–32.

Leoshko, Janice. "The Vajrasana Buddha." In *Bodhgaya: The Site of Enlightenment*. Edited by in Janice Leoshko. Marg Publications, 1988.

Lerner, Martin. *The Flame and the Lotus: Indian and Southeast Asian Art from the Kronos Collections*. Metropolitan Museum of Art, 1984.

Lerner, Martin, and Steven Kossak. *The Lotus Transcendent: Indian and Southeast Asian Art from the Samuel Eilenberg Collection*. Metropolitan Museum of Art, 1991.

Li, He. "Chinese Jade Art in the Ming and Qing Dynasties." In *Later Chinese Jades, Ming Dynasty to Early Twentieth Century*. Asian Art Museum of San Francisco, 2007.

Li, Yumin. "Shilun Tangdai xiangmo chengdao shi zhuangshi fo." In *Gugong xueshu jikan, The National Palace Museum Research Quarterly* 23, no. 3 (2006): 39–157.

Linrothe, Rob. *Collecting Paradise: Buddhist Art of Kashmir and Its Legacies*. Mary and Leigh Block Museum of Art and Rubin Museum of Art, 2014.

Lopez, Donald S. "Chapter Three: Art," 112–23. In *Buddhism: A Journey Through History*. Yale University Press, 2024.

Lutz, Albert. "Buddhist Art in Yunnan." *Orientations* (February 1992).

Mullin, Glenn H., with Jeff J. Watt. *Female Buddhas: Women of Enlightenment in Tibetan Mystical Art*. Clear Light Publishers, 2003.

Nara National Museum. *Buddhist Art Paradise: Jewels of the Buddhist Art Collection*. Nara National Museum, 2021.

Nishikawa, Kyōtarō, and Emily J. Sano. *The Great Age of Japanese Buddhist Sculpture AD 600–1300*. Kimbell Art Museum, 1982.

Pal, Pratapaditya. *The Arts of Nepal: Part I, Sculpture*. E. J. Brill, 1974.

Pal, Pratapaditya. *Asian Art at the Norton Simon Museum: Art from the Indian Subcontinent*. Yale University Press in association with the Norton Simon Art Foundation, 2003.

Pal, Pratapaditya. *Himalayas: An Aesthetic Adventure*. Art Institute of Chicago, 2003.

Pal, Pratapaditya. *The Ideal Image: The Gupta Sculptural Tradition and Its Influence*. Asia Society Galleries, 1978.

Pal, Pratapaditya. *Nepal: Where the Gods Are Young*. Asia House Gallery, 1975.

Pal, Pratapaditya. *The Sensuous Immortals: A Selection of Sculptures from the Pan-Asian Collection*. Los Angeles County Museum of Art, 1977.

The Palace Museum, ed. *Cultural Relics of Tibetan Buddhism Collected in the Qing Palace*. Forbidden City Press/Woods Publishing Company, 1992.

Pons, Jessie. "The Figure with a Bow in Gandharan Great Departure Scenes, Some New Readings." *Entangled Religions* 1 (2014).

Poster, Amy G. *From Indian Earth: 4,000 Years of Terracotta Art*. Brooklyn Museum of Art, 1986.

Prachoom, Kanohansawat. *Buddha Images*. Bangkok, 1969.

Rawson, Philip. *The Art of Southeast Asia*. Thames and Hudson, 1967. Reprinted 1995.

Ray, Nihar Ranjan, Karl Khandalavala, and Sadashiv Gorakshkar. *Eastern Indian Bronzes*. Lalit Kala Akademi, 1986.

Reischauer, Edwin O. *Ennin's Diary: The Record of a Pilgrimage to China in Search of the Law*. Ronald Press Company, 1955.

Rhie, Marilyn. *Early Buddhist Art of China and Central Asia*. Part 4, Vol. 12 (*Handbook of Oriental Studies*). Brill, 2002.

Rosenfield, John M. "On the Dated Carvings of Sarnath." *Artibus Asiae* 26 (1963).

Sakuri, Tokutarō, ed. "Origins of the Gangōji Monastery and Its Assets." In *Nihon Shisō Taikei 20: Jisha Engi*, 7–22. Iwanami Shoten, 1975.

Scheurleer, Pauline Lunsingh, and Marijke J. Klokke. *Ancient Indonesian Bronzes: A Catalogue of the Exhibition in the Rijksmuseum Amsterdam*. E. J. Brill, 1988.

Siudmak, John. *The Hindu-Buddhist Sculpture of Ancient Kashmir and Its Influences*. Brill, 2013.

Skilling, Peter. *Buddhism and Buddhist Literature of South-East Asia*. Ludwig Reichert Verlag, 2010.

Slusser, Mary. *Nepal Mandala: A Cultural Study of the Kathmandu Valley*. Vol. 2. Princeton University Press, 1982.

Sotheby's. *Chinese Art through the Eye of Sakamoto Goro: Early Buddhist Bronzes*. October 5, 2016.

Steinhardt, Nancy S. *Chinese Architecture in an Age of Turmoil, 200–600*. University of Hawaii Press, 2014.

Steinhardt, Nancy S. *Chinese Traditional Architecture*. China Institute, 1984.

Strahan, Donna. *Piece-Mold Casting: A Chinese Tradition for Fourth- and Fifth-Century Bronze Buddha Images*. Metropolitan Museum of Art; Yale University Press, 2010.

Strahan, Donna, and Blythe McCarthy. "Construction from the Inside Out: Early Chinese Lacquer Buddha Fabrication." National Museum of Asian Art, Smithsonian Institution, 2018. https://asia.si.edu/essays /construction-from-the-inside-out-early -chinese-lacquerbuddha-fabrication.

Strahan, Donna, and Blythe McCarthy, eds. *Research on Early Chinese Lacquer Buddhas: Proceedings of the Sixth Forbes Symposium at the Freer Gallery of Art*. London: Archetype Publications in association with the Freer Gallery of Art, Smithsonian Institution, 2023. https://doi.org/10.5479/10088 /116413.

Strong, John. "A Family Quest: The Buddha, Yaśodharā, and Rāhula in the Mūlasarvāstivāda Vinaya." In *Sacred Biography in the Buddhist Traditions of South and Southeast Asia*. Edited by Juliane Schober. University of Hawaii Press, 1996.

Tanabe, Saburosuke. *Buddha's Smile II— Transcending Time and Space*, 352–53. Edited by Tajima Mitsuru. London Gallery Tokyo, 2010.

Tanaka, Yoshiyasu. *Ancient Statues of the Infant Buddha*. Translated by Juliet Carpenter. Asuka Historical Museum, 1978. https:// www.nabunken.go.jp/english/e-catalogue /5.html

Tsiang, Hiuen [Xuanzang]. *Si-Yu-Ki: Buddhist Records of the Western World*. Translated by Samuel Beal. Chinese Materials Center, 1976.

Uhlig, Helmut. *On the Path to Enlightenment: The Berti Aschmann Foundation of Tibetan Art at the Museum Rietberg Zürich*. Museum Rietberg Zürich, 1995.

Von Schroeder, Ulrich. *Buddhist Sculptures in Tibet*. Vols. 1 and 2. Visual Dharma Publications, 2001.

Von Schroeder, Ulrich. *The Golden Age of Sculpture in Sri Lanka*. Visual Dharma Publications, 1992.

Von Schroeder, Ulrich. *Indo-Tibetan Bronzes*. Visual Dharma Publications, 1981.

Washizuka, Hiromitsu, et al. *Transmitting the Forms of Divinity: Early Buddhist Art from Korea and Japan*. Japan Society and Harry N. Abrams, 2003.

Weldon, David, and Jane Casey Singer. *The Sculptural Heritage of Tibet: Buddhist Art in the Nyingjei Lam Collection*. Laurence King Publishing, 2000.

Williams, Joanna. *The Art of Gupta India: Empire and Province*. Princeton University Press, 1982.

Wong, Dorothy. *Chinese Steles: Pre-Buddhist and Buddhist Use of a Symbolic Form*. University of Hawaii Press, 2004.

Wong, Dorothy. "The Light-Emitting Image of Magadha in Tang Buddhist Art." *Ars Orientalis* 50 (Miraculous Images in Asian Traditions) (2020): 33–54.

Wright, Arthur Frederick. "Fo-Tu-Teng, A Biography." *Harvard Journal of Asiatic Studies* 11 (December 1948).

Wu, Hung. "Buddhist Elements in Early Chinese Art (2nd and 3rd Centuries A.D.)." *Artibus Asiae* 47, no. 3/4 (1986).

Zhetan, Zhang. "A Study on Origin and Localization of Moving Buddha Image in Middle Age, Zhonggu fojiao xingxiang yishi de xingqi ji bentuhua." *Buddhist Studies* (2020): 158–71.

Zwalf, Wladimir. *Buddhism: Art and Faith*. British Museum, 1985.

Zwalf, Wladimir. *A Catalogue of the Gandhara Sculpture in the British Museum*. Vol. 2. British Museum Press, 1996.

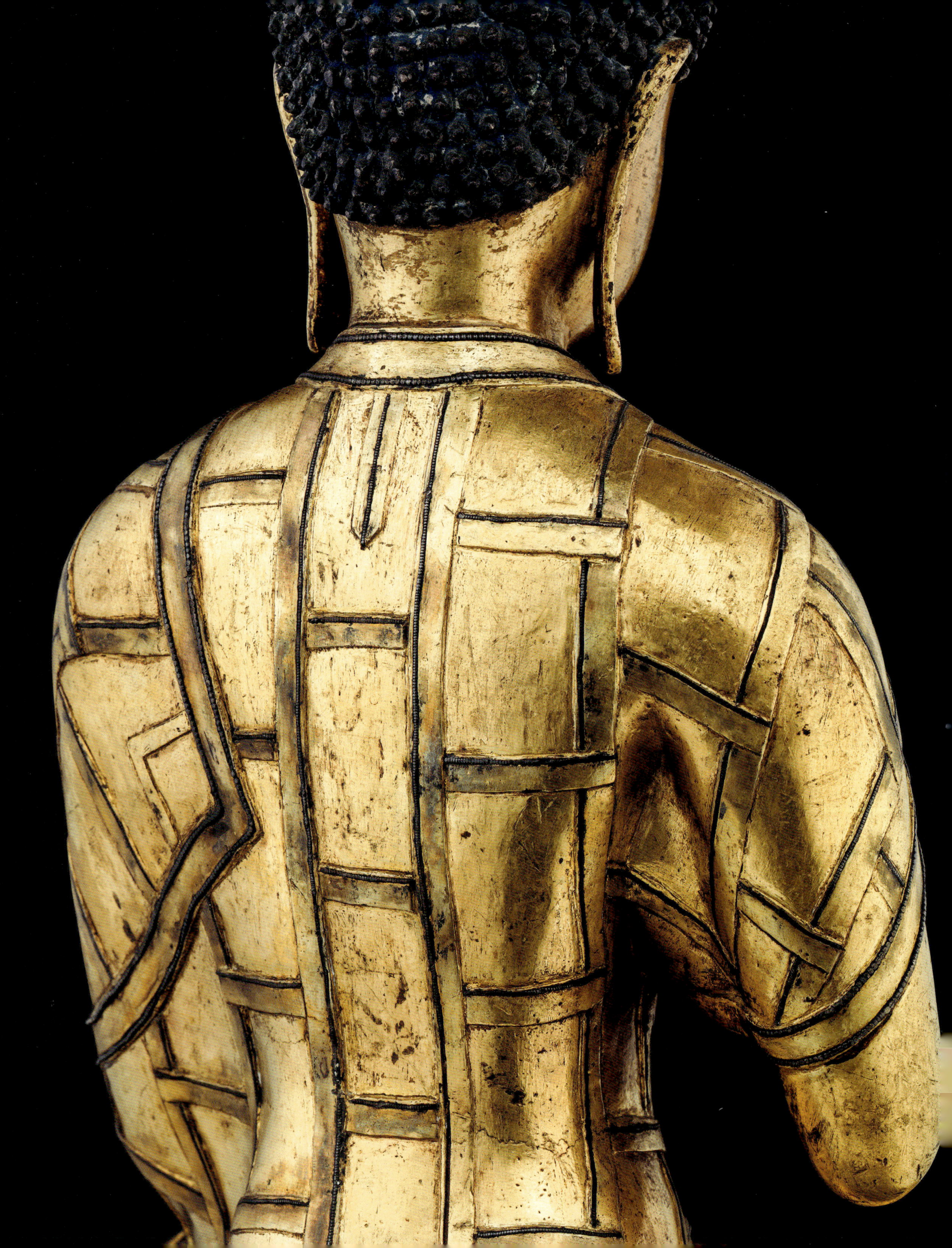

Contributors

Hao Sheng is consulting curator of Asian art at the Museum of Fine Arts, Houston.

Jane Casey is an art historian specializing in Himalayan art. She is the author of many publications, including *Taklung Painting: A Study in Chronology* (Serindia, 2023).

Susan L. Huntington, an art historian focusing primarily on South Asian Buddhist art, is Distinguished University Professor, Emerita, at the Ohio State University. With her late husband, John C. Huntington, she is cofounder of the John C. and Susan L. Huntington Photographic Archive of Buddhist and Asian art, a major online resource for the study of Buddhist art.

Karen Hwang is an art historian specializing in East Asian Buddhist art. She has worked at the Los Angeles County Museum of Art (LACMA) and taught at Wellesley College and Vassar College.

Michael Knight has a PhD in Chinese art history and archaeology from Columbia University. He began his curatorial career at the Seattle Art Museum in 1981. In 1996, he accepted the position of Senior Curator of Chinese Art at the Asian Art Museum of San Francisco. Since his retirement in 2014, he has served as a consultant for private collectors.

Donald S. Lopez is the Arthur E. Link Distinguished University Professor of Buddhist and Tibetan Studies in the Department of Asian Languages and Cultures at the University of Michigan.

Donna K. Strahan is Head of the Department of Conservation and Scientific Research at the National Museum of Asian Art, Smithsonian Institution, Washington, DC.

John Twilley is a research associate in the Department of Materials Science at Stony Brook University, New York, and serves as the Mellon Scientific Advisor to the Nelson-Atkins Museum of Art, Kansas City. His independent practice in conservation science focuses on the application of microanalytic and spectroscopic techniques to questions of attribution, authenticity, and conservation treatment for a wide spectrum of museums, galleries, and collectors.

David Weldon has worked in the fields of Indian, Himalayan, and Chinese Buddhist art since 1972, and has been a consultant to Sotheby's Indian and Himalayan Art Department since 1999.

This book accompanies the exhibition *Buddha | Nature* organized by and presented at the Museum of Fine Arts, Houston, from March 1 to May 10, 2026.

Published by the Museum of Fine Arts, Houston
Distributed by Yale University Press, New Haven and London
Produced by the Publications Department of
    the Museum of Fine Arts, Houston
Publisher in Chief: Heather Brand
Managing Editor: Megan Smith
Designed by Roy Brooks, Fold Four, Inc.
Typeset in Foco
Printed by Puritan Capital, New Hampshire

Front cover illustration: *Buddha Head* (detail) (cat. 21).
Frontispiece: *Buddha Maravijaya, Triumphing over Mara* (detail) (cat. 1).
Page 5: *Buddha Maravijaya, Calling the Earth to Witness* (detail) (cat. 15).
Page 6: *Avaloviteshvara as Acuoye Guanyin* (detail) (cat. 22).
Pages 38–39: *Buddha in Meditation* (detail) (cat. 4).
Page 126: *Buddha Shakyamuni* (detail) (cat. 16).
Back cover illustration: *Buddha in Meditation* (cat. 8).

Library of Congress Control Number: 2025942332

Authorized Representative in the EU: Easy Access System Europe, Mustamäe tee 50, 10621 Tallinn, Estonia, gpsr.requests@easproject.com

ISBN 978-0-300-28642-7

Copyright and Photography Credits